Memorials of Human Superstition; Imitated From the Historia Flagellantium of the Abbé Boileau, Doctor of the Sorbonne, ... By one who is not Doctor of the Sorbonne. The Third Edition

MEMORIALS

O F

HUMAN SUPERSTITION;

IMITATED FROM

The *HISTORIA FLAGELLANTIUM*
of the Abbé Boileau, Doctor of the Sorbonne,
Canon of the Holy Chapel, &c.

By One who is not Doctor of the Sorbonne.

Honi soit qui mal y pense.

THE THIRD EDITION.

INTRODUCTION.

THE Abbé Boileau, the author of the *Historia Flagellantium*, was elder brother to the celebrated Poet of that name. He filled, several years, the place of Dean of the Metropolitan Church of Sens, and was thence promoted to the office of one of the Canons of the Holy Chapel in Paris, which is looked upon as a great dignity among the French clergy.

While he was in that office (about the year 1700) he wrote, besides other books, that which is the subject of this work *. This book, in which the public expected, from the title of it, to find an history of the particular sect of Hereticks called Flagellants, only contained an aggregation of facts and quotations on the subject of self-disciplines and flagellations in general among Christians (which, if the work had been well executed, might have been equally interesting) and a mixture of alternate commendation and blame of that practice.

---

* The title of the book is *Historia Flagellantium, de recto & perverso flagrorum usu apud Christianos*, 12mo. Parisiis, apud J. Anisson, Typographiæ Regiæ Præfectum, MDCC.

The

The Theologians of that time, however, took offence at the book. They
judged that the author had been guilty
of feveral heretical affertions; for inftance, in faying, as he does in two or
three places, that Jefus Chrift had fuffered flagellation againft his will: and
they particularly blamed the cenfures
which, amidft his commendations of it,
he had paffed upon a practice that fo
many faints had adopted, fo many pontiffs and bifhops had advifed, and fo many
ecclefiaftical writers had commended.

In the fecond place, they objected to
feveral facts which the author had inferted in his book. as well as to the licenti-
oufnefs of expreffion he had fometimes
indulged; and they faid that fuch facts,
and fuch manner of expreffion, ought not
to be met with in a book written by a
good Chriftian, and much lefs by a Dean
of the Metropolitan Church of Sens, a
Canon of the Holy Chapel, and in fhort
by a man invefted with an eminent dignity in the Church; in which latter refpect they were perhaps right *.

* Our author, who was rather fingular in the
choice of his fubjects, had written another treatife
De tactibus impudicis prohibendis: and another on
the drefs of clergymen, wherein he attempted to
prove, that they might as well wear it fhort as long.

Among

Among the critics of the Abbé Boileau's book, were the Jefuits of Trevoux; the then conductors of a periodical review, called the *Journal de Trevoux.* The poet Boileau, taking the part of his brother, anfwered their criticifms by the following epigram:

Non, le livre des Flagellans
N'a jamais condamné, lifez le bien mes Peres,
 Ces rigidités falutaires
Que pour ravir le Ciel, faintement violens,
Exercent fur leurs corps tant de Chrétiens
  aufières.
Il blâme feulement cet abus odieux
 D'étaler & d'offrir aux yeux
Ce que leur doit toûjours cacher la bienféance,
Et combat vivement la fauffe piété,
Qui, fous couleur d'éteindre en nous la volupté,
Par l'aufiérité même & par la pénitence
Sait allumer le feu de la lubricité *.

 * The following is the literal tranflation of the above lines:

  " No, the book of the Flagellants never did condemn (read it well, my Fathers) thofe falutary feverities, which, in order to carry Heavens, through a holy violence, fo many rigid Chriftians exercife on their own bodies. It only animadverts upon that odious abufe of difplaying and offering to fight what decency always requires fhould be hidden, and zealoufly combats that falfe piety, which, under colour of extinguifhing luftfulnefs, through aufterity and penance themfelves knows how to kindle the fire of lewdnefs."

    The

The firft opportunity I had to fee the Abbé Boileau's book, which is pietty fcarce, but which I knew from the above epigram, and other books that mention it, was about ten years ago, in a town of Italy, where it was fhewn to me by a Quaker, an Englifhman, who lived theic; not a Quaker, however, of the common fort, that is, a fcrupulous obferver of the duties pieferibed by his feét; for he wore laced cloaths, and played admirably well on the flute.

Having fince met with another copy of the fame book, I judged that its fingularity, and the natuie of the faéts it contains, rendered it woithy to be laid before the public; and I had the thought of dreffing it in the vulgar tongue with the lefs reluétance, as, conformably to the confeffion I have made in the title-page, I have not the honour to be a doétor of the Sorbonne. However, I found, upon a more attentive examination of the book, that the obfcurity and want of meaning of that part of it which properly belongs to the author, who feems to have been as defcétive in point of clearnefs of head, as his brother the poet was remarkable for that qualification, rendered a tranflation impraéticable.

The

The fingular contradiction, for inftance, between moft of the conclufions the Abbé draws from the facts he relates, and the facts themfelves, is (when it is pof-fible to afcertain the meaning of fuch con-clufions) really matter of furprife. The critics of the Abbé, who were fenfible of this inconfiftency, had derived comfort from it, and hoped that the book would propagate but little herefy, fince hardly any body could underftand it. However, the very manner in which this author has compofed his work, wherein he contra-dicts not only the facts he relates, but even his own affertions, fometimes two or three times in the fame page, leads us to the difcovery of his real defign in writing it, and clears him from having enterrained any views of an heretical or dangerous nature. He only propofed, it appears, to compile together facts and quotations which amufed him, and which he thought would alfo amufe the public; and he terminated them (or fometimes whole ftrings of them) with feeming conclu-fions and random affertions, in order to make the reader judge that he had a feri-ous and even theological defign, in mak-ing his compilation.

Another caufe of furprife in the Abbé Boileau's book is, the extreme incohe-

rency

rency of the facts themselves he has link-
ed together. But in this respect, likewise, we discover, after a little examination, that his views were of a perfectly
harmlefs kind, and that this fingularity
was not owing to any deep, artful defign
of his own, as might at firft fight be
imagined, but only to the manner in
which he proceeded in his work. His
practice was, it appears, to lay down,
at the fame time, upon the paper,
all the facts to his liking he found
related in the productions of the fame
author; and at other times alfo, he introduced together all the ftories and
quotations the difcovery of which he
had made in the courfe of the fame
morning *.

A tranflation of a book thus made was
therefore, as hath been above faid, impracticable. And as a number of the
facts and quotations it contains are curious, either in themfelves, or on account
of the authors from whom they are extracted, I have at once enlarged my firft

----

* The fame manner of writing is alfo to be
met with in moft of the treatifes that were written
in England, France, and efpecially Germany,
about an hundred years ago, or more, when a
mechanical knowledge of Latin and Greek books,
and making compilations from them, was the
kind of learning in vogue

plan,

plan, and thought of writing another book with the materials contained in that of the Abbé Boileau.

With the facts and quotations, therefore, fupplied by the Abbé Boileau, I have undertaken to compofe thefe *Memorials of Human Superftition*. With thefe materials, the quantity or number of which I determined neither to increafe or decreafe, I have attempted to write a book; propofing to myfelf a tafk of much the fame nature with that kind of play which fometimes ferves to amufe companies of friends in winter evenings, in which fets of words, in appearance incompatible with one another, are propofed, and, without any of them being left out, or even difplaced, are to be made into fome confiftent fpeeches, by the help of intermediate arguments. Such tafk I have, as I fay, tried to perform, without fetting afide any of the facts contained in the Abbé Boileau's book : only I have taken great liberty with refpect to placing and difplacing fuch facts, as, without that indulgence, the tafk, on this occafion, was not to be performed. The work or problem, therefore, I propofed to myfelf, inftead of being that which more commonly occurs, and may be expreffed in the following

I terms,

terms, *Certain arguments being given, to find the neceſſary facts to ſupport them?* was this: *A certain number of facts, pretty well authenticated, being given, to find the natural concluſions and inductions which they ſuggeſt?*

To this paraphraſe thus made on the materials afforded by the Abbé Boileau, and to a few occaſional ſentences of his, which I have preſerved, I have added an ample Commentary, in which I have introduced only ſuch facts as either my own memory, or other authors, have ſupplied me with: ſo that the Abbé's work, a twelves book, printed on a very large type, has ſwelled into the majeſtic octavo which is now laid before the public.

In compoſing this octavo, two different parts I have performed. In the Text or Paraphraſe on the facts afforded by the Abbé, I have, keeping to the ſubject, and preſerving as much as I could the turn of my Author's book, expreſſed myſelf in that ſtyle and manner in which it was not unlikely a doctor of the Sorbonne, and a dean of the church of Sens, might have written: in the Commentary, I have followed my own inclination. Conformably to that which is often practiſed on the Stage, where the ſame player fills two different parts at the ſame time, by

ſpeedily

fpeedily altering his drefs, I have, in the
prefent work, acted in two different alternate capacities, as I changed fides: in the
text, I acted the part of a doctor of the
Sorbonne ; and then, quickly refuming
my former ftation, I expatiated and com-
mented, in the note, upon what the doctor had juft faid in the text.

Thus much for the manner in which
I have accomplifhed this work. In regard to giving any previous delineation
of the fubftance of it, it is what I find
fome difficulty in doing; and which,
befides, I think would be ufelefs, fince I
fuppofe the reader will (as readers commonly do) perufe this Preface only after
he has turned the laft leaf of the book :
taking it therefore for granted that the
reader knows, by this time, what the prefent performance is, I proceed to give an
account of my views in writing it.

In the firft place, I propofed to myfelf
the information of pofterity. A period
will, fooner or later, arrive, at which the
difciplining and flagellating practices now
in ufe, and which have been fo for fo
many centuries, will have been laid afide,
and fucceeded by others equally whimfical. And while the men of thofe days
will overlook the defects of their own
extravagant cuftoms, or perhaps even admire

mire the rationality of them, they will refuse to believe that the practices of which accounts are given in this work, ever were in ufe among mankind, and even matter of great moment among them. My defign, therefore, was effectually to remove all their doubts in that refpect, by handing down to them the flower and choice part of the facts and arguments on the fubject.

This book will likewife be extremely ufeful to the prefent age ; and it will in in the firft place be fo, the fubject being confidered in a moral light. The numerous cafes that are produced in this book, of difciplines which offenders of all claffes, kings as well as others, have zealoufly inflicted upon themfelves, will fupply a ftriking proof of that deep fenfe of juftice which exifts in the breafts of all men ; and the reader will from fuch facts conclude, no doubt with pleafure, that even the offenders of the high rank we have juft mentioned, notwithftanding the ftate by which they are furrounded, and the majeftic countenance which they put on, fometimes in proportion as they more clearly know that they are wrong, are inwardly convinced that they owe compenfation for their acts of injuftice.

Being

Being confidered in the fame moral light, this book will be ufeful to the prefent age, by the inftances it gives of corrections by which different offences againft the peace of mankind have been requited ; the confequence of which will be the preventing of fuch offences. Slanderous wits, for example, to mention only offenders of that clafs, writers of fatires, epigrams, and lampoons, dealers in bonmots, inventors of anecdotes, by reading the inftances of difciplines by which fuch ingenious paftimes have, on different occafions, been repaid, will naturally be led to recollect that all poffible flagellations (to ufe the expreffion of the Alguazil introduced in a certain chapter of Gil Blas) have not been yet inflicted ; and fudden confiderations like this, which this book will not fail to fuggeft to them, will be extremely apt to check them the inftant they are preparing to make their excurfions on the reputation of their neighbours ; and by that means the good name of many an innocent perfon will be preferved.

To the perfons themfelves who actually fuffer from the injuftice or wantonnefs of others, this performance will be of great fervice. Thofe, for inftance, who fmart under the lafh of fome infolent

lent

lent satirist, those who are disappointed in their expectations, those whose secrets have been betrayed, nay, even ladies, treacherously forsaken by those who had given them so many assurances of fidelity and eternal constancy, will find their misfortunes alleviated by reading the several instances and facts related in this book : they will take comfort from the thought, that what has already happened may happen again, and cheer themselves with the hope, that flagellations will sooner or later be the lot of those persons who cause their uneasiness.

Being considered in a philosophical light, this work will be useful to the present age, in the same manner as we have said it would be to posterity. The present generation, at least in this island, will find in it proofs both of the reality of the singular practices which once prevailed in their own country, and are still in full force in many others, and of the important light in which they have been considered by mankind. They will meet with accounts of bishops, cardinals, popes, and princes, who have warmly commended or blamed such practices; and will not be displeased to be moreover acquainted with the debates of the learned on the same subject, and with the honest,

though

though oppofite, endeavours, of a Cerebrofus and a Damian, a Gretzer and a
Gerfon.

To the critical reader this book will
likewife be ferviceable, by giving him an
infight into the manner of the debates
and arguments, and into the turn of the
erudition, of foreign Catholick divines,
at the fame time that the information
will be conveyed to him amidft other objects that will perhaps better amufe him:
to fecure this advantage, I have, as much
as I could, preferved the appearance of
the Abbé's book, ufing, for that purpofe, the titles of feveral of his chapters;
only taking care to keep more to the
fubject than himfelf has done.

To the fame critical reader this performance will alfo be recommendable, by
the numerous paffages from certain books
which it gives him an opportunity to
perufe. And the generality of readers
will not be difpleafed to meet with a
number of fhort fpecimens of the ftyle
of feveral authors whofe works they never would have read, though they were
once confpicuous on the particular line
which they followed; and to be thus
brought to fome flight acquaintance with
St. Auftin, St. Jerom, and Tertullian, of
whom they knew only the names; and
with

with St. Fulgentius, and Peter Chryfologus, of whom they knew nothing at all.

In fine, to thefe capital advantages poffeffed by this work, I have endeavoured to add the important one of affording entertainment; for entertainment is a thing which is not by any means to be defpifed in this world. In order the better to attain this end, I have avoided offending againft decency or religion; I had of myfelf too little inclination to be witty at the expence of either, efpecially the latter, to avail myfelf of the opportunities which the fubject naturally offered: and I fhould think it a great praife of this book, if I were hereafter informed that the graver clafs of readers have read with pleafure the lefs ferious part of it, and that the other clafs have gone with pleafure likewife through that part which is lefs calculated for amufement *.

* In order to give the reader a complete account of thefe *Memorials of Human Superftition,* I fhall add that the book was firft written in confequence of a wager or kind of challenge in a company of friends. Confideiable alterations were made in the fecond Edition, but very few have been made in this; fcaicely any thing material having been added, except a few facts concerning Henry the Fourth of France, and the inftance of the difcipline fubmitted to at Rome by the Emperor of Germany, Henry IV., which is introduced in page 256.

THE

HISTORY

OF THE

FLAGELLANTS.

CHAP. I.

The fubftance of the reafons given by the Abbé Boileau, for writing his Book. He feems to have been of opinion that voluntary flagellations were no very antient practice.

I AM not, I confefs, without fear that the defign I have formed of tracing the origin

*A

of thofe Flagellations which have in procefs of time been introduced among Chriftians, will be looked upon as a rafh undertaking, and that I may be accufed of having, in that refpect, fallen into the errors of the Proteftants, whether Lutherans, or Calvinifts.

In fact, thofe two Sects, under pretence of fhewing their obedience to the commands of God, who orders the Ifraelites *not to make incifions in their own flefh for the fake of the dead*, trample upon all laws concerning Penitence, extinguifh that kind of virtue which confifts in repreffing the luftful appetites of the flefh, and ridicule thofe mortifications and penances to which Tertullian advifes us to fubmit.

Indeed, I am far from wifhing to favour the relaxed Doctrine of Heretics. That kind of enthufiaftic fury which the Calvinifts manifefteft, in the laft Century, againft the laborious exercifes of the Monaftic life, rather heightens, in my opinion, the glory of the Catholic Church. I think that the manner of the antient Anchorites of Syria, of Thebaid, and of Egypt, the purity of their virtue, and the furprifing penances to which they fubmitted, deferve our utmoft reverence, however impoffible it may be for us to imitate them.

7

I have no other object in view, on this occasion, than to bring back those happy times of the primitive Church, in which the true Science of conquering luftful appetites flourished among our holy Forefathers. All I propose to myself, is, to render it manifest to every candid Reader, that those methods of doing Penance, which are in our days called *Difciplines* *, were unknown in the happy

* The word *Difcipline* originally fignified in general, the cenfures and corrections which perfons who were guilty of Sins, received from their Superiors, and when *Flagellation* was to be part of thofe corrections, it was exprefsly mentioned; and they called fuch Difcipline, as the Reader will fee in the Sequel of this Book, " the difcipline of the whip," *(difciplina flagelli)*. As Flagellation grew afterwards to be the common method of doing penance that prevailed among perfons in religious Orders, the bare word *difcipline* became in courfe of time the technical word to exprefs that kind of chaftifement · thus, the Reader will find hereafter an inftance in which Flagellation, when too long continued, is called " the madnefs of too long difcipline," *(longioris difciplinæ infania)*. And at laft, thofe kinds of whips made of knotted and twifted cords, commonly ufed for the above

C   pious

happy periods of the primitive Church. By Difciplines I mean here to fpeak of thofe voluntary Flagellations which Penitents inflict upon themfelves with their own hands; lafhing their own backs, or pofteriors, either with fcourges or whips, or willow and birch rods. A practice this, which, we are not to doubt, prevails much in the Societies of modern Monks and Nuns, efpecially among thofe who, under pretence of reformation, have abolifhed their antient Rules, and fubftituted new Conftitutions in their ftead.

But before I enter upon this fubject, I muft inform the Reader of two facts, which it is neceffary he fhould know, at the fame time that they are undeniable, and confirmed by every

pious exercifes, have alfo been called by the fame name; and the word *difcipline* has become in French, for inftance, the appropriated word to exprefs the inftrument of religious flagellation. Thus, in Moliere's Play, called the *Tartuffe*, or the Hypocrite, Tartuffe tells his Man, " Laurent, " lock up my hair-cloth, and difcipline, and pray " that Heaven may always illuminate you."

Laurent, ferrez ma haire avec ma difcipline,
Et priez que toujours le Ciel vous illumine.

TART. A. III. Sc. 2.

every day's practice. The first is, that Penitents, as we have above-mentioned, both inflict those Disciplines on themselves with their
own hands, and receive the same from other
persons, either with scourges, or rods, or
whip-cords. The second is, that those chas-
tisements are inflicted on them, either on the
bare back or shoulders, or on the posteriors:
the former method is usually called the *upper*,
and the latter, the *lower* discipline *.

Now,

* *Sursùm* & *deorsùm disciplina.*——All the Women (as the Writer of this Commentary has been
told, when in Catholic Countries) who make self-
flagellation part of their religious exercises, whether they live in or out of Convents, use the *lower
discipline,* as defined above : their pious and merci-
ful Confessors having suggested to them, that the
upper discipline may prove dangerous, and be the
cause of hurting their breasts, especially when they
mean to proceed in that holy exercise with unusual
fervour and severity. A few Orders of Friars,
among whom are the Capuchins, also use the lower
kind of discipline, but for what reason the Commentator has not been as yet informed.

Perhaps it will be asked here, how Priests and
Confessors have been able to introduce the use of
such a painful practice as flagellation, among the

persons

Now, that this latter kind of Difcipline is
a contrivance of modern times, is what I pofitively

perfons who choofe to be'directed by them in religious matters, and how they can enforce obedience to the prefcriptions they give them in that refpect. But here it muft be remembered, that *Fe-
nance* has been made a Sacrament among Catholics, and that *Satisfaction*, as may be feen in the
Books that treat of that fubject, is an effential
part of it, and muft always precede the *Abfolution*
on the part of the Confeffor. Now, as Confeffors have it in their power to refufe this Abfolution, fo long as the Penances or Satisfactions of
any kind, which they have enjoyed to their Penitents, have not been accomplifhed, this confers
on them a very great authority, and though, to a
number of thofe who apply to them, who care but
little for fuch Abfolution, or in cafe of refufal are
ready to apply to other more eafy Confeffors, they
fcarcely prefcribe any other kind of *Satisfaction*
than faying a certain number of prayers, or fuch
like mortification, yet, to thofe perfons who think
it a very ferious affair when a Confeffor in whom
they truft, continues to refufe them his abfolution,
they may enjoin almoft what kind of penance they
pleafe. And indeed fince Confeffors have been
able to prevail upon Kings to leave their kingdoms
and

tively aver. It was unknown, as I ſhall de-
monſtrate to the Reader, among the firſt Chriſtians ; and it is moreover repugnant both to
true Piety, and to Modeſty, for ſeveral rea-
ſons which I ſhall deduce hereafter. I pro-
poſe, beſides, to ſhew that this practice is an
offspring of Idolatry and Superſtition ; that it
ought to be baniſhed from among Chriſtians
as an erroneous and dangerous exerciſe ; and
that it has only been introduced into the Chriſtian Church by ignorant perſons, under the
ſpecious appearance of Piety and more perfect Mortification.

Painters, it ſeems, have not a little helped
to eſtabliſh and ſtrengthen the practices we
mention, by their pictures, of which Pope
Gregory the Great ſays, in his Epiſtle to Se-
renus Biſhop of Marſeilles, that they were
" the Libraries of ignorant Chriſtians." In
C 3
fact,

and engage in perilous wars and croiſades to the
Holy Land, and to induce young and tender
Queens to perform on foot pilgrimages to very diſ-
tant places, it is not difficult to underſtand how
they have been able gradually to prevail upon numbers of their Devotees of both Sexes, to follow
practices which they had been ſo fooliſh as to
adopt for themſelves, and to practiſe, at their own
choice, either the lower, or the upper, diſcipline.

fact, we fee they have never reprefented any of the antient Anchorites, without leaving fome fpare corner on their canvas, whereupon to place either whips or rods; inftruments of which thofe holy Hermits had not probably made the leaft ufe during their lives, and about which they perhaps had never fo much as entertained a thought.

A number of able Writers in the laft century have, it muft be confeffed, alfo contributed to bring into credit the practice we mention. Confidering voluntary flagellations in the fame light as they did all methods in general of mortifying the flefh, they commended them, and procured them to be admitted. My defign here is not by any means to queftion the good intentions of fo refpectable perfons, who held the firft rank among the Society of the Fathers Jefuits, and were looked upon, if I may fo exprefs myfelf, like fo many Heroes in the Republic of Letters: but yet, on the other hand, I cannot be perfuaded that it is unlawful to animadvert upon the ignorance and impudence of Painters, of which Lucian fays that they were " as licentious as the Poets *," and to endeavour, if poffible,

to

---

* Dial. Ὑπὲρ τᾶ, Εἰκόνι—Καὶ τὸ παλαιὸς ἔτος ὁ λόγος, ἀνελθὼν

to obtain from the Prelates of the Church, that, fince pictures are the books of ignorant Chriftians,

ἀνευθύνες εἶναι Ποιητὰς καὶ Γϱαφέας. The Greek word ἀνευθύνες, ufed here, literally fignifies that Poets and Painters are not obliged to give any account of their actions. Horace has alfo expreffed a thought of the fame kind with regard to them, in his *Ars Poetica*, " Painters and Poets have always equally enjoyed the power of daring every thing."

Pictoribus atque Poëtis
Quidlibet audendi femper fuit æqua poteftas.

A. P. v. 9, 10.

The complaints of our Author with refpect to the loofe which Painters have been ufed to give to their own fancy, when they have treated religious fubjects, are well grounded; and perfons who have travelled in Catholic Countries cannot but have taken notice of the freedom that prevails in their Church-pictures : hence a number of ftories are related among them of Nuns, or other Women, who have fallen in love with naked figures of Angels and Saints, and of Men who have been led into extravagances by the paffion they had conceived for certain ftatues, or pictures. As to errors concerning facts merely, and faults againft the *Coftume*, which our Author feems more parti-

C 4

cula.ly

Chriſtians, no Fables and lies be repreſented in them; and that ſuch as contain notorious falſehoods be baniſhed from thoſe Churches and Chapels in which Jeſus Chriſt, who was truth itſelf, is daily adored. At leaſt this will be admitted, that truth has no need of the aſſiſtance of falſehood to protect it · ſupported by its own ſtrength, it ſets at defiance the attacks of both Folly and Sophiſtry.

cularly to allude to, in this Chapter, they are certainly very frequent in the works of Painters : even the firſt among them, ſuch as Paul Veroneſe and others, are reproached with capital ones. On this occaſion the Writer of this Commentary thinks he may relate what he himſelf has ſeen in a Country Church in Germany, in which a Painter, who had intended to repreſent the Sacrifice of Iſaac, had ſo far availed himſelf of the *poteſtas quidlibet audendi*, mentioned above, that he had repreſented Abraham with a blunderbuſs in his hand, ready to ſhoot his ſon, and an Angel, ſuddenly come down from Heaven, pouring water on the pan.

CHAP.

C H A P. II.

No perfons, under the antient Law, inflicted on
themfelves, with their own hands, voluntary
flagellations, or received them from the hands
of other perfons.

FLAGELLATION, there is no doubt, is
a method of coercive punifhment very
antiently ufed among Men. We find it mentioned in the Old Teftament, in the fifth chapter of *Exodus :* it is faid in that chapter, that
the Minifters of Pharaoh, who required from
the Ifraelites a certain number of bricks every
day, having found them to have failed in fupplying the ufual number, ordered them to be
flogged; and that the latter complained of this
harfh ufage.

V. 14. " And the officers of the children
" of Ifrael, which Pharaoh's Tafk mafters had
" fet over them, were beaten *, and de-
" manded,

---

* The words of the Vulgate in this place, are,
flagellati funt, which fignify, were lafhed with rods
or whips : and in v. 16. *flagellis cædimur,* which
has the fame meaning.

" manded, Wherefore have you not fulfilled
" your talk in making brick, both yefterday
" and to-day, as heretofore ?"

15. " Then the Officers of the children of
" Ifrael came and cried unto Pharaoh, faying,
" Wherefore dealeft thou thus with thy fer-
" vants ?"

16. " There is no ftraw given unto thy
" fervants, and they fay to us, Make brick :
" and behold we are beaten, but the fault is
" in thine own people."—Now, I think that
no commentary is neceffary to prove that the
flagellations mentioned here were not in any
degree voluntary on the part of thofe who underwent them.

We alfo find mention made in Leviticus of
the punifhment of Flagellation : this is the
punifhment awarded, in the nineteenth chapter, againft thofe who fhould be guilty of the
fin of Fornication. " And whofoever lieth
" carnally with a woman that is a bond-maid,
" betrothed to an hufband, and not at all re-
" deemed, nor freedom given her, fhe fhall
" be fcourged ; they fhall not be put to death,
" becaufe fhe was not free."

The Hebrew words in the text, which are
commonly tranflated by thefe, *fhall be fcourged*, are juftly tranflated fo ; though in the verfion

fion of the LXX. they are only tranflated by
the words, *fhall be punifhed* *; for the punifhment

* The Hebrew words in the text are כקרת
החיה ; the Greek words for thefe, in the LXX.
are, ἐπισκοπὴ ἔσαι αὐτοῖς.—As I do not underftand
Hebrew, I fhall not try to make any remark on
the above Hebrew words, but truft for that to the
fagacioufnefs of the reader, however, with refpect
to the Greek words that follow them, 1 think I
fhould be greatly wanting in my duty to the Public, in my capacity of Commentatoi, if I did not
communicate to them an obfervation with which
thofe words fupply me, which is, that there is a
material error in the paffage above recited, in our
common tranflation of the Bible; for the Reader
may fee that the punifhment of fcourging, in cafe
of fornication, is confined, in that paffage, to the
Woman folely, whereas the word αὐτοῖς, which
is a plural word, fhews that both the Man and
Woman were to be punifhed alike, and inflead of
fhe fhall, as our Bible is worded in that paffage, it
ought to be, *they fhall* be fcourged. This remaik
on the above fingular alteration of the true fenfe
of the Bible, to the prejudice of Women (fuppofing it is not an error of the pref ... atuially
leads me to take notice here of th. .i, .. 'pofi
tion

ment ufed on thofe occafions was inflicted, as the learned Vatable obferves, with thongs of ox-leather, that is to fay, with fcourges. To this I think it is needlefs to add, that the Ifraelites did not voluntarily impofe on themfelves the abovementioned fcourgings, and that they never were fuffered by any of them but much againft their will.

In the xxvth chapter of Deuteronomy, the number of lafhes which Offenders of any kind were to receive, was limited to forty. V. 2. " And it fhall be, if the wicked may be wor-" thy to be beaten, that the Judge fhall caufe " him to lie down, and to be beaten before " his face, according to a certain number."

3. " Forty

tion of Men towards Women in general, in all that relates to the mutual intercourfe of the Sexes : a difpofition that has induced them in modern times to impofe humiliating penalties on fuch Women as are guilty of fins which the Men themfelves commit with the utmoft freedom, and thus to eftablifh a mortifying difference, in that refpect, between the two fexes, inflead of that amiable equality which obtained between them under the Jewifh law, according to which the Man and Woman who had committed together the fin of Fornication, were lafhed with equal numbers of ftripes

3. " Forty ftripes he may give him, and
" not exceed; but if he fhould exceed, and
" beat him above thefe with many ftripes,
" then thy brother fhould feem vile unto
" thee."

Now, it is evident from the above paffage,
that the Ifraelites were very far from approving any cruel flagellations, like thofe which
Monks in our days inflict on themfelves with
whip-cords filled with knots, or fometimes
armed with nails or needles ; fince they
were even forbidden to fuffer their Brother to
be too cruelly lafhed in their prefence. Nor
was it the incifions made on the bodies of innocent perfons before the altar of Moloch, or
at the funerals of the dead, which God meant
here to prevent; He even prefcribed ten-
dernefs to the fufferings of a convicted offender,
though he deferved the ftripes that were
inflicted on him. Therefore, if the law of
God forbad any cruel excefs in the chaftifing
of perfons who were guilty of crimes, much
more did it difapprove that Men fhould unmercifully lafh and flay themfelves with rods
and whip-cords. Indeed, the modern practice of lafhing and whipping one's felf to the
effufion of blood, is by no means intitled to
our admiration. How could it be poffible

3   that

that an unhappy Friar, who lives in certain modern Monafteries, fhould not have his fkin torn from head to foot, fince it is a conftant practice among them to difcipline themfelves three or four times every week, during the whole time that the *Miferere*, the *De Profundis* *, and the *Salve Regina*, are finging, with a melodious, though flow, voice; and that too fo heavily, and in fuch earneft, that the rattling of the blows refounds on all fides?

Several perfons, however, ftill infift that religious flagellations were in ufe among the ancient Jews, and draw, it muft be confeffed, ftrong arguments from the words of David,

in

---

* The *Miferere* is the 51ft Pfalm, and the *De Profundis* is the 130th, which is none of the fhorteft.

The finging of the *Miferere* feems to be particularly appropriated, among Catholics, to regulate both the duration of religious flagellations, and the *time* to which they are to be performed, as we may conclude from the above paffage of our Author, and alfo from a paffage of M. de Voltaire in his *Candide*, in which he fays, that, when *Candide* was flagellated at Lifbon, by order of the Inquifition, he was all the while entertained with a *Miferere en faux bourdon*, which is a kind of Church Mufic.

in Pfal. lxxiii. 14 : " *For all the day long have* " *I been plagued, and chaftened every morn-* " *ing *.*" But if we confider attentively thefe expreffions of the Prophet, we fhall find that they do not by any means fignify that he lafhed himfelf with a fcourge every day, and all the day long. Thofe ftripes of which he fpeaks are to be underftood only in a figura- tive fenfe, and they only mean thofe misfor- tunes and tribulations which are frequently the lot of the righteous in this world : and indeed we fee that David exclaims elfewhere, ' *For I* ' *am ready to halt, and my forrow is continu-* ' *ally before me.*'

Befides, we are to obferve that St. Auftin, a Writer of the higheft authority, paraphrafes the above-mentioned paffage of Pf. lxxiii. in the following manner : " I am never free " from afflictions from God ; I difcharge my " duty, and yet I am beaten, &c." Indeed the above is only the rational meaning of the paffage in queftion ; and we cannot with any degree

---

* The expreffions of the *Vulgate* are, *fui fla-gellatus, I have been whipped.* The *Vulgate* of the Old Teftament is a very ancient Latin verfion of it from the Hebrew, corrected afterwards by St. Jerom, which is followed in all Catholic Countries.

degree of probability infer from it (as certain perfons do) that the practice of fcourging one's felf voluntarily, and lafhing one's hide with rods and whip cords, was in ufe among the ancient Hebrews, and that fuch a whimfical notion ever entered their heads. It is true that Philo *the Jew*, and Eufebius of Cæfarea, relate, that the Effeans, or *Therapeutæ* (whether they were a particular fect of the Jews, or are to be ranked among the firft Chriftians, is not clear) were celebrated on account of the macerations which they practifed; but then we are intirely ignorant of the methods which they ufed in order to mortify themfelves, and we are no where told that they employed for that purpofe either *difciplines* or whips.

Yet, this cannot be difallowed, that after the two Rabbins, *Mayr*, and *Affe the Son*, had compiled the Babylonian Talmud *, that is to fay,

* The Talmud is the Tradition, or *unwritten* law of the Jews, the Law of Mofes being their *written* Law. This Tradition has, in procefs of time, been fet down in writing, and two different Collections have been made of it: the one, in the Jerufalem School, about three hundred years after Jefus Chrift, which is called the *Jerufalem* Talmud,

fay, about the 476th year from the birth of our Lord, new practices began to prevail among the Jews. Fafcinated, I do not know by what kind of fuperftition, they began to ufe, contrary to their former cuftoms, a fort of voluntary difcipline; though, we are to obferve, they never inflicted fuch difcipline on themfelves with their own hands. We are informed of the above fact, in the Treatife intitled *Malkos*, in the 3d Chapter of which it is faid, that the Jews, after they had finifhed their prayers and confeffed their fins (which were exercifes they derived from their ancef-tors) ufed to lafh one another with fcourges.

John Buxtorf the Father, a Proteftant Au-thor, in his Book of the *Judaic Synagogue*, printed at Bafil in the year 1661, defcribes the above practice of the Jews at fome length, and fays, That there are conftantly two Men in every Jewifh fchool, who withdraw from the reft of the Company, and retire into a particular place of the room where they are

Talmud, the other, in the Babylonian School, five hundred years after Jefus Chrift, and is called the *Babylon* Talmud. The latter is that which is ufually read among the Jews, and when they fim-ply fay, the *Talmud*, they mean the Babylon Talmud.

D

met; that the one lays himself flat on the ground with his head turned to the North, and his feet to the South (or his head to the South, and his feet to the North); and that the other, who remains standing, gives him thirty-nine blows upon his back with a strap, or thong of ox-leather. In the meanwhile, the Man who is lashed, recites three times over the thirty-eighth verse of Psal. lxxviii. This verse, in the Hebrew language, contains just thirteen words; at every word the Patient recites, he receives a lash from the other Man; which, when he has recited the whole verse three times over, makes up the prescribed number of thirty-nine; and at every time he says the last word, he strikes his own breast with his fist *. This operation being concluded,

---

* Buxtorf, the Author from whom the above facts are drawn, is mentioned with great praise in the *Scaligerana*, which is a Collection, or mixture, of Notes, partly French, partly Latin, found in the papers of J. Scaliger, and printed after his death. Buxtorf is called, in one of these Notes, the only Man learned in the Hebrew language, and Scaliger adds, that it is surprising how the Jews can love him, though he has handled them-

cluded, the *Agent* in his turn becomes the *Patient*, and places himſelf in the ſame ſitua-tion as the other had done, who then uſes him in the ſame brotherly manner in which the former had uſed him, and they thus mutually chaſtiſe each other for their ſins, and *rub one another*, Buxtorf obſerves, *like Aſſes*.

Perhaps the Reader will be ſurpriſed that the Rabbins have limited the number of the ſtripes inflicted in the manner above-deſcribed, to thirty-nine, ſince the Law of Moſes had extended their number to forty; but to this the Rabbins anſwer, that it is owing to the peculiar manner in which the puniſhment of ſtripes was inflicted in antient times. The ancient Jews, they ſay, uſed a ſcourge made of three thongs; one of which was very long, and went round the body of the perſon who was ſcourged, and the two others were a good deal ſhorter. Thirteen blows with this *three-thonged* ſcourge were given to the Patient; which, according to the Rabbins' manner of explaining the law, made thirty-nine ſtripes in

ſo ſeverely, which ſhews that he has been impar-tial in his accounts. *Merum quomodo Buxtorſius à Judæis ametur, in illâ tamen Synagogâ Judaicâ illos call. perſtringit.*

all: now, if one ſtroke more had been given him, he would have received forty-two, which would have been contrary to the law of Moſes, which ſays, " Forty ſtripes he may give him, " and not exceed *."

* It is to be ſuppoſed, that the Jew Prieſts had been well feed for the above benign interpretations they gave of the law of Moſes.

C H A P. III.

Voluntary flagellations were unknown to the first Chriftians. An explanation is given of the paffage of St. Paul: I chaftife my body, and keep it under fubjection +.

FLAGELLATIONS are mentioned fo often as eleven times by the Holy Writers of the New Teftament.

Of

+ As the difputes concerning religious flagellations have been carried on with great warmth on both fides, the two parties have ranfacked the Scriptures for paffages that might fupport their refpective opinions, and the fupporters of flagellations have been particulaly happy in the difcovery of the paffage of David, mentioned in the preceding Chapter, and that of St. Paul which is recited here. By the former paffage, the fupporters of flagellations pretend to fhew, that they were in ufe fo early as the time of David; and that the Prophet underwent a flagellation every morning: by the latter paffage, they endeavour to prove that

D 3

Of thefe, five relate to Jefus Chrift.   The firft is in the *xixth chapter* of the Gofpel according

felf-fcourgings were practifed by St. Paul, and of courfe by the fiift Chriftians.   As the literal meaning of the above two paffages is wholly on the fide of the fupporters of flagellations, this, as it always happens in controverfies of that kind, has given them a great advantage over their opponents, who have been reduced, either to plead that the expreffions urged againft them were only to be underftood in a figurative fenfe, or to endeavour, by altering the original paffage, to fubftitute others in their ftead.   The latter is the expedient on which our Author has chiefly relied in this chapter, and he ftrives to fubftitute another word, to the word ὑπωπιάζω, ufed by St. Paul when he faid, he *cheftifed* his *flefh*; which is to be found in all the common Editions of the Greek New Teftament.   And indeed it muft be confeffed, that the above word is of itfelf extremely favourable to the promoters of felf-flagellation, little lefs fo than the words of Afaph, *fui flagellatus (I have been whipped)* mentioned in the foregoing Chapter, its precife meaning being the fame as *I bruife or difcolour with blows*   it comes from the word ὑπώπιον, which fignifies a livid mark left under the eye by a

cording to St. Matthew, v. 19; and in the *xxvith* of the fame, v. 26. In the *xvth chapter* of St. Mark's Gofpel, v. 33. In the *xviith chapter* of the Gofpel according to St. Luke, v. 33; and in the *xixth chapter* of the

blow: on which the Reader may obferve (which, no doubt, will be matter of agreeable furprife to him) that what is called in plain Englifh a *black-eye*, was expreffed in Greek by the word ὑπώπιον. Befides trying to fubftitute another word to that attributed to St. Paul in the common Greek Editions of the New Teftament, our Author produces feveral paffages from Greek and Latin Fathers, to fhew that they thought that St. Paul meant no more than to fpeak of his great labours, abftinence, continence, &c.

The principal end of this Chapter is, therefore, to difcufs the interefting queftion, whether St. Paul ufed to flagellate himfelf· and I have preferred to give the above compendious account of the conteft on the fubject, rather than introduce the long difcuffion of Greek words, and ufe the whole ftring of paffages from Greek and Latin Fathers, contained in the Abbé Boileau's Book. By that means, the prefent Chapter has, for the fake of the Reader, been fhortened to ten pages, inftead of thirty, it muft otherwife have contained.

Gofpel according to St. John, v. 1 *. No juft conclufion, as the Reader may fee, can be drawn from the above-mentioned paffages, in fupport of voluntary flagellations, and of thofe *Difciplines* which Monks now-a-days inflict on t'emfelves; fince it is plain that our Saviour did not whip himfelf with his own hands: and we might as well fay that we ought to inflict death upon ourfelves, and nail ourfelves to a crofs, as that we ought to lacerate our own flefh with fcourges, becaufe Jefus Chrift was expofed to that kind of punifhment.

The other fix paffages of the New Teftament in which whipping is mentioned, are, firft, in St. John's (c. ii. v. 15.) *And when He had made a fcourge of fmall cords, he drove them out of the Temple, and the fheep, and the oxen; and poured out the changers of money, and overthrew the tables.* The fecond chapter is in the fifth chapter of the Acts (v. 40.) *And when they had called the Apoftles and beaten*

---

* " And fhall deliver him to the Gentiles to " mock and to fcourge and to crucify him." St. *Matth.* c. xx. v. 19. . . . . " Then Pilate took " Jefus, and fcourged him." St. *John*, c. xix. ver. 1.

them with scourges, they commanded that they should not speak in the name of Jesus; and let them go. The third place in which scourgings are mentioned, is the sixth chapter of the second Epistle to the Corinthians (v. 15.) St. Paul in that Chapter places *Stripes* among the different methods of persecution which were used against the ministers of the Gospel; and he moreover relates the sufferings to which he himself had been exposed. *Of the Jews five times received I forty stripes save one*: and in the next verse he says, *Thrice was I beaten with rods, once was I stoned, thrice I suffered shipwreck; a night and a day I have been in the deep.* Fifthly, in his Epistle to the Hebrews (xi. 36.) the same Apostle says, speaking in general terms, *And others had trials of cruel mockings and scourgings, yea, moreover of bonds and imprisonments.* Now, from all these passages no authority whatever can be derived to justify the practice of voluntary flagellation. All the persecuted persons above-mentioned suffered those beatings with rods, and those scourgings, much against their will.

The sixth and last passage in which whipping is mentioned, in the New Testament, is therefore the only one from which any specious conclusion may be drawn in support of the practice of voluntary flagellation: it is contained in the first Epiftle to the Corinthians (ix. 22); St. Paul in it fays, *I chaftife my body, and keep it under fubjection.* Indeed this paffage is well worth examining attentively. Several men of great authority have given it as their opinion, that the Apoftle exprefsly meant to fay, by the above words, that it was his practice to lafh himfelf, in order to overcome his vicious inclinations. Among others, James Gretzer, an able Theologian and one of the Fathers Jefuits, vehemently afferts that the Greek words in the text literally fignify, " I imprint on my own body the ftripes or " marks of the whip, and render it livid by " dint of blows;" and the fame Father fupports his affertion by the authority of *Septalius* and *Guaftininius,* two celebrated Interpreters of Ariftotle, who, in their Commentaries, quote *Gallienus* as having ufed the Greek word in queftion (ὑπωπιαζω) in the fame fenfe which he (Father Gretzer) attributes to St. Paul. To thefe authorities Gretzer moreover adds thofe of St. Irenæus, St. Chryfoftom, Paulinus, and Theophylactus, who (he fays) have all explained the above paffage in the fame manner as himfelf does: fo that, if we were to credit all the comments of Father Gretzer, there would, indeed, remain little doubt but that St, Paul meant to fay, he fuftigated himfelf with his own hands; and that he was thereby left an example which all faithful Chriftians ought in duty to imitate.

But yet, if, fetting afide, for the prefent, all authorities on this head, we begin with examining attentively into the real meaning of the Greek word which is the fubject of the prefent controverfy, we fhall fee that it cannot have that fignification which Father Gretzer pretends.   In fact, let us examine if that word occurs in any other place of the New Teftament, and in what fenfe it is employed. We meet with it in the eighteenth Chapter of St. Luke, wherein Jefus Chrift fays, in the manner of a Parable, that a Widow ufed to teaze a Judge with her frequent complaints, who was thereby compelled at laft to do her juftice; and he makes him fpeak in the following words: " Becaufe this Widow trou-
" bles me, I will avenge her, left by her con-
" tinual coming, fhe *weary* me (ὑπωπιάζῃ
" μέ.)   Now, who can imagine that this Judge entertained any fear that the Woman fhould flagellate him? Yet, we muft think fo, if the Greek word ufed in the Text (which is the very fame as that employed by St. Paul, and on which Father Gretzer builds his fyftem)

fhould always fignify, as that Father pretends, to beat, or lafh. If a literal explanation of that word, therefore, is in many cafes improper and ridiculous, it follows that it is frequently to be underftood in a figurative fenfe, and that it is then only employed to exprefs that kind of hard ufage either of one's felf, or of others, which is exercifed without any mixture of real violence, or bodily fufferings. To this add, that St. Paul himfelf, when, on other occafions he really means to fpeak of blows and actual ftripes, never once makes ufe of the word in queftion.

Befides, if in order rightly to underftand the meaning of St. Paul, we confult the holy Fathers and Interpreters (which certainly is a very good method of inveftigating the truth), we fhall fcarcely find one who thought that St. Paul either beat or lafhed himfelf, and in the above paffage meant to fpeak of any fuch thing as voluntary Flagellation. St. Iræneus, Bifhop of Lyons, though he has tranflated the words in queftion into thefe, " *I chaftife my own body, and render it livid,*" has made no mention whatever of either fcourges, whips, or rods.—St. Chryfoftom likewife fuppofes, that the Apoftle in the above paffage, only fpoke of the pains and care he took, in order to preferve

his temperance, and conquer the paffions of
the flefh ; and that it was the fame as if he had
faid, " I fubmit to much labour, in order to
" live according to the rules of Temperance.
" I undergo every kind of hardfhip, rather
" than fuffer myfelf to be led aftray" It muft
be confeffed, however, that Benedictus Haeftenus, in his *Difquifitiones Monafticæ*, quotes a
paffage from the above Author's 34th Homily,
by which he pretends to prove that felf-flagellations were in ufe in that Father's time ; but
the words which Haeftenus has quoted in Latin are not to be found in the original Greek
of St. Chryfoftom's Homilies, and are therefore
to be attributed to fome modern Flogging-
Mafter (Μαςιγοφόρος) who has lent them to him,
by a kind of pious fraud. Other paffages to
prove our affertion, might be quoted from the
words of Theodoret, Bifhop of Cyrus, of Oe-
cumenius, as well as feveral other Greek Fathers.

The Latin have alfo underftood St. Paul's
words in the fame fenfe that the Greek Fathers
have done. Indeed I do not find one among
them but who thought that St. Paul did not
actually lafh himfelf with his own hands. St.
Ambrofius, Bifhop of Milan, expreffes himfelf
on the fubject in the following words. ' He

' who fays (meaning St. Paul) I chaftife my
' body, and bring it into fubjection, does not
' fo much *grieve (contriftatur)* for his own
' fins, which after all could not be fo very nu-
' merous, as for ours.'

St. Fulgentius, Bifhop of Rufpe, and an
illuftrious Difcipline of St. Auguftin, on this
occafion treads in the footfteps of his excellent Mafter, giving the fame fenfe as him to
the words of St. Paul. The following is the
manner in which St. Fulgentius explains thofe
words, in his Epiftle *on Virginity*, addreffed to
Proba. " The fpiritual Spoufe of Virgins
" does not feek in a Virgin a body practifed
" in carnal pleafures; but rather wifhes fhe
" fhould have chaftifed it by abftinence. This,
" the Doctor of the Gentiles ufed to practife
" on his own body. *I chaftife* (fays he) *my*
" *body, and keep it under fubjection.* And
" again, *in watchings often, in thirft and hun-*
" *ger, in faftings often:* let therefore the Vir-
" gin of Chrift forbear to feek after pleafures
" which, fhe fees, are equally with-held from
" the widow."

To all the above proofs, I know it will be
objected that St. Petrus Chryfologus, archbifhop of Ravenna, is clearly of opinion that
St. Paul lafhed himfelf with his own hands.

The following is the manner in which he expreſſes himſelf on this head, at leaſt if we are
to credit the account given of his words by
that great Patron of flagellations, Father
Gretzer, in his Book printed at Ingolſtadt in
the year 1609. " This St. Paul uſed to do,
" who wrote in the following words the title-
" deed of his own Servitude, *I render my bo-*
" *dy livid, and bring it into ſubjection :* like a
" faithful Slave, himſelf ſupplied the rod,
" *(vindictam)* and ſeverely laſhed his own
" back, till it grew livid *." Now, who
would not from theſe words, thus ſtanding
alone, as Father Gretzer recites them, conclude
that St. Paul really uſed to cover his back
with ſtripes ? But, if we conſult the original
itſelf, we ſhall ſee that St. Chryſologus meant
no more than to borrow a ſimile from the puniſhment uſually inflicted on Slaves; which
puniſhment he mentions in the beginning of
the very paſſage we diſcuſs here, and of which
Father Gretzer has artfully quoted only the
concluſion. " After all (ſays *Peter Chryſo-*

---

* *Hoc implebat* Paulus, *qui ſervitutis ſuæ titulos
ſic ſcribebat.* Lividum facio corpus meum, & ſer-
vituti ſubjicio. *Præbebat vindictam bonus ſervus,
qui ſe ſque ad livorem. ſic agens, jugiter verberabat.*

" *logus*) if the Servant does not awake early
" the next day, and rife before his Mafter,
" whether he be weary or not, he will be tied
" up and laffied.   If the Servant therefore
" knows what he owes to another Man, the
" Mafter is thence taught what himfelf owes
" to the Lord of Lords, and is made fenfible
" that he alfo is fubject to a Mafter."   ' This
' is what St. Paul practifed, who wrote the
' title-deeds of his own fervitude, and ex-
' pofed himfelf to thirft, hunger, and naked-
' nefs.   Like a good flave, he himfelf fup-
' plied the rod, and feverely lafhed himfelf.'

If we examine into the works of St. Hie-
rom, St. Auftin, Pope Gregory the Great,
and other Latin Fathers, we fhall find that
they alfo underftood, that St. Paul had expreffed himfelf in a figurative manner.   And
it is only by mifquotations, or arts of the
like kind, that Father Gretzer, Cardinal De-
mian, and others, have attempted to prove
that felf-flagellations were in ufe fo early as the
time of St. Paul among Chriftians.

CHAP. IV. .

The ufe of Flagellations was known among the ancient Heathens. Several facts and obfervations on that fubject.

IT is not to be doubted, that flagellations had been invented, and were become, in early times, a common method of punifhment in the Pagan world. Even before the foundation of Rome, we meet with inftances which prove that it was the ufual punifhment inflicted on Slaves. Juftin, in his Epitome of Trogus Pompeius, relates that the Scythians more ea-fily overcame their rebellious Slaves with fcourges and whips, than with their fwords. ' The Scythians being returned (fays Juftin) ' from their third expedition in Afia, after ' having been abfent eight years from their ' Wives and Children, found they now had a ' war to wage at home againft their own ' Slaves. For, their Wives, tired with fuch ' long fruitlefs expectation of their Hufbands, ' and concluding that they were no longer de- ' tained by war, but had been deftroyed, mar-

E

‘ ried the Slaves who had been left to take
‘ care of the cattle ; which latter attempted to
‘ ufe their Mafters, who returned victorious,
‘ like Strangers, and hinder them, by force of
‘ arms, from entering the Country.　The war
‘ having been fupported, for a while, with
‘ fuccefs pretty nearly equal on both fides, the
‘ Scythians were advifed to change their man-
‘ ner of carrying it on, remembering that it
‘ was not with enemies, but with their own
‘ Slaves, that they had to fight ; that they
‘ were to conquer by dint, not of arms, but
‘ of their right as Mafters ; that inftead of
‘ weapons, they ought to bring lafhes into the
‘ field, and, fetting iron afide, to fupply them-
‘ felves with rods, fcourges, and fuch like in-
‘ ftruments of flavifh fear.　Having approved
‘ this counfel, the Scythians armed themfelves
‘ as they were advifed to do ; and had no
‘ fooner come up with their enemies, than
‘ they exhibited on a fudden their new wea-
‘ pons, and thereby ftruck fuch a terror into
‘ their minds, that thofe who could not be
‘ conquered by arms, were fubdued by the
‘ dread of the ftripes, and betook themfelves
‘ to flight, not like a vanquifhed enemy, but
‘ like fugitive flaves.’

Among the antient Perfians, the punifhment of whipping was alfo in ufe : it was even

frequently inflicted on the Grandees of the Kingdom by order of the King, as we find in *Stobæus*, who moreover relates in his forty-second Difcourfe, ' That when one of them ' had been flagellated by order of the King, ' it was an eftablifhed cuftom, that he fhould ' give him thanks as for an excellent fa- ' vour he had received, and a token that the ' King remembered him.' This cuftom of the Perfians was however in fubfequent times altered : they began to fet fome more value on the fkin of Men ; and we find in Plutarch's *Apophthegms of Kings*, ' That Artaxerxes, fon ' of Xerxes, firnamed the *Longhanded*, was ' the firft who ordered that the Grandees of ' his kingdom fhould no longer be expofed to ' the former method of punifhment; but ' that, when they fhould have been guilty of ' fome offence, inftead of their backs, only their ' clothes fhould be whipped, after they had ' been ftripped of them.'

We alfo find, that it was a cuftom in antient times, for Generals and Conquerors, to flog the Captives they had taken in war; and that they moreover took delight in inflicting that punifhment with their own hands on the moft confiderable of thofe Captives. We meet, among others, with a very remarkable proof of this practice, in the Tragedy of So-

phocles, called *Ajax Scourgebearer* (Μαςιγοφόρος) : in a Scene of this Tragedy Ajax is introduced as having the following converfation
with Minerva.

MINERVA.

‘ What kind of feverity do you prepare for
‘ that miferable man ?’

AJAX.

‘ I propofe to lafh his back with a fcourge
‘ till he dies.’

MINERVA.

‘ Nay, do not whip the poor Wretch fo
‘ cruelly.’

AJAX.

‘ Give me leave, Minerva, to gratify, on
‘ this occafion, my own fancy; he fhall have
‘ it, I do affure you, and I prepare no other
‘ punifhment for him.’

The punifhment of flagellation was alfo
much in vogue among the Romans ; and it
was the common chaftifement which Judges
inflicted upon Offenders, efpecially upon thofe
of a fervile condition. Surrounded by an apparatus of whips, fcourges, and leather-ftraps,
they terrified Offenders, and brought them to
a fenfe of their duty.

4

Judges, among the Romans, as has been just now mentioned, used a great variety of instruments for inflicting the punishment of whipping. Some consisted of a flat strap of leather, and were called *Ferulæ*; and to be lashed with these *Ferulæ*, was considered as the mildest degree of punishment. Others were made of a number of cords of twisted parchment, and were called *Scuticæ*. These *Scuticæ* were considered as being a degree higher in point of severity than the *ferulæ*, but were much inferior, in that respect, to that kind of scourge which was called *Flagellum*, and sometimes *the terrible Flagellum*, which was made of thongs of ox-leather, the same as those which Carmen used for their Horses. We find in the third Satyr of the first Book of *Horace*, a clear and pretty singular account of the gradation in point of severity that obtained between the above-mentioned instruments of whipping. In this Satyr, Horaee lays down the rules which he thinks a Judge ought to follow in the discharge of his office; and he addressed himself, somewhat ironically, to certain persons who, adopting the principles of the Stoics, affected much severity in their opinions, and pretended that all crimes whatever being equal, ought to be punished in the same manner. ' Make such a rule of conduct to

E 3.

' yourself (fays Horace) that you may always
' proportion the chaftifement you inflict to the
' magnitude of the offence; and when the
' Offender only deferves to be chaftifed with
' the whip of twifted parchment, do not ex-
' pofe him to the lafh of the horrid leather
' fcourge; for, that you fhould only inflict
' the punifhment of the flat ftrap on him who
' deferves a more fevere lafhing, is what I am
' by no means afraid of *.'

The choice between thefe different kinds of
inftruments, was, as we may conclude from
the above paffage, left to the Judge, who ordered that to be ufed which he was pleafed
to name; and the number of blows was
likewife left to his difcretion; which fometimes were as many as the Executioner could
give. ' He (fays Horace in one of his Odes)
' who has been lafhed by order of the Trum-
' virs, till the Executioner was fpent †.'

* ———— Adfit
Regula peccatis quæ pœnas irroget æquas,
Nec Scuticâ dignum horribili fectere Flagello,
Nam, ut Ferulâ cædas meritum majora fubire
Verbera, non vereor. Lib. I. Sat. I. v. 117.

† Sectus flagellis hic Triumviralibus
Præconis ad faftidium. Lib. V. Ode IV. v. 11,12

Besides this extensive power of whipping exercised by Judges among the Romans, over persons of a servile condition, over Aliens, and those who were the subjects of the Republic, Masters were possessed of an unbounded one with regard to their Slaves, over whose life and death they had moreover an absolute power. Hence a great number of instruments of flagellation, besides those above-mentioned, were successively brought into use for punishing Slaves. Among those were particular kinds of cords manufactured in Spain, as we learn from a passage in an Ode of Horace, the same that has just been quoted, and was addressed to one *Menas*, a freed-man, who had found means to acquire a great fortune, and was grown very insolent. ' Thou (says ' Horace) whose sides are still discoloured (or ' burnt) with the stripes of the Spanish ' cords *.'

A number of other instances of this practice of whipping Slaves, as well as other different names of instruments used for that purpose, may be found in the antient Latin Writers, such as Plautus, Terence, Horace, Martial, &c. So prevalent had the above prac-

---

* *Iberitis per uste funibus latus.*

Lib. V. Ode IV. v. 3.

E 4

tice become, that Slaves were frequently denominated from that particular kind of flagellation which they were moft commonly made
to undergo.   Some were called *Reftiones*, becaufe they were ufed to be lafhed with cords ;
others were called *Bucædæ*, becaufe they were
ufually lafhed with thongs of ox-leather; and
it is in confequence of this cuftom, that a
Man is made to fay in one of Plautus's Plays,
' They fhall be *Bucædæ* (that is to fay, fcourg-
' ed with leather-thongs) whether they will or
' no, before I confent to be *Reftio*,' or fo
much as beaten with cords *.   And Tertullian, meaning in one of his Writings to exprefs Slaves in general, ufes words which fim-
ply fignify ' thofe who are ufed to be beaten,
' or to be difcoloured with blows †.'

---

* *Erunt Bucædæ invitò, potius quàm ego fim Reftio.*   Moftell. Act. IV. Sc. II.

† *Verberones, Subverbuftos.*—The latter word
literally fignifies, *burnt with blows* · a figurative
expreffion commonly ufed among the Romans,
when they fpoke of flagellations : thus, the words
flagrum and *flagellum*, had been derived from the
word *flagrare*, which fignifies *to burn*, and Horace,
in a paffage that will be quoted in page 66, fays,
to be burnt with rods *(virgis uri)* for, *to be lafhed.*

Nay, so generally were whipping and lash-
ing confidered among the Romans, as being
the lot of Slaves, that a whip, or a fcourge,
was become among them the emblem of their
condition. Of this we have an inftance in the
fingular cuftom mentioned by *Camerarius*,
which prevailed among them, of placing in
the triumphal car, behind the Triumpher, a
man with a whip in his hand ; the meaning of
which was to fhew, that it was no impoffible
thing for a Man to fall from the higheft pitch
of glory into the moft abject condition, even
into that of a Slave.

Suetonius alfo relates a fact which affords
another remarkable inftance of this notion of
the Romans, of looking upon a whip as a
characteriftic mark of dominion on the one
hand, and of flavery on the other. ' Cicero
' (fays Suetonius, in the life of Auguftus)
' having accompanied Cæfar to the Capitol,
' related to a few friends whom he met there,
' a dream which he had had the night before.
' It feemed to him, he faid, that a graceful
' Boy came down from Heaven, fufpended
' by a golden chain ; that he ftopped before
' the gate of the Capitol, and that Jupiter
' gave him a whip (*flagellum*). Having af-
' terwards fuddenly feen Auguftus, whom (as
' he was ftill perfonally unknown to feveral of

' his near relations) Cæfar had fent for and
' brought along with him to be prefent at the
' ceremony, he affured his friends that he was
' the very perfon whofe figure he had feen
' during his fleep.' Juvenal likewife, in one
of his Satyrs, has fpoken of Auguftus conformably to the above notion of the Romans.
' The fame (fays he) who, after conquering
' the Romans, has fubjcćted them to his
' whip *.'

* *Ad fua qui domitos diduxit flagra Quirites.*

Juv. Sat. X. v. 99.

This notion of the Romans, of looking upon
a fcourge as a charaćteriftic appendage of dominion, was fo general among them, as is obferved
above, that they moreover fuppofed the gods
themfelves to be fupplied with whips, and even
Venus had alfo been thought to be furnifhed with
one. In confequence of this fuppofition, Horace,
who, as we may conclude from thence, had caufe
to be diffatisfied with fome trick his Miftrefs had
played him, or perhaps only with her impertinence
in general, defires Venus to chaftife her with her
whip, " Do, Queen, (fays he, addreffing Venus)
" do, for once, give arrogant Chloe a touch with
" your fublime whip."

Regina, fublimi flagello
Tange Chloen femel arrogantem.

Od. 26. Lib. III. ad Ven.

But, befides all thofe inftruments of flagellation ufed for punifhing Slaves, which have been mentioned above, and as if the terrible *flagellum* had not been of itfelf fufficiently fo, new contrivances were ufed to make the latter a ftill more cruel weapon; and the thongs with which that kind of fcourge was made, were frequently armed with nails, or fmall hard bones. They alfo would fometimes faften to thofe thongs fmall leaden weights: hence fcourges were fometimes called *Aftragala*, as Hefychius relates, from the name of thofe kinds of weights which the Ancients ufed to wear hanging about their fhoes. Under the tortures which thofe different inftruments inflicted, it was no wonder that Slaves fhould die: indeed this was a frequent cafe; and the cruelty, efpecially of Miftreffes towards their female Slaves, grew at laft fo fuch a pitch, that a provifion was made in the Council of Elvira to reftrain it; and it was ordained, that if any Miftrefs fhould caufe her Slave to be whipped with fo much cruelty as that fhe fhould die, the Miftrefs fhould be fufpended from Communion for a certain number of years. The following are the terms of the above Ordinance, in the fifth Canon. " If a Miftrefs, in a fit of anger and madnefs, fhall

lash her female Slave, or cause her to be lashed, in such a mnner that she expires before
the third day, by reason of the torture she has
undergone; inasmuch as it is doubtful whether it has designedly happened, or by chance;
if it has designedly happened, the Mistress
shall be excommunicated for seven years; if
by chance, she shall be excommunicated for
five years only; though, if she shall fall into
sickness, she may receive the Communion *."

∗ The absolute dominion possessed by Masters
over the persons of their slaves, led them to use a
singular severity in the government of them. So
frequently were flagellations the lot of the latter,
that appellations and words of reproach drawn
from that kind of punishment, were, as hath been
above observed, commonly used to denominate
them, and expressions of this kind occur in the
politest writers: thus, we find in the Plays of Terence, an Author particularly celebrated for his
politeness and strict observance of decorum, Slaves
frequently called by the words *Verberones*, *Fla-
griones*, or others to the same effect.

As for Plautus, who had been the Servant of a
Baker, and who was much acquainted with every
thing that related to Slaves, and their flagellations
in particular, he has filled his scenes with nick-

names of Slaves, drawn from this latter circumstance; and they are almoft continually called in
his Plays, *flagritribæ* (a verbis, *flagrum* & *terere*)
plagipatidæ, *ulmitribæ*, &c. befides the appellations
of *Bucædæ* and *Reftiones*, above-mentioned.

Sometimes the flagellations of Slaves, or the
fear they entertained of incurring them, ferved
Plautus as incidents for the conduct of his plots;
thus, in his *Epidicus*, a Slave who is the principal
character in the Play, concludes upon a certain
occafion, that his Mafter has difcovered his whole
fcheme, becaufe he has fpied him, in the morning, purchafing a new fcourge at the fhop in
which they were fold. The fame flagellations
in general, have moreover been an inexhauftible
fund of pleafantry for Plautus. In one place, for
inftance, a Slave, intending to laugh at a fellow-
flave, afks him how much he thinks he weighs,
when he is fufpended naked, by his hands, to the
beam, with an hundred weight (*centupondium*) tied
to his feet; which ·was a precaution taken, as
Commentators inform us, in order to prevent the
Slave who was flagellated from kicking the Man
(*Virgator*) whofe office it was to perform the operation. And in another place, Plautus, alluding
to the thongs of ox-leather with which whips were
commonly made, introduces a Slave engaged in
deep reflection on the furprizing circumftance of

" dead bullocks, that make incurfions upon living Men."

Vivos homines mortui incurfant boves !

But it was not always upon their Slaves only that Mafters, among the Romans, inflicted the punifhment of flagellation · they fometimes found means to ferve in the fame manner the young Men of free condition, who infinuated themfelves into their houfes, with a defign to court their Wives. As the moft favourable difguife on fuch occafions, was to be dreffed in Slaves clothes, becaufe a Man thus habited was enabled to get into the houfe, and go up and down without being noticed, Rakes engaged in amorous purfuits, ufually chofe to make ufe of it, but, when the Hufband either happened to difcover them, or had had previous information of the appointment given by his faith- ful Spoufe, he feigned to miftake the Man for a run-away Slave, or fome ftrange Slave who had got into his houfe to commit theft, and treated him accordingly. Indeed the opportunity was a moft favourable one for revenge ; and if to this confideration we add that of the fevere temper of the Romans, and the jealous difpofition that has always prevailed in that country, we fhall eafily conclude that fuch an opportunity, when obtain- ed, was feldom fuffered to efcape, and that many a Roman Spark, caught in the above difguife, and engaged in the laudable purfuit of feducing his

2

neighbour's wife, has, with a *centupondium* to his feet, been fadly rewarded for his ingenuity. A misfortune of that kind actually befell Salluft the Hiftorian. He was caught in a familiar intercourfe with Fauftina, wife to Milo, and daughter of the Dictator Sylla. The hufband caufed him to be foundly lafhed (*loris bene cæfum*), nor did he releafe him till he had made him pay a confiderable fum of money. The fact is related by Aulus Gellius, who had extracted it from Varro. To it was very probably owing the violent part which Salluft afterwards took againft Milo, while the latter was under profecution for flaving the Tribune Clodius, and the tumult he raifed on that occafion, which prevented Cicero from delivering the fpeech he had prepared.

An allufion is made to the above practices in one of Horace's Satyrs. He fuppofes in it, that his Slave, availing himfelf of the opportunity of the *Saturnalia*, to fpeak his mind freely to him, gives him a lecture on the bad courfes in which he thinks him engaged, and ufes, among others, the following arguments.

‘ When you have ftripped off the marks of
‘ your dignity, your equeftrian ring, and your
‘ whole Roman drefs, and from a Man invefted
‘ with the office of Judge, fhew yourfelf at once
‘ under the appearance of the Slave Dama, dif-

' graced as you are, and hiding your perfumed
' head under your cloak, you are not the Man
' whom you feign to be : you are at leaft intro-
' duced full of terror, and your whole frame
' fhakes through the ftruggles of two oppofite paf-
' fions. In fact, what advantage is it to you,
' whether you are cut to pieces with rods, or
' flaughtered with iron weapons ?'

Tu cum projectis infignibus, annulo Equeftri
Romanoque habitu, prodis ex judice Dama,
Turpis, odoratum caput obfcurante lacernâ
Non es quod fimulas ; metuens induceris, atque
Altercante libidinibus tremis offa pavore.
Quid refert uri virgis, ferroque necari ?

Lib. II. Sat. 7.

The above uncontrouled power of inflicting
punifhments on their Slaves, enjoyed by Mafters
in Rome, was at laft abufed by them to the greateft degree. The fmalleft faults committed in their
families by Slaves, fuch as breaking glaffes, fea
foning difhes too much, or the like, expofed them
to grievous punifhments ; and it even was no un-
ufual thing for Mafters (as we may judge from the
defcription of *Trimalcion's* entertainment in the
Satire of Petronius) to order fuch of their Slaves
as had been guilty of faults of the above kind, to
be ftripped, and whipped in the prefence of their
guefts, when they happened to enteitain any at
their houfes.

Women in particular feem to have abufed this power of flagellation in a ftrange manner; which caufed expiefs provifions to be made, at different times, in order to reftrain them, of which the Canon above-quoted is an inftance.   It was often fufficient, to induce the Roman Ladies to caufe their Slaves to be whipped, that they were diffatisfied with the prefent ftate of their own charms; or, as Juvenal expreffes it, that their nofe difpleafed them. and when they happened to fancy themfelves neglected by their hufbands, then indeed their Slaves fared badly.   This latter obfervation of Juvenal, Dryden, in his tranflation of that Author's Satires, has expreffed by the following lines :

‘ For, if over night the hufband has been flack, ⎫
‘ Or counterfeited fleep, or turn'd his back,   ⎬
‘ Next day, be fure, the fervants go to wrack.’ ⎭

Here follows the literal tranflation of the paffage of Juvenal, in which he defcribes in a very lively manner, the havock which an incenfed Woman ufually made on the above occafion.   " If " her hufband has, the night before, turned his " back on her, woe to her waiting Woman, " the dreffing Maids lay down their tunicks; " the errand Slave is charged with having return-

F

" ed too late; the ſtraps break on the back of
" ſome , others redden under the laſh of the lea-
" ther ſcourge, and others, of the twiſted parch-
" ment."

Si noƈte maritus
Averſus jacuit, periit Libraria , ponunt
Coſmetæ tunicas; tardè veniſſe Liburnus
Dicitur ; hic frangit ferulas , rubet ille flagellis,
Hic ſcuticâ.　　　　　　　　　　Juv. Sat. VI.

The wantonneſs of power was carried ſtill farther by the Roman Ladies, if we may credit the
ſame Juvenal It was a cuſtomary thing with ſeveral among them, when they propoſed to have
their hair dreſſed both with nicety and expedition,
to have the dreſſing Maid who was charged with
that care, ſtripped naked to the waiſt, ready for
flagellation, in caſe ſhe became guilty of any fault
or miſtake, in performing her taſk. The following is the paſſage in Juvenal on that ſubjeƈt. " For,
" if ſhe has determined to be dreſſed more nicely
" than uſual, and is in haſte, being expeƈted in
" the public gardens, the unfortunate Pſecha*s*
" then dreſſes her head, with her own hair in the
" utmoſt diſorder, and her ſhoulders and breaſts
" bare. Why is that ringlet too high ?—The
" leather thongs inſtantly puniſh the crime of a
" hair, and an ill-ſhaped curl."

Nam fi conftituit folitoque decentiùs optat
Ornari & properat, jamque expectatur in hortis,
Componit crinem, laceratis ipfa capillis,
Nuda humeros, Pfechas infœlix, nudifque mamillis:
Altior hic quare cicinnus ? taurea punit
Continuà flexi crimen, facinufque capilli.

These abuses which Masters, in Rome, made of the power they poffeffed over their Slaves, were at laft carried by them to fuch a pitch, either by making them wantonly fuffer death, or torturing them in numberlefs different ways, that, in the beginning of the reign of the Emperors, it was found neceffary to reftrain their licence.

Under the reign of Claudius (for it is not clear whether any provifion to that effect was made under Auguftus) it was ordained, that Mafters who forfook their Slaves when fick, fhould lofe all right over them, in cafe they recovered; and that thofe who deliberately put them to death, fhould be banifhed from Rome.

Under the Emperor Adrian, the cruelties exercifed by *Umbricia*, a Roman Lady, over her female Slaves, caufed new laws to be made on that fubject, as well as the former ones to be put in force, and Umbricia was, by a *refcript* of the Emperor, banifhed for five years. *(l. 2. in fine, Dig. L. I. t. 6.)*

New laws to the fame ends were likewife made under the following Emperors, among which Civilians make particular mention of a *conſtitution* of Antonius Pius *(Divus Pius)* ; and in ſubſequent times, the Church alſo employed its authority to prevent the like exceſſes, as we may ſee from the Canon above-recited *(Si quæ domina*, &c) which was framed in the Council held at Elvira, a ſmall Town in Spain, that has been ſince deſtroyed. But the diſorder was of ſuch a nature as was not to be cured ſo long as the cuſtom itſelf of ſlavery was allowed to ſubſiſt ; and it has been remedied at laſt, only by the thorough abolition of an uſage which was a continual inſult on Humanity . an advantage which (to be, once at leaſt, very ſerious in the courſe of this learned and uſeful Work) we are indebted for, to the eſtabliſhment of Chriſtianity, whatever other evils certain Writers may reproach it with having occaſioned.

CHAP. V.

The subject continued.

THE punishment of flagellation was thought among the Antient Heathens, as we have just seen, to possess great efficacy to mend the morals of persons convicted of offences, and insure the honesty and diligence of Slaves. Nor were Schoolmasters behind-hand either with Judges or Masters, in regard to whipping those persons who were subjected to their authority.

Of this we have an undoubted proof in one of the Epistles of Horace ; and it moreover appears that he had had, when at school, the bad luck of being himself under the tuition of one who had strong inclination to inflict that kind of chastisement. ' I remember ' (says he) that the flogging *Orbilius*, who ' when I was a boy, used to dictate to us the ' verses of Livius Andronicus—.'

* . . . . *Memini quæ plagosum mihi parvo*
    Orbilium dictare.—Lib. II. Ep. 1. v. 70.

F 3

Quintilian has alſo mentioned this practice of Schoolmaſters of whipping their Diſciples; and the ſeverity which they uſed, as well as other conſiderations, induced him to diſapprove of it intirely. The following are his expreſſions on that ſubject. ' With reſpect to
' whipping School-boys, though it be an eſta-
' bliſhed practice, and Chryſippus is not averſe
' to it, yet I do not in any degree approve it.
' Firſt, it is a baſe and ſlaviſh treatment; and
' certainly if it were not for the youth of thoſe
' who are made to ſuffer, it might be deem-
' ed an injury that might call for redreſs.
' Beſides, if a Diſciple is of ſuch a mean
' diſpoſition that he is not mended by cen-
' ſures, he will, like a bad Slave, grow equal-
' ly inſenſible to blows. Laſtly, if Maſters
' acted as they ought, there would be no oc-
' caſion for chaſtiſement; but the negligence
' of Teachers is now ſo great, that, inſtead
' of cauſing their Diſciples to do what they
' ought, they content themſelves with puniſh-
' ing them for not having done it. Beſides,
' though you may compel the obedience of a
' Boy, by uſing the rod, what will you do with
' a young Man, to whom motives of a quite
' different nature muſt be propoſed? Not to
' add, that ſeveral dangerous accidents which
' are not fit to be named, may be occaſioned

‘ either by the fear or the pain attending ſuch
‘ puniſhments. Indeed, if great care is not
‘ taken in chooſing Teachers of proper diſ-
‘ poſitions, I am aſhamed to ſay to what de-
‘ gree they will ſometimes abuſe their power
‘ of·laſhing: but I ſhall dwell no longer on
‘ that ſubject, concerning which the Public
‘ knows already too much *.’

After theſe diſmal accounts of Diſciples
flogged by their Teachers, and of the cruel
ſeverity uſed by the latter, the Reader will
not certainly be diſpleaſed to read inſtances of
Teachers who were flogged by their Diſciples.

A very remarkable inſtance of this kind
occurs in the caſe of that Schoolmaſter of the
Town of *Falerii*, who is mentioned in the
fifth Book of the Decad of Livy. The Town
of *Falerii* being beſieged by the Romans, under the command of the Dictator Camillus,
a Schoolmaſter in that Town, thinking he
would be ſplendidly rewarded for his ſervice,
one day led, by treachery, and under pretence
of making them take a ſhort walk out of the

---

* . . . . “ *Jam ſi minor in diligendis cuſtodum &*
præceptorum moribus fuit cura, pudet dicere in qua
proba nefandi homines iſto jure cædendi abutantur;
non morabor in parte hac, nimium eſt quod intelligi-
tur.”—Inſtitut. Orat. Lib. I. Cap. 3.

F 4

gates of the Town, the children of the moſt
conſiderable families, who had been entruſted
to his care, to the Roman camp, and delivered them up to the Dictator.   But the latter, incenſed at his perfidy, ordered him to be
ſtripped naked, with his hands tied behind
his back, and having ſupplied the children
with rods, gave the Schoolmaſter up to them,
to drive him back in that condition to their
Town *.

Another inſtance of the like kind is alſo to
be met with in more modern times.   The
Tutor's name was _Sadrageſillus_, and his Diſ-
ciple was _Dagobert_, ſon of _Clotaire_, King of
France, who reigned about the year of Jeſus
Chriſt, 526.   The tranſaction is related in the

* " _Denudari deinde Ludi-magiſtrum juſſit, eum-
que pueris tradidit reducendum Falerios, manibus poſt
tergum illigatis; virgas quoque eis dedit, quibus pro-
ditorem agerent in urbem verberantes._"

The inhabitants of _Falerii_ were ſo ſtruck with
the juſt conduct of the Dictator (Livy adds) that
a total change of their diſpoſitions towards the
Romans was the conſequence, and the Senate
having been aſſembled thereupon by the Magiſtrates, they came to the reſolution of opening their
gates, and ſurrendering to the Romans; which
was ſoon after effected.

following manner by *Robert Gaguin*, in his
History of France. ‘ Dagobert (fays he)
‘ having received from his Father a Tutor
‘ who was to inftruct him in the worldly fci-
‘ ences, and whom the King had made Duke
‘ of Aquitain, the young Man, who did not
‘ want parts for one of his years, foon per-
‘ ceived that *Sadragefillus* (fuch was the Pe-
‘ dagogue's name) was much elated with
‘ pride on account of his newly-acquired dig-
‘ nity, fo that he began to fail in the refpect
‘ he owed to him, and grew remifs in the
‘ difcharge of his duty. The Prince having
‘ once invited him to dine with him, and Sa-
‘ dragefillus having not only placed himfelf
‘ at table oppofite the Prince, but alfo offered
‘ to take the cup from him as if he had been
‘ his companion, the Prince ordered him to
‘ be foundly whipped with rods, and caufed
‘ his beard, which he wore very long, to be
‘ cut off.’ The above fact is alfo related
by *Tilly*, Scrivener of the Parliament of Paris, in his *Chronicles* of the Kings of France.

In fine, to the paffages above-produced
concerning the Flagellations of Children,
from which we find that very great men have
much differed in their opinions in regard to
them, we may add, that King Solomon, that

Oracle of Wifdom, has, without referve, declared in favour of that mode of correction.
‘ He that fpareth the rod, hateth his fon ;
‘ but he that loves him, chaftifes him be-
‘ times.’ The Greek Philofopher Chryfippus has afterwards manifefted the fame opinion. And Petrarch, who may be called
here a modern Author, has alfo adopted the
opinion of King Solomon ; and, notwithftanding Quintilian’s arguments on the fubject,
has fided with the antient Moralift and Sage .
“ Correct your fon (fays Petrarch) in his
“ tender years, nor fpare the rod : a branch,
“ when young, may eafily be bent at your
“ pleafure *.”

----

* From the above-mentioned paffages of king
Solomon, Livy, and other antient authors, down
to Petrarch, we may fafely conclude that the practice of flagellating children has been followed in
the world during a number of fucceffive centuries ,
and we know from undoubted authorities, that
the fame practice continues in our days to prevail,
efpecially among Schoolmafters. Nay more, very
refpectable Writers inform us, that Schoolmafters
ftill poffefs the fame ftrong inclination to excit
their authority that way, as they did in the times
of Horace and Quintilian.

Thus, Mr. *Henry Fielding*, a Writer who, better than moft others, knew the manners of Men, in his *Hiftory of a Foundling*, reprefents *Thwackum* the Schoolmafter, as having, upon every occafion, recourfe to his rod, and defcribes him to us as a true fucceffor of the *plagofus Orbilius.*

Mr. Gay, another writer, who, too, was deeply verfed in the knowledge of Mankind, expreffes himfelf with ftill more precifion on that head, and lays it down as an undoubted maxim, that the delight of a Schoolmafter is to ufe his whip. The opinion of that Author on the fubject is contained in a fong written by him   this fong was compofed in honour of *Molly Mog*, an Innkeeper's daughter, at Oakingham in Berkfhire : the verfes are fifteen in all , and the name of *Molly Mog* is to be found in each of them, with a rhyme to it.

> The School-boy's defire is a play-day,
>   The Schoolmafter's joy is to flog,
> The milk-maid's delights are on May-day ,
>   But mine are in fweet Molly Mog.

However, the refearches of our Author on the prefent deep fubject, as well as mine in my humble capacity of Commentator, can bear no comparifon, I think, in point of fagacioufnefs, with the difcovery made by Thomas Perez, the Uncle

of Diego, who relates his own hiftory in the third
volume of the Adventures of Gil Blas, and who
takes that occafion to mention the great abilities
of his Uncle as an Antiquary. " If it had not
" been for him (fays he) we fhould ftill be igno-
" rant that children, in Athens, cried when their
" Mothers whipped them."

C H A P. VI.

Flagellations of a religious and voluntary kind were practised among the ancient Heathens.

WE have hitherto only treated of involuntary Flagellations, and such as were in all cases inflicted by force on those who suffered them. But besides Flagellations of this kind, there were others of a voluntary sort among the Heathens, to which those who underwent them, freely and willingly submitted, and which may indeed create our surprise in a much greater degree than the former.

Thus, at Lacedæmon, there was a celebrated Festival, which was kept annually, and was named the *Day of Flagellations*, on account of the ceremony that was performed in it, of whipping before the altar of Diana a number of Boys, who freely submitted to that painful treatment; and this Festival has been mentioned by a great number of Authors.

Plutarch, for instance, in his Book of the *Customs of the Lacedæmonians*, relates, that

he had been an eye-witnefs of the celebration
of the folemnity we fpeak of. ' Boys (fays
' he) are whipped for a whole day, often to
' death, before the altar of Diana the Or-
' thian; and they fuffer it with chearfulnefs,
' and even joy: nay, they ftrive with each
' other for victory; and he who bears up the
' longeft time, and has been able to endure
' the greateft number of ftripes, cairies the
' day. This folemnity is called *The Conteft*
' (or race) *of Flagellations*; and is celebrated
' every year.'

Cicero, in his Tufculana, has alfo mentioned this cuftom of the Lacedæmonians.
' Boys (fays he) at Sparta are lafhed before
' the Altar in fo fevere a manner, that the
' blood iffues from their body. While I was
' there, I feveral times heard it faid that Boys
' had been whipped to death; none of whom
' ever uttered the leaft complaint, or fo much
' as groaned.' And in another place Cicero
likewife fays, ' Boys, at Sparta, utter no
' complaint, though lacerated by repeated
' lafhes.' Nay more; Mozonius, in *Stobæus*,
relates that the Spartan Boys were rather
pleafed with thefe flagellating folemnities.
' The fons of the Lacedæmonians make it
' very evident (fays Mozonius) that ftripes do
' not appear to them either fhameful or hard

' to be borne, fince they allow themfelves to
' be whipped in public, and take a pride
' in it.'

The Scholiaft or Commentator of Thucy-
dides relates the fame things of the Lacedæmonian young men ; and fays that thofe among
them who could bear the greateft number of
lafhes, acquired much glory by it. ' And
' indeed (fays he) the *Flagellations* are per-
' formed at particular times during a certain
' number of days ; and thofe who receive the
' greateft number of ftripes, are accounted
' the moft manly.'

The Parents of the young men who were
thus publickly whipped, were commonly prefent during the performance of the ceremony ;
and fo far were they from difcouraging their
Sons from going through it, that, as Lucian
relates, they deemed it a fhameful piece of
cowardice in them, if they feemed ro yield to
the violence of the lafhes, and in confequence
of this notion they exhorted them to go ftoutly through the whole trial. ' Indeed (conti-
' nues Lucian) a number of them frequently
' died in the *conflict*, thinking it was unwor-
' thy of them, fo long as they continued to
' live, to yield to blows and bodily pain, in
' fight of their friends and relations.' ' And
' to thofe who die upon thofe occafions, Sta-

‘ tues, as you will fee, are erected at Sparta,
‘ in the public places."

Seneca, in his Treatife upon *Providence*,
has alfo mentioned thofe fingular *Flagellations*
which took place at Lacedæmon, as well as
the conduct of the Lacedæmonian Fathers on
thofe occafions. ‘ Do not you think (fays
‘ he) that the Lacedæmonians hate their chil-
‘ dren, who try their tempers by having them
‘ lafhed publickly? Their very Fathers ex-
‘ hort them firmly to bear the lafhes of the
‘ whips; and intreat them, when torn to
‘ pieces and half dead, ftill to continue to of-
‘ fer their wounds to other wounds.’

In fine, with fo much folemnity were the
flagellating ceremonies and trials we mention
performed, that a Prieftefs, as Silenus of
Chios relates, conftantly prefided over them,
holding up a fmall ftatue of the Goddefs in
her hand while the young Men were lafhed;
and, to crown all, Priefts were eftablifhed to
infpect the ftripes and marks of the blows,
and draw omens from them. ‘ I am witnefs
‘ (fays Lucian) that there are Priefts appoint-
‘ ed to infpect the lafhes and ftripes *.’ To

---

* Pag. 1002. Litt. C. μαντικὸς ἦν μαρτύρομαι δὲ, ἢ μὴν
καὶ ἱερέας αὐτῷ ἀποδειχθήσεσθαι μαϲίγων ἢ καυτηρίων.

this it may be added, that thefe extraordinary
ceremonies of the Lacedæmonians, which are
here defcribed, were preferved among them,
notwithftanding the numerous revolutions
which their Republic underwent, to very late
times; and Tertullian mentions them as continuing, in his days, to be regularly celebrated every year. 'For (fays that Author)
'the Feftival of *The Flagellations* is ftill in
'thefe days looked upon as a very great fo-
'lemnity at Lacedæmon. Every body knows
'in what Temple all the young Men of the
'beft families are lafhed in the prefence of
'their Relations and friends, who exhort
'them to bear to the laft this cruel ceremony *.'

Even Philofophers among the Greeks, I
mean particular fects of them, had adopted
the practice of voluntary Flagellation. Lucian relates in one of his Dialogues, that there
were Philofophers in his time, 'who trained
'young Men to endure labour, pain, and
'want; and who made the practice of virtue
'confift in thefe aufterities. A number of

* *Pag.* 158. *Edit. Rig.* *Namque hodiè apud
Lacedæmonas folemnitas maxima eft* διαμασιγωσις, *id
eft, flagellatio. Non latet in quo Sacro ante aram nobiles quique adolefcentes flagellis afficiantur, adftanti-
bus parentibus atque propinquis, & uti perfeverrrirt
adhortantibus.*

' them would bind themſelves; others whip-
' ped themſelves; and thoſe who were the
' moſt tender, flead their outer ſkin with in-
' ſtruments of iron made for that purpoſe.'

However, auſterities of this kind were only practiſed by particular Sects of Philoſo-
phers, as hath been above obſerved; and the
generality of them were ſo far from adopting
ſuch practices, that a great many ridiculed
them. Of this we have an inſtance in the
Book of the *Life of Apollonius Tyanæus*, written by Philoſtrates. In this Book, Apollonius
is ſaid to have ſpoken in the following manner to *Theſpeſion*. ' Flagellations are practiſed
' before the altar of Diana Scythia, becauſe
' the Oracles have ordered it ſo; now, I think
' that it would be folly to reſiſt the will of the
' Gods. If ſo (Theſpeſion anſwers) you
' ſhew, O Apollonius, that the Gods of the
' Greeks poſſeſs but little wiſdom, ſince they
' preſcribe to Men who think they are free, to
' laſh themſelves with whips.'

Nor was the practice of thoſe Flagellations
to which the perſons who underwent them
willingly ſubmitted, confined to the Nations
of Greece; but the ſame had alſo been
adopted in other Countries. It obtained
among the Thracians, as we find in Arte-
midorus. ' The young Men of noble fami-

' lies among the Thracians (fays that Author)
' are on certain occafions cruelly lafhed.'

Voluntary Flagellations were alfo in ufe
among the Egyptians. It even feems that this
practice took its origin among them; and
they ufed them as a method of atoning for
their fins, and appeafing the incenfed Deity.
Herodotus has left us an account of the manner in which they commonly performed their
flagellations, in the account he has given of
the Feftival which they celebrated in honour
of the great Goddefs. ' After preparing
' themfelves by fafting (he fays) they begin
' to offer Sacrifices, and they mutually beit
' each other during the time that the offerings
' are burning on the Altar: this done, the
' viands which remain after the facrifice is
' accomplifhed, are placed upon tables before
' thofe who compofe the Affembly.'

The fame Herodotus fays on another occafion, ' I have already related in what manner
' the Feftival of Ifis is celebrated in the city
' of Bufiris. While the Sacrifice is perform-
' ing, the whole Affembly, amounting to fe-
' veral thoufands of both Men and Women,
' beat one another.' To this Herodotus adds,
that ' he is not allowed to mention the reafon
' why thofe beatings were performed *.'

† In Euterpe, Lib. II. Cap. 42. pag 113.
Ἑι᾿ ὅτι δὲ τύ- ῶονται, ἤ μοι ὅσιόν ἐσι λέγιιν.

Among the Syrians, we likewife find that the ufe of voluntary Flagellations had been adopted; and their Priefts practifed them upon themfelves with aftonifhing feverity. Apuleius, in his *Metamorphofis* of the Golden Afs, relates the manner in which thefe Priefts both made incifions in their own flefh, and lafhed themfelves voluntarily.

‘ In fine, they diffect their own arms with
‘ two-edged knives, which they ufe eonftantly
‘ to carry about them. In the mean while,
‘ one of them begins to rave and figh, and
‘ feems to draw his breath from his very
‘ bowels. He at laft feigns to fall into a
‘ kind of phrenetic fit, pretending that he is
‘ replete with the fpirit of the Goddefs ; as
‘ if the prefence of the Gods ought not to
‘ make Men better, inftead of rendering them
‘ difordered and weak. But now, behold
‘ what kind of favour the Divine Will is go-
‘ ing to beftow upon him. He begins to vo-
‘ ciferate, and, by purpofely contrived lies,
‘ to upbraid and accufe himfelf in the fame
‘ manner as if he had been guilty of having
‘ entertained bad defigns againft the myfteries
‘ of their holy Religion. He then proceeds
‘ to award a fentence of punifhment againft
‘ himfelf; and at the fame time grafping his
‘ fcourge, an inftrument which thofe Priefts

‘ conſtantly wear about them, and which is
‘ made of twiſted woollen cords armed with
‘ ſmall bones, he laſhes himſelf with repeated
‘ blows ; all the while manifeſting a wonder-
‘ ful, though affected firmneſs, notwithſtand-
‘ ing the violence and number of the ſtripes.’
From all that is above related, it is pretty evident that thoſe Syrian Prieſts uſed (or ſeemed
to uſe) themſelves, in this cruel manner, only
with a view to raiſe admiration in the minds of
weak and ſuperſtitious perſons by this extraordinary affectation of ſuperior ſanctity, and
thereby to cheat them out of their money.
At leaſt this is the conjecture made by Philip-
pus Beroaldus, in his Commentaries on the
Metamorphoſis of the Golden Aſs, who ſays,
that thoſe Prieſts were no better than Jugglers,
or rather Cheats, who only aimed at catching
the money of the Fools who gazed at them *.

* Whether thoſe Prieſts whipped themſelves in
earneſt, or only made a feint ſo to do, as Beroaldus ſuſpects, is difficult to determine ; but with
reſpect to the inciſions which they pretended to
make in their own fleſh, there is juſt ground to
think that they only impoſed upon their ſpecta-
tors, ſince a law was made by the Emperor Com-
modus, which Dr. Middleton has quoted in his
Letter from Rome, by which it was ordered that

Nay, the opinion of the merit of voluntary or religious Flagellations, was in antient times grown so universal, that we find them to have also been practised among the Romans, who had adopted notions on that subject of the same kind with those of the Syrians and the Egyptians, and thought that the Gods were, upon particular occasions, to be appeased by using scourges and whips. An instance of this notion or practice is to be met with in the Satyricon of Petronius, in which *Encolpus* relates, that, being upon the sea, the people of the ship flagellated him, in order, as they thought, to prevent a storm. ' It was re-
' solved (he says) among the Mariners, to give
' us each forty stripes, in order to appease the
' tutelar Deity of the ship. No time ac-
' cordingly is lost; the furious Mariners set
' upon us with cords in their hands, and en-
' deavour to appease the Deity by the effusion
' of the meanest blood: as to me, I received
' three lashes, which I endured with Spartan
' magnanimity *.'

thofe Priests should be made really to suffer the amputations which they pretended they made on themselves. *Bellonæ servientes brachia verè exsecare præcepit.* Lamprid. in Com.

* " *Itaque ut Tutela navis expiaretur, placuit*

l

But the moſt curious inſtance of religious Flagellations, among the Romans, and indeed

quadragenas utrique plagas imponi. Nulla ergo fit mora; aggrediuntur nos furentes nautæ cum funibus, tentantque viliſſimo ſanguine Tutelam placare, & ego quidem tres plagas Spartanâ nobilitate concoxi."— Pet. Arb. Sat. L. II.——The Story, as it is to be found in Petronius, is this. *Encolpus* and *Giton* had embarked, unawares, on the ſhip of one *Lycas*, to whom Encolpus had formerly given offence, and on board the ſame ſhip was alſo a Lady named *Tryphena*, who owed a grudge to Giton, by whom ſhe thought ſhe had on a former occaſion been ſlighted. Encolpus and Giton no ſooner diſcovered in whoſe ſhip they were, than they were afraid of being ill-uſed, and attempted to diſguiſe themſelves in the dreſs of Slaves, and for that purpoſe cut off their hair, a thing which (though they did not know it) was the worſt of omens during a voyage, as it never was done but in a ſtorm, in order to make offerings to the incenſed Deities of the ſea. Somebody ſpied Encolpus and Giton while they were performing the above operation; the rumour of ſuch a nefarious act, in fair weather, ſoon ſpread about the ſhip, and the crew thereupon uſed our two paſſengers in the manner above related. Encolpus (as himſelf ſays) bore the three firſt blows with great magnanimity,

G 4

among all other Nations, is that of the ceremony which the Romans called *Lupercalia*; a ceremony which was performed in honour of the God Pan, and had been contrived in Arcadia, where it was in use so early as the times of King Evander, and whence it was afterwards brought over to Italy. In this Festival, a number of Men used to dance naked, as Virgil informs us: ' Here (says he) the ' dancing *Salii*, and naked *Luperci* *.' And Servius, in his Commentary upon this verse of Virgil, explains to us who these *Luperci*

but Giton, who was of a more tender frame, screamed so loud at the first blow, that Tryphena heard him, knew his voice, ran upon the deck, and instead of being moved by the sight of his nakedness, insisted upon the whole number of blows being given him: other passengers then took the part of the two culprits, which brought on a battle between them and the crew: at last the affair was compromised, and Encolpus and Giton were released. As for the latter, a Maid slave found means afterwards to fit him with a wig, and paste false eyebrows to his forehead, which made him appear as charming as ever, and Tryphena's favour was restored to him

* " *Hic exultantes Salios nudosque Lupercos.*" Æn. Lib. III.

were. They were (he fays) Men who, upon
particular folemnities, ufed to ftrip themfelves
ftark naked; in this fituation they ran about
the ftreets, carrying ftraps of leather in their
hands, with which they ftruck the Women
they met in their way. Nor did thofe Women run away from them; on the contrary,
they willingly prefented the palms of their
hands to them, in order to receive their blows;
imagining, through a fuperftitious notion received among the Romans, that thefe blows,
whether applied to their hands or to their bel-
ly, had the power of rendering them fruitful,
or procuring them an eafy delivery.

The fame facts are alfo alluded to, by Juvenal, who fays in his fecond Satire, ‘ Nor
‘ is it of any fervice to her, to offer the palms
‘ of her hands to a nimble *Lupercus* †.’ And
the antient Scholiaft on Juvenal obferves on
this verfe, that barren Women, in Rome,
ufed to throw themfelves into the way of the
Luperci when become furious, and were beaten
by them with ftraps †.

Other Authors, befides thofe above, have
mentioned this feftival of the Lupercalia.

* “ *Nec prodeft agil: palmas præbere Luperco.*”
Juv. Sat. II.

† “ *Steriles mulieres fibi uantibus Lupercis fe offe-
rebant, & fcrula verberabantur.*”

Among others, *Feſtus*, in his Book on the *Signification of words*, informs us, that the *Luperci* were alſo ſometimes called *Crepi*, on account of the kind of noiſe *(crepitus)* which they made with their ſtraps, when they ſtruck the Women with them : ' For it is a cuſtom ' among the Romans (continues the ſame Au- ' thor) for Men to run about naked during ' the feſtival of the Lupercalia, and to ſtrike ' all the Women they meet, with *ſtraps*.'

Prudentius, I find, has alſo mentioned the ſame feſtival in his Roman Martyr : ' What is ' the meaning (ſays he) of this ſhameful ce- ' remony ? By thus running about the ſtreets ' under the ſhape of Luperci, you ſhow that ' you are perſons of low condition. Would ' you not deem a Man to be the meaneſt of ' Slaves, who would run naked about the ' public ſtreets, and amuſe himſelf with ſtrik- ' ing the young Women *?'

* From the above ſentiments delivered by Pru- dentius, we might be induced to think that only perſons of low condition, in Rome, or even Slaves alone, uſed to *run*, in the feſtival of the Lupercalia , yet this does not ſeem to have been the caſe, and the lines of Prudentius appear to have contained more declamation than real truth.

For *Luperci* were in very early times formed

All the Flagellations we have abovementioned were performed in public Solemnities,

into two bands, which were called by the names of the moft diftinguifhed families in Rome, *Quintiliani* and *Fabiani*, and to thefe was afterwards added a third band, called *Juliani*, from J. Cæfar's name. Marc Antony, as eveiy one knows, did not fcruple to *run* as one of the *Luperci*, having once harangued the people in that condition : and if he was afterwaids inveighed againft, on that account, by feveral perfons, and among others by Cicero, his perfonal enemy, it was owing to his being Conful, when he thus ran among the *Luperci* : a thing which, it was faid, had never been done by any Conful before him.

The feftival in queftion (which may furprife the Reader) continued to be celebrated fo late as the year 496, long after the eftablifhment of Chriftianity, and perfons of noble familities not only continued to run among the *Luperci*, but a great impiovement was moreover niade about thofe times in the ceremony, the Ladies, no longer contented with being flapt on the palms of their hands, as formerly, began to ftrip themfelves naked, in order both to give a fuller fcope to the *Lupercus* to difplay the vigoui and agility of his arm, and enjoy, themfelves, the entertainment of a more compleat flagellation. The whole cere-

I

or with religious views of some kind or other; but there were other instances of voluntary fustigations (as we learn from the ancient Authors) in which those who performed them were actuated by no such laudable motives; or at least, had no precise intention that has been made known to us. Such were the Flagellations mentioned by St. Jerom, in his Observations on the Epitaph of the Widow *Marcella*. In these Observations St. Jerom informs us, that there were Men in Rome silly enough to lay their posteriors bare in the public Markets, or open Streets, and to suffer themselves

mony being thus brought to that degree of perfection, was so well relished by all parties, that it continued to subsist (as has just now been observed) long after the other ceremonies of Paganism were abolished, and when Pope Gelasius at last put an end to it, he met with a strong opposition from all orders of Men, Senators as well as others. The general discontent became even so great, that the Pope, after he had carried his point, was obliged to write his own Apology, which Baronius has preserved. one of his arguments, among others, was drawn from the above practice of the Ladies, of stripping themselves naked in public in order to be lashed.——*Apud illos, nobiles ipsi currebant, & matronæ nudato corpore vapulabant.*

to be lashed by a pretended Conjuror. 'It 'is no wonder (says he) that a false Diviner 'lashes the buttocks of those blockheads in 'the middle of the Streets, and in the Mar-'ket-place *.'

And these Conjurors not only lashed the persons who desired them to do so, but they, at other times, would also lash themselves, as we learn from Plautus, though an early Wri-ter; for those Flagellations we mention were, it seems, an old practice among the vulgar in Rome. 'Pray, is it not (says an Actor in 'one of this Author's Plays) is it not the Con-'juror who lashes himself †?'

Another proof of the practice of those both active and passive flagellations which prevailed among the People in Rome, is also to be drawn from the above-mentioned Book of Festus, on the *Signification of words* Festus, explaining in that Book the signification of

* "Nec mirum si, in places & foro rerum vena-lium, fictus dico us studiorum verberet nates." Lib. II. adv. Juv. Cap. XIX. & Lib. I. Apolog. adv. Austin. Cap IV.—Recte à non nates, sed nares (subjungit Author noster) legendum estimaverunt Erasmus & M. V. Routimur sed ex Codicibus Ma-nuscriptis, nates in nates, denuò emendaverunt Gre-vius, & doctissimus Jesu 1a H. Rosweidus.

† Num obsecro, num Aeolus qui ipsus se verberas?

the word *Flagratores*, says, that this word sig-
nified ' those who allowed themselves to be
' whipped for money.' And M. Dacier, a
person of consummate learning in all that relates to Antiquity, says, in his Notes on the
above Author, that the word *Flagratores* sig-
nified likewise ' those who whipped others.'
he adds, that this was the more common acceptation of the word *.

Besides the flagellations just mentioned, which
perhaps were also owing to some superstitious
notion or other in those persons who practised them, we find, in antient Authors, instances of lashings and whippings performed
in a way perfectly jocular, and as a kind of
innocent pastime. None is more remarkable
than that which is related by Lucian of the
Philosopher Peregrinus. This Peregrinus (Lucian observes) was a Cynic Philosopher of a
very impudent disposition. He lived in the
time of the Emperor Trajan: after having
embraced the Christian Religion, he returned
to his former Sect: and then used frequently
to lash himself in public in rather an indecent
manner. ' Surrounded by a croud of Spec-
' tators, he handled his *pudendum* (αἰδοῖο)

---

* *Immò potius ii videntur fuisse qui flagris cæ-
debant.*

‘ which he exhibited as a thing, he said, of
‘ no value. He afterwards both gave himself,
‘ and received from the Byftanders, lafhes up-
‘ on his pofteriors, and performed a number
‘ of other juvenile tricks equally furprizing
‘ as thefe.’

We alfo find in Suetonius another inftance
of fportive lafhings or flappings among the
Ancients; and thefe, too, practifed upon no
lefs a perfon than a Roman Emperor. The
Emperor here alluded to, was the Emperor
Claudius. ‘ When he happened (fays Sueto-
‘ nius) to fall afleep after his dinner, which
‘ was a cuftomary thing with him, they threw
‘ ftones of olives or of dates at him, in order
‘ to awaken him; or fometimes the Court
‘ Buffoons would roufe him, by ftriking him,
‘ in a jocular way, with a ftrap or a fcourge *.’

In fine, I fhall conclude this Chapter with
an inftance of voluntary flagellation among the
Ancients, which was not only free either from
the fuperftition or wantonnefs above mentioned, but was moreover produced by rational,
and, we may fay, laudable motives. The inftance I mean, is that of the flagellations

---

* “ *Quoties poft cibum obdormifceret, quod ei ferè
quotidiè accidebat, olearum & palmularum offibus in-
ceffebatur : interdùm ferula flagrove velut per ludum
excitabatur à Capreis.*”

beſtowed upon himſelf by a certain Philoſo-
pher, mentioned by Suidas. The Philoſo-
pher's name was *Superanus :* he was a Diſciple
of Laſcaris; though paſt the age of thirty
years, he had taken a ſtrong reſolution of ap-
plying himſelf to Science, and began at that
time to read the works of the moſt famous
Orators. So earneſt was he in his deſign of
ſucceeding in thoſe ſtudies which he had undertaken, that ' he never grudged himſelf
' either the rod or ſharp lectures, in order to
' learn all that Schoolmaſters and Tutors
' teach their Pupils. He even was more than
' once ſeen, in the public Baths, to inflict up-
' on himſelf the ſevereſt corrections *.'

---

* This *Superanus,* who conſidered whipping as
a neceſſary circumſtance to make a complete education, has been followed in that opinion by no
leſs a man than the celebrated Loyola, the Founder of the Order of the Jeſuits. Ignatius of
Loyola, after having led a military life, took it
into his head, though paſt thirty years of age, to
begin his ſtudies, and in order to render his courſe
of learning as complete as poſſible, he inſiſted, on a
certain occaſion, on the Maſter inflicting the correction of the School upon him, in the preſence of

all the Boys. Some Writers have advanced, that Loyola was thirty-three years old, when he underwent the above flagellation, while others fay, he was thirty-feven. On the other hand, certain Proteftant Authors, in order to rob the Saint of the praife of humility he acquired on that occafion, pretend, that when he defired to undergo the above correction, he knew that the Profeffor had, of himfelf, refolved to inflict it upon him. The queftion is alfo examined in *Bayle's* Dictionary, whether Ignatius of Loyola was ferved in the manner above-recited, at Bay-onne, or in the *Montaigu* School, at Paris.

Moliere, in his *Bourgeois Gentilhomme*, introduces juft fuch another character as Superanus and Loyola. M. Jourdain, though a Man of a mid-dle age, and without education, takes it into his head to be on a fudden a learned Man and a fine Gentleman: and in confequence of this fancy, fills his houfe with Fencing Mafters, Dancing Mafters, Mafters of Mufic, Mafters of Philofo-phy, and Mafters of every kind. His Wife and Maid Servant, being very angry to fee their ap-partments full of duft, and their floors covered with dirt, take him to tafk on that account, and the Wife, who is a fort of blunt, vulgar Woman, among other peevifh expreffions of her difplea-fure, afks him, " Do you mean, at your age, to get yourfelf whipped, one of thefe days ?"—To

H

which Mr. Jourdain, like a true *Superanus*, an-
fwers, " Why not ' Would to God I were whipped this very inftant before all the world, and
knew what is to be learnt at School."

Madame JOURDAIN.

*N' irez vous point un de ces jours vous faire don-
ner le fouët, à votre âge ?*

M. JOURDAIN.

*Pourquoi non ? Plût à Dieu d'avoir tout à l'heure
le fouët, devant tout le monde, & favoir ce qu'on ap-
prend au Collège.*

From the extenfive ufe of flagellations that took
place among the antient Heathens, the Abbé Boileau ten or twelve times draws the conclufion in
different parts of his Book, that the fiift Chriftians
held that mode of punifhment in deteftation, and
never adopted it for themfelves. However, the
other Catholic Divines are very far from admit-
ting this conclufion, noi by any means grant that,
becaufe certain practices were adopted by the antient Heathens, it follows that the firft Chriftians
abftained from them. They, on the contrary,
fay that the Abbé himfelf ought to know, that
Chriftians have imitated feveral ceremonies of the
Pagans, which they have fanctified by the intentions with which they perfoim them, and on
this fubject they quote Polydore Vergil, who remarks, that the cuftom adopted by Prelates, of
giving the outfide of their hand to be kiffed, when

they officiate in their Pontifical dreſſes, the cuſtom of making prayers for the dead on the ſeventh day after their burial, the offering of pictures to thoſe Saints by whoſe aſſiſtance dangers have been eſcaped, &c. &c. are practices derived from the Heathens.

They moreover add, that even the Temples of the Pagans have been converted by Chriſtians, to their own uſe; and on this occaſion they alledge, among other inſtances, that of Pope Gregory the Great, who wrote to St. Auguſtin, Apoſtle of England (or rather to Melitus, with an injunction to inform the Apoſtle) that he muſt not demoliſh the temples of the idols in the above kingdom, but that he ought to preſerve thoſe which are well built *(benè conſtructa)*, and after purifying them with holy water, and by placing relicks, appropriate them to the uſe of the Church.

C H A P.   VII.

Containing the most ingenious arguments of the
Abbé Boileau. The practice of scourging one's-
self was unknown to the first Fathers of the
Church; and also to the first Anchorites, or
Hermits.

FLAGELLATIONS of different kinds
being univerfally practifed among the Heathens, this circumftance muft needs have given
but little encouragement to the firft Chriftians,
to imitate fuch mode of correction; and we
may take it for granted that they had not
adopted it.   Indeed, we find that no mention
is made of it in the writings of the firft, either Greek or Latin Fathers; for inftance, in
the Epiftles of St. Ignatius, the Apologies of
Juftinius, the Apoftolic Canons, the Conftitutions attributed to Clement the Roman, the
works of Origen, the *Stromats* of Clement
of Alexandria, and all the works in general
of Eufebius of Cæfarea, of St. Chryfoftom,
of St. Bafil, and of St. Bafil of Seleucia.   In
all the above Authors, no mention, I fay,

is made of flagellations; at least, of those of
a voluntary kind; unless we are absolutely to
explain in a literal manner passages in which
they manifestly spoke in a figurative sense:
we may therefore safely conclude, that the
first Christians had no notion of those cruel
exercises which prevail in our days, and that
to flay one's hide with scourges or rods, as is
in these times the practice of numberless Devotees, in or out of religious Orders, were
practices unknown among them.

So far, indeed, were the first Christians from
approving the practice of self-flagellations,
that they seem on the contrary to have entertained a notion, that their very quality of
Christians freed them from any kind of flagellation whatever, as we may learn from the
inscription in Latin verses that had been placed
by them upon the column to which Jesus
Christ was fastened when he was whipped:
the following is the translation of that inscription: ' In this House our Lord stood bound;
' and, being fastened to this column, like a
' slave, offered his back to the whip. This
' venerable column is still standing, continu-
' ing to support the fabric of the Temple, and
' teaches us to live exempt from every kind
' of flagellation.'

" *Vinctus*

" *Vinctus in his Dominus stetit ædibus, atque*
    Columnæ
Annexus, tergum dedit ut servile flagellis.
Perstat adhuc, templumque gerit veneranda Co-
    lumna,
Nosque docet cunctis immunes vivere flagris."

Now, if the first Christians had been used
to inflict daily discipline upon themselves, or
to receive it from other persons, it is altogether improbable that they would have said
that they were exempt from every kind of flagellation. The above lines, it may not be
amiss to observe, were thought to have been
written by Prudentius, who lived about the
latter end of the fourth century. Fabri-
cius, in his Edition of the Christian Poets,
ascribes the same lines to one Amœnus, who
lived in the eighth Century; and, on the
other hand, Johannes Siccardus says, that Se-
dulius, who lived under the reign of Theodo-
sius junior, is the Author of them. Be it as
it may, it does not much matter on this occasion to know who has written them; it is suf-
ficient to observe that they are very useful to
confirm the assertion, as to the novelty of voluntary flagellations * .

* Our Doctor of the Sorbonne and Abbé
Boileau (whose meaning is here faithfully laid

Arguments have alfo been derived by the promoters of flagellations, from thofe which

before the reader) fpeaks with much confidence of the proofs he derives in fupport of his opinion, fiom the above Latin lines, which he adds he thinks he has done *well* and *wifely* to produce; and I have poftponed to the end of his argument, to make any remark upon the fubject, in order to let him enjoy his triumph a little longer. However, his whole reafoning is no more than a quibble on the fenfe of the word *flagrum*; which indeed fignifies a whip, but alfo fignifies a luftful paffion: both come from the verb *flagrare*, to burn; and *flagrare amore*, to burn with love: hence the word *flagrans delictum*, which is faid of a Man who is caught in the act of debauching another Man's wife, or as fome Civilians exprefs it, *alienam Uxorem fubagitans* · from the above expreffion the French have made the words *flagrant délit*, which have the fame meaning, and they fay of a Man under the above circumftances, that he is caught *en flagrant délit*. The real meaning of the Latin lines above-quoted, is, therefore, that Chriftians ought to be free, not fiom every kind of *flagellation*, but fiom luftful paffions. Thofe lines, it may be obferved, together with the quibble contained in them, of which our Author has availed himfelf to fupport his private opinion, are

H 4

Jefus Chrift was made to fuffer, in order to prove that they were practifed upon themfelve, by the firft Chriftians. But though it may be a meritorious action to endure whipping with as much patience as Jefus Chrift, and for caufes of the fame kind as he did, yet it is no proof that the firft Chriftians had any thought of expofing themfelves voluntarily to a punifhment which had been impofed upon him by force. Befides, the firft Chriftians could not poffibly be induced by their defire of imitating Jefus Chrift's whipping (fuppofing they really had fuch defire) to flagellate themfelves in the cruel manner that has fince prevailed; for they did not think that the flagellation undergone by our Lord was in a very high degree painful, and they looked upon it as having been but an inconfiderable part of the punifhment he was made to fuffer. In fact, St. Chryfoftom and St. Auftin, as the Reader may fee in their works, relate that Pi-

in the fame tafte with the other productions of Monks, during the times of the *middle age*, and of the general decay of literature, when finding out quibbles and puns, and fucceeding in compofing acroftics, anagrams, and other *difficiles nugæ*, engroffed the whole ambition of Verfificators though, to fay the truth, worfe lines than the above have been written in that kind of ftyle.

late ordered Jefus Chrift to be fcourged after the manner, not of the Romans, among whom the punifhment of whipping was inflicted with great feverity, but of the Jews, who never fuffered the number of forty ftripes to be exceeded. And though the truth in that refpect has afterwards been better known, yet, it was only in latter times that the difcovery was made, and that St. Bridget, a holy Nun, by means of a revelation fhe had on that fubject, was informed, and thereby enabled to inform the world, that the two holy Fathers were wrong in their opinions, and that Jefus Chrift had really been flagellated with great cruelty *.

* Inftances of revelations, like thofe of St. Bridget, concerning the perfon of Jefus Chrift and his fufferings, are very frequent among Nuns; and, to fay the truth, it is no wife furprifing that they fhould, at times, have vifions of this kind. As thofe Women who are deftined to live in the condition of Nuns, are commonly, not to fay always, made to take their vows at an early age, that is, at a time when their paffions are moft difpofed to be inflamed, and when an object of love may be looked upon as one of the neceffaries of life, this, together with the circumftance of their clofe confinement, induces a number of them to

Befides thofe Fathers who have been quoted
above, as having made no mention of flagella-

contract a real and ardent love for the perfon of
Jefus Chrift, whofe pictures they fee placed almoft in every corner, who is, befides, exprefsly
called their Hufband, whofe Spoufes they are
faid to be, and to whom, at the final and folemn clofing of their vows, they have been actually betrothed, by having a ring put on their fin-
ger. To the mind of fuch of thofe unfortunate
young Women as have once begun to indulge
fancies of this kind, the image of their beloved
Spoufe is continually prefent, under fome one of
the figures by which he is reprefented in the abovementioned pictures; and his flagellations, and
other hardfhips he was made to undergo, are,
among other things, the objects of their tendereft
concern : hence the numberlefs vifions and revelations which Nuns, like St. Bridget, have at all
times had upon thofe fubjects : and feveral among
them, whofe love was more fervent, or who
thought themfelves intitled to fome particular diftinction from their Spoufe, have even fancied,
on certain occafions, that they had been favoured
with a vifible impreffion of his facred *Stigmats*,
that is, of the marks of the five main wounds
which he received when he was put to death. The
idea of thofe vifible marks or *Stigmats* of Jefus

tions in their writings, except in a figurative manner, there are others no lefs commendable for their learning, who have been equally fi- lent on that fubject. St. Jerom, among others, deferves to have particular notice taken of him; and he once had, we are to ob- ferve, a very natural opportunity of mention- ing voluntary flagellations, if he had had any notion of fuch a practice. I mean here to fpeak of the letter he wrote to Deacon Sabi- nus, in order to admonifh him of his fins, and exhort him to repent of them. This Sabinus was a moft profligate man, who was publicly known to have been guilty of the crime of adultery, and who had, in one inftance, carri- ed his wickednefs fo far as to attempt to ravifh a girl in the very manger in which Jefus Chrift had received the adoration of the three Eaf- tern Kings. St. Jerom exerts the utmoft powers of his eloquence in order to bring that

Chrift's wounds, we may obferve, was, in the firft inftance, a contrivance of St. Francis, who pre- tended that they had been imprefled on his body during a vifion he had in a remote place; and he prevailed upon his Monks, and other adherents, to confider them as emblems of a clofe affinity be- tween him and our Lord, and as a kind of order of knighthood that had been conferred on him.

man to a fenfe of his crimes, and engage him
to do a fuitable penance for them, and yet he
makes no mention whatever about whipping
or difcipline. Now, is it in any degree credible that he would, on fuch an occafion, have
been filent as to the ufe of whips, leather-
thongs, or fcourges, if they had been commonly in ufe, and avowed by the Church?

The fupporters of flagellations, however,
urge that the fame St. Jerom, in his Epiftle to
Euftachius, fays, fpeaking of himfelf, ' I re-
' member to have many a time fpent the
' whole day in loud lamentations, and to have
' only ceafed to beat my breaft when the ad-
' monitions of our Lord reftored tranquillity
' to me.' But this very paffage, which is
made ufe of to prove that voluntary flagellations were in ufe during the times of the primitive Church, manifeftly proves the contrary,
and that St. Jerom was an utter ftranger to
the ufe either of fcourges or rods. It is true,
he lamented, as he fays, for his fins, and beat
his breaft, in order to expel by this natural
method of venting his grief, the wicked
thoughts with which he felt himfelf agitated;
but in doing this, he employed, and could
employ, only his fifts: the fhort diftance between his arms and his breaft made it alto-

ther impracticable for him to use rods, thongs, straps, sticks, scourges, besoms, or whips.

Nor is any argument to be drawn from what is related of the same St. Jerom, that the Angels once fustigated him in the presence of God, and covered him with stripes, because he was fired with an ardent desire of acquiring the style and eloquence of Cicero : for it is evident, that this flagellation was imposed upon him by force, and as an involuntary chastisement. Besides (which would make it completely unjust to draw any inference from this fact) St. Jerom only suffered the flagellation in question in a dream, as himself with great wisdom observes, in his Apology against Ruffinus : ' I was asleep (says he) when I pro- ' mised before the tribunal of God never to ' engage in the study of worldly letters ; so ' that the sacrilege and perjury he charges me ' with, amount to no more than the violation ' of a dream.'

If we peruse the History of the Lives of the ancient Anchorites of the East, we shall find great reason to think that they likewise were strangers to the practice of self-flagellation. Theodoret, Bishop of Cyrus, who distinguished himself so honourably in the fifth Council of Chalcedon, has, for instance, written the lives of thirty of these Solitaries, who

7

were particularly celebrated on account of the great aufterities and mortifications which they practifed, and who were afterwards on that account raifed to the dignities of Priefts or of Bifhops; and yet, he has made no mention of their ufing either rods or whips, in the numerous and different penances which they performed.

Thus, we are informed in the Book of Theodoret, that St. James of Nifibe (who was afterwards made a Bifhop) had voluntarily deprived himfelf, during his whole life-time, of the ufe of fire. He lay upon the ground; he never wore any woollen clothes, but only ufed goat-fkins to hide his nakednefs.

It is related in the fame book, that St. Julian only ate bread made of millet, and that he abftained from the ufe of almoft every kind of drink. St. Martianus never ate but once in a day, and that very fparingly too; fo that he continually endured the tortures of hunger and thirft: this holy Man had, befides, a Difciple who never touched either bread or meat.

St. Eufebius ufed to wear an iron chain round his body; his continual faftings and other kinds of macerations rendered him fo lean and emaciated, that his girdle would continually flide down upon his heels; and

4

Publius *the elder*, voluntarily fubmitted to mortifications of the fame kind.

Simeon only fed upon herbs and roots. St. Theodofius the Bifhop ufed to wear a hair-cloth around his body, and iron chains at his hands and feet. St. Zeno never refted upon a bed, nor looked into a Book. Macedonius, during forty years, never ufed any other food than barley, and was not afterwards raifed to the dignity of Prieft, but againft his own con-fent. Bifhop Abrahames never tafted bread during the whole time of his being a Bifhop, and carried his mortifications fo far, as to for-bear the ufe of clear water.

The fame Theodoret, continuing to relate the life of the holy Hermits, fays, that fome of them ufed to wear iron fhoes, and others were conftantly burdened with cuiraffes inwardly armed with points. Some would willingly expofe themfelves to the fcorching heat of the fun in fummer days, and to the nip-ping cold of winter evenings : and others (continues Theodoret) as it were buried them-felves alive in caverns, or in the bottom of wells; while others made their habitations, and in a manner roofted, upon the very tops of columns.

Now, among all thofe numerous and fingu-lar methods of felf-mortification which Theo-

doret defcribes as having been conftantly practifed by the above-named holy Hermits, we
do not find, as hath been above obferved, any
mention made of flagellations : methods of
doing penance, thefe, which it is hardly credible, Theodoret would have neglected to mention, if thofe holy Men had employed them '.

---

* Among thofe Solitaries who, as is abovementioned, fixed their habitations upon the tops
of columns, particular mention is made of one
who was afterwards, on that account, denominated St. Simeon *Stylites*, from the Greek word
Στυλος, a column. This St. Simeon Stylites was a
native of Syria, and the column upon which he
had chofen to fix his habitation, was fixty cubits
high. Numbers of people reforted to it from all
parts, in order to confult him upon different fubjects, and he delivered his oracles to them from
his exalted manfion. One of his methods of
mortifying himfelf was, to make frequent genuflexions ; and he made them fo quickly, it is faid,
and in fuch numbers, that a perfon, who one day
fpied him from fome diftance, and attempted to
count them, grew tired, and left off when he had
told two thoufand.

The exiftence of the above Hermit, as well as of thofe mentioned by our Author, together with the hard penances to which they fubmitted, feem in general to be facts pretty well afcertained, and the amazing hardfhips which the *Fakirs* in the Eaft Indies, ftill continue in thefe days to impofe upon themfelves, make the above accounts appear the lefs incredible. However, they have been fince wonderfully magnified in the Compilations of Lives of Saints, and Hiftories of miracles, efpecially in that called the *Golden Legend*, which is the moft remarkable of all, and was compiled a few Centuries ago by one *Jacobus de Voragine*, and has been fince tranflated into feveral languages. it is a thick folio book, bound in parchment, which is found at all the Inns in Catholic Countries

The life of a Hermit ftill continues to be followed by feveral perfons. Thofe who make profeffion of it, are Men who, like the firft Anchorites of the Eaft, choofe to live by themfelves, in places more or lefs remote from Towns, without being tied by any vows; they only wear a particular kind of habit, and perform certain religious duties.

Whatever may be the real or affected fanctity of a few of them, the whole tribe of Hermits, however, have not efcaped the common misfor-

I

tune of Friars and Nuns, who have numbers of amorous stories circulated on their account , often for no other reason, we are charitably to suppose, than the additional degree of relish which they derive from the contrast between the facts they contain, and the outward Life and professions of those of whom they are related.　Thus, the cele-brated *La Fontaine* has made the contrivance of a certain Hermit, for obtaining possession of a young Woman who lived in a neighbouring cottage, the subject of one of his *Tales.*　And *Poggio* has related another story of an Hermit, which I think wor-thy of a place here, since this book is designed no less for the entertainment than the information of the Reader.

The Hermit in question lived in the neigh-bourhood of Florence.　He was a great favourite with the Ladies, and the most distinguished at Court flocked daily to the place of his retreat. The report of the licentious life he led, reached the ears of the Grand Duke, who ordered the Man to be seized and brought before him　and as it was well known he had been connected with the first Ladies at Court, he was commanded by the Secretary of State to declare the names of all the Ladies whose favours he had received . when he named three or four, and said there were no more. The Secretary insisted upon his telling the whole truth, and as he was very hard upon him, the Hermit named a few more, affuring that now he had told all. The Secretary then gave him threats, and again infifted with great warmth upon his declaring the names of all the Ladies , when the Hermit, fetching a deep figh, faid, *Well then, Sir, write down your own* which words confounded the Secretary, and afforded much merriment to the Grand Duke and his Courtiers.

CHAP. VIII.

*A few more of the Abbé Boileau's arguments are
    introduced. It does not appear that self-fla-
    gellation made a part of the duties prescribed
    in the first Monasteries, during the times of
    the first establishments of that kind. The
    only positive instances of flagellations suffered by
    Saints, or the Candidates for that title, in the
    days we speak of, are those which the Devil
    has inflicted upon them.*

IN the antient Monasteries of Egypt, and
    of the East, that is to say, in the first re-
gular religious establishments which took place
among Christians, it does not seem that self-
flagellations were in use, and that they had
any notion of those frequent lashings and
scourgings with which Monasteries have since
resounded.

In fact, we find that that Rule which commonly goes under the name of St. Anthony,
who lived about the year 300, and was the
very first professor of Monastic Life, is entirely silent on that subject. The same is to be

obferved of the Rules framed by the Abbot Ifaiah, who lived in much the fame time as St. Anthony; of thofe compofed by the Fathers Serapion, Macarius, Paphnutius, another Macarius, and feveral other very antient Rules, framed in the Monafteries of the Eaft, which the learned Lucas Holftenius, Librarian of the Vatican, has publifhed in his *Code of Rules*.

The Rules of the firft religious Orders founded in the Weft, have been likewife filent as to the voluntary ufe of thongs and whips. The firft Rule, for inftance, prefcribed to the Benedictines, that antient Weftern Order, does not mention a word about felf-flagellation : and the fame filence is to be obferved in the Rules framed by Ovifiefius, Abbot of Tabennæ, by St. Aurelian, Bifhop of Arles, by St. Ifidorus, Bifhop of Sevil, by St. Tetradius, and a number of others, whofe Rules Holftenius has likewife collected. From thence we may therefore conclude, that Chriftians, in thofe times, had no notion of thofe beatings and fcourgings which are now fo prevalent; and that the *upper* and the *lower* difciplines were alike unknown among them *.

---

* Conclufions againft the antiquity of the *upper* and the *lower* difciplines, are frequent in the Abbé Boileau's book; though I have thought it unne-

The only Author of weight, in the days we fpeak of, who feems to have made any

ceffary to lay them all before the reader. Againft the latter kind of difcipline, he has been particularly zealous, and, befides his ufual charge of novelty, he has, on one occafion, taxed it with being a remnant of idolatry and Pagan fuperftition. This imputation has much difpleafed a French Curate, who wrote an anfwer to him: he thought it reflected on thofe Saints who practifed the difcipline in queftion, and he animadverted on the Abbé in the following terms. *Quelle plus grande injure peut-on faire aux Saints & aux Saintes qui fe difciplinent par en bas, que de dire qu'ils font des idolatres & des fuperftitieux ? . . . Peut on les deshonorer davantage, ces Saints, que d'en parler comme fait M. Boileau ?* 'Can a greater infult be put upon thofe Saints of 'both Sexes who practife the lower difcipline, 'than faying that they are fuperftitious perfons 'and idolaters ? Is it poffible to fhew more difre- 'fpect to thofe Saints, than fpeaking of them as 'Monf. Boileau does ?'

With refpect to the filence of the firft Monaftic Rules, concerning voluntary flagellation, it may be obferved that it has been amply compenfated in fubfequent ones. The *Carmes* are to difcipline themfelves twice a week, and the Monks of *Monte Caffino*, once at leaft, the *Urfuline* Nuns,

mention of voluntary flagellations being practised in the antient Monasteries, is St. John
Climax, who, according to some accounts,
lived in the middle of the fourth, and, according to others, only in the sixth Century.
This Author relates, that, in a certain Monastery, ' some, among the Monks, watered
' the pavement with their tears; while others,
' who could not shed any, beat themselves *.'
Several Writers have laid great stress on that
passage, and quoted it as an undoubted proof
of the antiquity of the practice of voluntary
flagellation ; yet I will take the liberty to diffent from their opinion, since other Writers
have judged that St. John Climax only spoke
in a figurative manner, and have translated
the above passage, by saying that ' those monks

every Friday, the Carmelite Nuns, on Wednes-
days and Fridays ; the Nuns of the Visitation,
when they please, the English Benedictines, a
greater or less number of times, weekly, according to the season of the year, the Celestines, on
the eve of every great festival; and the Capuchin
Friars are to perform a lower discipline every
morning in the week, &c. &c.

* Ὁι μὲν ἐν ἐκείνοις τὸ ἔδαφο, τοῖ, δ'ερυσιν ἔβρεχον, ὁι δὲ
δακρύων ἀπορῖντε· ἑαυτὰς κατέκοπτοι.

I 4

‘ who could not fhed tears, lamented them.
‘ felves *.’

* The above paffage of St. Climax, like thofe
of David and St. Paul, difcuffed in the 2d and
3d Chapters, has caufed much difputation between
the Affertors, and the Oppofers, of the doctrine of
the antiquity of voluntary flagellations.   The
Abbé Boileau has taken much pains, in his text, to
prove that St. John Climax, notwithftanding the
precifion of the expreffion he has ufed, only
meant to fpeak in a figurative fenfe, and he has
for that purpofe produced a number of authorities
from different books, and entered into a long
grammatical differtation on the Greek words ufed
by that Saint, in which he at laft bewilders
himfelf, and fays the very reverfe of what he
had promifed to prove.   He has alfo beftowed fome pains on different paffages of other
Greek fathers, which are as pofitive as that quoted
from St John Climax; and among others, upon
one of St. Cyril, Patriarch of Alexandria, who
expreffes himfelf with great clearnefs, and fays,
he *whips himfelf*, and exhorts his friends to do the
fame.

However, notwithftanding the great precifion
of the words ufed by the above good Fathers, whether in fpeaking of themfelves, or of other perfons, we are not perhaps intirely to refufe to ad-

Regard for truth, however, obliges us to mention one or two inſtances of flagellations, which are to be found in the hiſtory of the antient Eaſtern Anchorites, written by Theodoret, who has been abovementioned; but thoſe inſtances are ſuch, that certainly no argument can be derived from them, to prove that voluntary flagellations were in uſe in the times in which thoſe Anchorites lived.

One of thoſe inſtances is to be found in the life of Abrahames. It is related in it, that the

mit the aſſertions of the Abbé Boileau, that they only ſpoke in a figurative ſenſe. It is not abſolutely impoſſible that the paſſages which are quoted from them, though ever ſo expreſsly mentioning *flagellations, beatings, and ſcourgings*, were no more, after all, than canting ways of expreſſion, like thoſe commonly uſed by men who affect pretenſions to ſuperior ſanctity, who take every opportunity of magnifying their ſufferings, or thoſe of their friends, though often of an imaginary kind. However, on this important ſubject, I ſhall leave the Reader to determine · I will only obſerve, that the moſt zealous Supporters of ſelf-flagellation confeſs, that the ſame was never ſo much practiſed among the Eaſtern as among the Weſtern Chriſtians, as they had adopted ſeveral other means of ſelf-mortification.

Chriftian populace having attempted to feize
the fheets in which the body of that Saint was
wrapped, the lictors drove them back with
whips.   Now, it is obvious to every one, that
the lafhes which thefe lictors beftowed, to and
fro and at random, upon thofe men who befet
them, were not willingly received by the latter.   And the fame may certainly with equal
truth be obferved of the flagellations inflicted
upon the people (which is the fecond inftance
mentioned by Theodoret) by the Collectors of
the public Tributes, who, he fays, uled to
collect them with fcourges and whips *.

* Sir Robert Walpole's Excife Scheme made a
wonderful noife in this Nation, but we may fafely fuppofe, that if flagellations, like thofe abovementioned, had been made part of the project,
the noife would have been ftill greater.

A fact, fupplied by the Abbé Boileau himfelf,
will be introduced in a fubfequent Chapter, from
which it appears, that Theodoret was not unac-
quainted with the practice of felf-flagellation. The
filence of that Author on the fubject, in certain
parts of his writings, only fhews that that practice was not yet become, in his time, that fettled
method of atoning for paft fins, which has been
fince adopted, and that a fcourge had not yet been
made a neceffary part of the furniture of Devotees

To thofe inftances of involuntary flagellations, during the times of the Eaftern Anchorites, and the firft Monks, we may, I think, fafely add thofe which the Devil, jealous of their merit, has inflicted upon them : a cafe which has frequently happened, if we are to credit the Writers of thofe times.

In the life of St. Anthony, which was written by St. Athanafius, we read that that Saint was frequently fet upon, and lafhed in his cell, by the Infernal Spirit.

St. Hilarion was alfo often expofed to the fame misfortune ; as we are informed by St. Jerom, who wrote an account of his life. ' This wanton Gladiator (fays St. Jerom, ' fpeaking of the Devil) beftrides him, beat- ' ing his fides with his heels, and his head ' with a fcourge *.'

A great many other Saints, which it would be too tedious to mention, have been expofed to the like treatment ; and the prieft Grimlaïcus, the Author of an antient Monaftic Rule, obferves that Devils will often infolently lay hold of Men, and lafh them, in the fame manner as they ufed to ferve the bleffed Anthony.

That the above-mentioned inftances of the wantonnefs of the Devil, with refpect to

* *Infidet dorfo ejus feftivus Gladiator, & latera calcibus, cervicem flagello verberans.*

Saints, were not willingly fubmitted to by the latter, needs not, I think, to be fupported by any proof: it muft certainly have been with great reluctance, that they felt themfelves expofed to the lafh of fo formidable a Flagellator *.

---

* Inftances of flagellations beftowed by the Devil, occur frequently in the Books in which the Lives of Saints, either antient or modern, are recited, whether it was that thofe Saints, after having dreamed of fuch flagellations, fancied they had in reality received them, and fpoke accordingly, or that they had fome fcheme in view, when they made complaints of that kind. St Francis of *Affifa*, for inftance, as is related in the Golden Legend, received a dreadful flagellation from the Devil the very firft night he was in Rome, which caufed him to leave that place without delay. And, to fay the truth, it is not at all unlikely that, having met there with a colder reception than he judged his fanctity intitled him to, he thought proper to decamp immediately, and when he returned to his Convent, told the above ftory to his Monks

Among thofe Saints who received flagellations, or vifits in general, from the Devil, St. Anthony

is however the moft celebrated. At fometimes the
Devil, as is mentioned above, flagellated him vigoroufly, and at others, employed temptations of
quite a different kind, in order to feduce him:
thus, he affumed in one inftance, the fhape of a
beautiful young Woman, who made all imagina-
ble advances to the Saint: but, happily, all was
to no purpofe. The celebrated Engraver *Calot*
has made one of thofe vifits of the Devil to St.
Anthony, the fubject of one of his Prints, which
is infcribed *The Temptation of St. Anthony*; and he
has reprefented in it fuch a numerous fwarm of
Devils of all fizes, pouring at once into the Saint's
cavern, and exhibiting fo furprifing a variety of
faces, poftures, and ludicrous weapons, fuch as
fquirts, bellows, and the like, that this Print may
very well be mentioned as an inftance, among
others, of the great fertility of the imagination of
that Engraver.

Befides the perfecutions which St. Anthony fuffered from the Devil, he has the farther merit of
having been the firft Inftitutor of the Monaftic
life, feveral other Hermits having in his time
chofen to affemble together, and lived under his
direction; and though he has not exprefsly been
the Founder of any particular Order, yet it is
glory enough for him to have been the Father of
the whole family of Friars and Nuns. In more
modern times, however, his relicks having been

brought from Egypt to Conftantinople, and thence transferred to *Dauphiné*, in France, a Church was built on the fpot where they were depofited, and a new Order of Friars was a little after eftablifhed, who go by the name of Monks of St. Anthony. Thefe Monks form a kind of Order diftinct from all others, but yet they have no lefs ingenuity than the other Monks for procuring the good of their Convent, as may be judged from the following ftory, which, I think, I may venture to relate as a conclufion both of this Note, and of the whole Chapter.

The Story I mean, is contained in the Book of the *Apologie pour Hérodote*, which was written about the year 1500 by *Henry Etienne*, on purpofe to fhew that thofe who intirely reject the facts related by Herodotus, on account of their incredibility, treat him with too much feverity, fince a number of facts daily happen, which are altogether as furprifing as thofe that are found in that Author.

Before relating the ftory in queftion, the Reader ought to be informed, that St. Anthony is commonly thought to have a great command over fire, and a power of deftroying, by flafhes of that element, thofe who incur his difpleafure; the common people have been led into this belief, by conftantly feeing a fire placed by the fide of that Saint, in the reprefentations that are made of him, though this fire is placed there for no other reafon than becaufe the Saint is thought to have the power of curing the *eryfipelas*, which is alfo called the *facred fire (ignis facer)*, in the fame manner as St. Hubert cures the Hydrophoby, St. John the Epilepfy, and other Saints other diforders. A certain Monk of St. Anthony (to come to our point) who was well acquainted with the above prepoffeffion of the vulgar concerning the power of his Saint, ufed on Sundays to preach in public, in different villages within a certain diftance from his Convent. One day he affembled his congregation under a tree on which a magpye had built her neft, into which he had previoufl, found means to convey a fmall box filled with gunpowder, which he had well fecured therein, and out of the box hung a long thin match, that was to burn flowly, and was hidden among the leaves of the tree. As foon as the Monk, or his Affiftant, had touched the match with a lighted coal, he began his fermon. In the mean while the magpye returned to her neft, and finding in it a ftrange body which fhe could not remove, fhe fell into a paffion, and began to fcratch with her feet, and chatter unmercifully. The Friar affected to hear her without emotion, and continued his fermon with great compofure, only he would now and then lift up his eyes towards the top of the tree, as if he wanted to fee what was the matter. At laft, when he judged the fire was very near reaching the gunpowder, he pretended to be quite out of patience, he curfed the magpye, and wifhed St. Anthony's fire might confume her, and went on again with his fermon, but he had fcarcely pronounced a few periods, when the match on a fudden produced its effect, and blew up the magpye with her neft; which miracle wonderfully raifed the character of the Friar, and proved afterwards very beneficial both to him and his Convent.

CHAP. IX.

Corrections of a flagellatory kind, inflicted by force, were however, though in very early times, the common method of correcting offences of a religious nature; and the power of inflicting them was possessed alike by Bishops, and the Heads of Monasteries *.

IT must be confessed, however, that though self-flagellations made no part of the rules or statutes belonging to the different monastic Orders, founded in those early ages of Christianity, the same cannot be said of that method of correction, when imposed by force

---

* The whole substance of the Abbé Boileau's arguments (so far as it has been possible to make them out) is contained in the three first Chapters of this Work, and in those two which precede this: the Author is now to continue the text part of the Book, without any farther prospect of assistance from the Abbé's observations and directions; except in the last Chapter, in which they are once more to meet, and to lay again their wise heads together.

K

upon fuch Monks as had been guilty of offences, either againſt the diſcipline of the Order, or againſt piety: an extenſive power of
inflicting ſuch ſalutary corrections, having,
from the earlieſt times, been lodged in the
hands of Abbots, and the *Superiors* of Convents.

Nay more, we find that Biſhops, during
the very firſt times of Chriſtianity, aſſumed
the paternal power we mention, even with regard to perſons who were bound to them by
no vow whatever, when they happened to
have been guilty either of breaches of piety,
or of hereſy. Of this, a remarkable proof
may be deduced from the 59th Epiſtle of St.
Auguſtin, which he wrote to the Tribune Marcellinus, concerning the *Donatiſts*. St. Auguſtin expreſſes himſelf in the following
words: ‘ Do not recede from that paternal di-
‘ ligence you have manifeſted in your re-
‘ ſearches after offenders; in which you have
‘ ſucceeded to procure confeſſions of ſuch
‘ great crimes, not by uſing racks, red-hot
‘ blades of iron, or flames, but only by the
‘ application of rods. This is a method of
‘ coercion which is frequently practiſed by
‘ Teachers of the fine Arts upon their Pupils,
‘ by Parents upon their Children; *and often*

' also by Bishops *upon those whom they find to*
' *have been guilty of offences* ∗.'

Another proof of this power of flagellation, assumed by Bishops in very early times,
may be derived from the account which Cyprianus has given of Cesarius, Bishop of Arles; who says, that that Bishop endeavoured
as much as possible, in the exercise of his
power, to keep within the bounds of moderation prescribed by the law of Moses. The

---

∗ " *Noli · perdere paternam diligentiam quam in
ipsâ inquisitione servasti, quando tantorum scelerum
conf.ssionem eruisti, non extendente equuleo, non sul-
cantibus ungulis, non urentibus flammis, sed virga-
rum verber.bus. Qui modus coercionis & à magistris
artium liberalium, & ab ipsis parentibus, & sæpè
etiam in judiciis solet ab Episcopis adhiberi.*"——
This Letter of St. Augustin, addressed to a Man
invested both with military and civil power, as the
Tribune Marcellinus was, in order to exhort him
to employ violence and whipping against those who
differed from him in their opinions, is an additional proof of a melancholy truth that has often
been noticed, which is, that those who exclaim
most bitterly against persecution, when exercised
against them, and are the most ready to claim to-
leration in their own favour, are not always the
most willing to grant the same favour to others.

following are Cyprianus's words. ' This holy
' Man took conftant care, that thofe who were
' fubjected to his authority, whether they were
' of a free, or a fervile condition, when they
' were to be flagellated for fome offence they
' had committed, fhould not receive more
' than thirty-nine ftripes. If any of them,
' however, had been guilty of a grievous
' fault, then indeed he permitted them to be
' again lafhed a few days afterwards, though
' with a fmaller number of ftripes.'

From the two paffages above, we are informed that the power of whipping, poffeffed
by Bifhops, extended to perfons of every
vocation, indifcriminately; and with much
more reafon may we think that thofe perfons
who made profeffion of the Ecclefiaftical Life,
were fubjected to it. In fact, we fee that even
the different dignities which they might poffefs in the Church, did not exempt them from
having a flagellation inflicted upon them by
their Bifhops, when they had been guilty of
offences of rather a grievous kind; and Pope
St. Gregory the Great moveover recommended to the Bifhops of his time, to make a
proper ufe of their authority. In his fixty-
fixth Epiftle, he himfelf prefcribes to Bifhop
Pafchafius, the manner in which he ought
to chaftife Deacon *Hilary*, who had calum-

4

niated Deacon *John.* ' Whereas (he fays)
' guilt ought not to pafs without adequate fa-
' tisfaction, we recommend to Bifhop Pafcha-
' fius to deprive the fame Deacon Hilary of
' his office, and, after having caufed him to
' be publickly lafhed, to confine him to fome
' diftant place; that the punifhment inflicted
' upon one, may thus ferve to the correction
' of many.'

This power of inflicting the brotherly correction of whipping, was alfo poffeffed by the
Abbots and Priors in all the antient Monafteries; though, at the fame time, it was exprefsly provided by the *Rules* of the different
Orders, that the fame fhould be affumed by
no other perfons. ' Let no Man, except the
' Abbot, or him to whom he has intrufted
' his authority, prefume to excommunicate, or
' flog, a Brother.'

When the faults committed by Monks were
of a grievous kind, the Abbot was not only
charged to correct them by means of his dif-
cretionary power of flagellation; but he was
moreover exprefsly directed to exert that
power with rigour. In the *Rule* framed by
St. *Fructuofus,* Bifhop of *Braga,* it is ordained with refpect to a Monk who is convicted of
being *a Liar, a Thief, or a Striker,* ' That
' if, after having been warned by the elder

K 3

'Monks, he neglects to mend his manners,
'he shall, on the third time, be exhorted, in
'the presence of all the Brethren, to leave off
'his bad practices. If he still neglects to re-
'form, let him be flagellated with the utmost
'severity *.' The above Rule of St. Fruc-
tuosus is mentioned by Ecbert, in his Collection of Canons, which, together with the
Councils of England, has been published by
Spelman.

St. Ferreol, Bishop of *Usez*, has framed a
Rule for Monks, which, like that above,
makes severe provisions against such Monks
as are addicted to the practice of thieving.
'With regard to the Monk who stands con-
'victed of theft, if we may still call him a
'Monk, he shall be treated like him who is
'guilty of adultery for the second time; let
'him therefore be chastised with the whip,
'and with great rigour too: the same punish-
'ment ought to be inflicted upon him as up-
'on a fornicator, since it may be justly sus-
'pected that his lewdness has induced him to
'commit theft †.'

---

* Cap. XVI. De mendace, fure, & percussore
Monacho . . . . *Si nec sic se emendaverit, flagelletur
acerrimè.*

† " *Furti scilicet consuum, si adhuc vocare possu*

Committing indecencies with other Monks,
or with Boys, were offences which the Statutes

mus Monachum, quaſi adulterum fecundum, flagello
fubdi & magnâ coerceri afflictione jubemus; dantes
illi unam cum fornicante fententiam, quia & ipfe fu-
ratus eſt ut luxuriaretur."

It is a little furprifing that repeated adultery is,
in the above Rule, exprefsly placed on a level with
fimple fornication. Whether the Framer of this
Rule has done fo purpofely, and thought that
adultery ought to be treated with indulgence, on
account of the uncommon temptation he fuppofed Men were under to commit it, or has only
been very carelefs in his manner of expreffing
himfelf, I fhall not attempt to difcufs. Yet, left
the Reader fhould thence be led to entertain too
bad an opinion of the tenets and morals of Monks
in general, I fhall obferve, that all are not in the
fame way of thinking with refpect to adultery, as
the Framer of the above Rule feems to have been.
As a proof of this, the inftance, I think, may be
produced of that Monk, mentioned in one of the
Epigrams of the Poet Rouffeau, who was a great
enemy to that fin : one day preaching againft
it, he grew fo warm in his arguments, and
took fo much pains to convince his Congregation
of his own abhorrence of it, that at laft he broke
out into the following folemn declaration · ' Yea,
' my Brethren. I had rather, for the good of my

K 4

of Convents likewife directed to be punifhed by severe flagellations; and the above St. Fructuofus, Bifhop of Braga, ordered that the punifhment fhould, in the above cafe, be inflicted publickly. ' If a Monk (it is faid ' in his Rule) is ufed to teaze Boys and young ' Men, or is caught in attempting to give ' them kiffes, or in any other indecent action, ' and the fact be proved by competent wit- ' neffes, let him be publickly whipped *.'

' foul, to have to do with ten Maidens every ' month, than in ten years touch one married ' Woman.'

The following is the Epigram of Rouffeau, which is written in *Marotic* verfes; a kind of jo- cular ftyle among the French, which admits of old words and turns of phrafe.   •

> *Un Cordelier prêchoit fur l'adultère,*   &—s
> *Et s'échauffoit le Moine en fon harnois*
> *A démontrer par maint beau commentaire*
> *Que ce péché bleffoit toutes les loix.*
> *Oui, mes Enfans, dit il, hauffant la voix,*
> *J'aimerois mieux, pour le bien de mon ame,*
> *Avoir à faire à dix filles par mois*
> *Que de touch r en dix ans, une femme.*

* " *Monachus parvulorum & adolefcentulorum confectator, vel qui ofculo vel de quâlibet occafione turpi deprehenfus fuerit inhiare, comprobatâ patenter, per accufatores veriffimos, five teftes, causâ, publicè ver- beretur.*"

Refusing to make proper satisfaction to the Abbot for offences committed, or in general persevering in denying them, were also grievous faults in the eye of the first Founders, or Reformers, of Monastic Orders. In the Rule framed fifty years after that of St. Benedict, in order to improve it, the following direction was contained. ' If the Brothers who have ' been excommunicated for their faults, per- ' severe so far in their pride, as to continue, ' on the ninth hour of the next day, to re- ' fuse to make proper satisfaction to the Ab- ' bot, let them be confined, even till their ' death, and lashed with rods.' Nor is the Rule of the abovementioned Bishop of Braga less severe against those Monks whose pride prevents them from making a proper confession of the offences they may have committed. ' To him (it is said in that Rule) who, ' through pride and inclination to argue, con- ' tinues to deny his fault, let an additional ' and severer flagellation be imparted.'

The habit of holding wanton discourses, or solliciting the Brethren to wickedness, was also deemed by the Founders of religious Orders to deserve severe flagellations; and St. Pacom ordered in his Rule, which, it was said, had been dictated to him by an Angel, that such as had been guilty of the above faults, and

had been thrice admonifhed, fhould be publickly lafhed before the gate of the Convent.

Attempts to efcape from Monafteries, were,
even in very early times, punifhed by flagellation.   We read in Sozomenius, that St. Macarius of Alexandria, Abbot of Nitria in
Thebaid, who had five thoufand Monks under his direction, ordered that chaftifement to
be inflicted upon thofe who fhould attempt to
climb over the walls of the Monafteries. ' If
' any one continues in his wickednefs, and
' fays, I can no longer bear to ftay here, but
' I will pack up my things, and go where
' God will direct me *; let any one of the
' Brothers inform the Prior, and the Prior the
' Abbot, of the fact; let then the Abbot af-
' femble the Brothers, and order the offender
' to be brought before them, and chaftifed
' with rods.'

The holy Founders of religious Orders have
alfo been very fevere, in their provifions, againft
fuch Monks as feek for familiarities with the
other Sex.   In the Rule of the Monaftery of
Agaunus, it was ordained, that, ' If any
' Monk had contracted the bad habit of look-
' ing on Women with concupifcence, the Ab-

* . . . . . *Hic ego durare non poffum, fed acci-
piam cafulam, & eam ubi voluerit Dominus.*

2

' bot ought to be informed of the fact, and
' beſtow upon the Monk a corrective diſci-
' pline; and that, if he did not mend his
' manners in conſequence thereof, he ought
' to be expelled from the Society as a ſcabby
' ſheep, leſt he ſhould ruin others by his ex-
' ample.' The above Monaſtery had been
built by Sigiſmond, King of Burgundy, to
the honour of CXX. Martyrs of the Theban
Legion, of which St. Maurice was the Commander, under the reign of the Emperor
Maximinus.

The above-quoted Rule of St. Fructuoſus,
is no leſs ſevere againſt thoſe Monks who ſeek
for the Company of Women. In the XVth
Chapter, which treats *of the lewd and quar-
relſome* *, it is ordered, that, ' if after hav-
' ing received proper reprehenſions, they per-
' ſiſt in their wicked courſes, they ſhall be
' corrected by repeated laſhings.' And St.
Columbanus, who is the firſt who inſtituted
the Monaſtic Life in France, and has written
a Rule as a ſupplement to that of St. Benedict, alſo expreſſes himſelf with great ſeverity
againſt ſuch Monks as are convicted of having barely converſed with a Woman in the
abſence of witneſſes; for though there are

* Cap. XV. *De laſcivis & clamoſis.*

faults for which he orders only six lashes to be given, yet, in the case here mentioned, he prescribes two hundred. ‘ Let the Man who ‘ has been alone with a Woman, and talked ‘ familiarly to her, either be kept on bread ‘ and water for two days, or receive two hun- ‘ dred lashes *.’

----

* “ *Qui solus cum solâ fœminâ sine personis certis loquitur familiariter, maneat sine cibo, duobus diebus, in pane & aquâ, vel ducentis plagis afficiatur.*”

This Article, in which the Founder of a religious Order expressly rates the hardship of living upon bread and water for one day, at that of receiving an hundred lashes, is somewhat surprising. And supposing the generality of Readers should agree that the loss of a good dinner has really been over-rated by the good Father, his decision on that head, may then serve as one proof of that remarkable love of good eating and drinking which prevails among Monks ; a disposition with which, to say the truth, they have long ago been charged. On this occasion, I shall quote the two following lines in Monkish style, recited by Du Cange in his Glossary, in which the love of good cheer is said to be one of the three things that prove the ruin of Monks : these lines only mention the *black* Monks; but this has been done, we may suppose, for the sake of the measure, and their meaning was, no doubt, also intended to be applied to the *Grey* and *White*.

Sunt tria nigrorum, quæ vastant res Monachorum,
Renes & venter, & pocula sumpta frequenter.

Other modern Latin Writers have also exerted their wit at the expence of the Clergy : some have pretended that the word *Sorbona* (the Sorbonne) comes from *forbendo* * , and others have derived the word *Præsbiter* (a Priest), from *præ aliis bibens ter* †, &c. &c.

As an instance of the love of Monks for entertainments, I shall relate the following story, which is extracted from a Monkish Book, and may serve to give the reader some insight into the manner in which Monks live among themselves, and the internal polity of their Convents

A certain Friar, in a Convent of the Benedictine Order, found means to procure, besides plenty of good wine, a certain number of dishes extremely nice and well seasoned, several of which were expresly forbidden by the Institutes of the Order; and he invited a select party of Brothers to partake of his fare. As they could not, with any degree of safety, carry on the entertainment

---

* Which signifies, to *sip*, or to *swallow*.
† He who drinks thrice times before the others.

in the cell of any of them, they thought of re-pairing to one of the cellars of the Houfe, where they hid themfelves in one of thofe wide and fhal-low tuns (about eight or nine feet in diameter, and three or four deep) which ferve in the making of wines. The Abbot, in the meanwhile, mif-fing fo many of the Monks from the Convent, went in fearch of them through all the different apartments: being unable to find them, he at laft went down into the cellars, and foon per-ceived whereabout they lay : he ftepped up to the place, and, on a fudden, made his appearance over the edge of the tun. The Monks were pro-digioufly alarmed at this unexpected appearance of the Abbot, and there was none among them but who would have gladly compromifed the affair, by giving up his remaining fhare of the entertain-ment, and fubmitting to inftant difmiffion. But the Abbot, contrary to all hope, put on a mild and chearful look. he kindly expoftulated with the Monks on their having made a fecret of the affair to him ; expreffed to them the great pleafure it would have been for him to be one of their par-ty ; and added, that he fhould ftill be very glad to be admitted to partake of the entertainment. The Monks anfwered, by all means : the Abbot there-upon leaped into the tun, fat down among them, partook of their excellent wine and well-feafoned dishes with the greatest freedom, in just the same manner as it is said the late Sir James Lowther would of the dinner of his servants in his own kitchen, and, in short, spent an hour or two with them in the tun, in the most agreeable and convivial manner.

At last, the Abbot thought proper to withdraw; and as soon as he had taken his leave, some of the Monks began to admire his extraordinary condefcenfion; while the others were not without fears that it foreboded some misfortune. Indeed, the latter were in the right; for the Reader must not think that the Abbot had acted in the manner above-described, out of any sudden temptation he had felt at the fight of the jollity of the Friars, or of the dainties that composed their entertainment · by no means; his design had only been, by thus making himself guilty along with them, to be the better able to shew them afterwards the way to repentance, and thereby derive good from evil. In fact, the next day, a chapter having been summoned, the Abbot desired the Prior to fill his place, while himself took his feat among the reft of the Monks. Soon after the Chapter was met, he stepped forward into the middle of the Affembly, accused himself of the fin he had committed the day before, and requested that discipline might be inflicted upon him. The Prior objected much to a discipline being inflicted on the Abbot; but the latter having infifted, his requeft was complied with. The other Monks were at firft greatly aftonifhed; but feeing no poffibility of keeping back on that occafion, they ftepped into the middle of the Chapter, and likewife confeffed their fin; when the Abbot, by means of a proper perfon he had felected for that purpofe, got a lufty difcipline to be inflicted upon every one of his late fellow-banqueters.

CHAP. X.

*Strictness of certain Superiors of Convents, in
exerting their power of flagellation. The
same is abused by several of them.*

THE Reader has seen, in the preceding
Chapter, that the punishment of flagellation was extended to almost every possible
offence Monks could commit; and the dur -
tion of the flagellations was, moreover, left
pretty much to the discretion of the Abbot,
whether in consequence of the generality of
the terms used in the Statutes, or through
some express provision made for that purpose.
In the ancient Constitutions of the Monastery
of Cluny, for instance, which St. Udalric
has collected in one volume, several kinds of
offence are mentioned, for the punishment of
which it is expressly said, that the Offender
shall be lashed *as long as the Abbot shall think
meet.*

That Abbots and Priors have at all times
well known how to exert those discretionary

L

and flagellatory powers we mention, there is
no manner of doubt. On this occafion, the
two following ftories may be related.

The firft is that of the difcipline which
the Prior of a certain Monaftery, who lived
in the times of Charles Martel (A. 750) inflicted on fome Carpenters who were employed by him in the fervice of the Convent, and
who having too carelefsly marked the proper
fize of a certain piece of timber, with their
ftring rubbed with chalk, made afterwards a
miftake in fawing it. The fact, as it is recited in the life of St. Pardulph, is as follows.

‘ One *Liframnus*, the then Prior of the
‘ Monaftery, refolved to build a few wooden
‘ fteps, in the Chapel of St. Albinus the Mar-
‘ tyr. After the Carpenters had meafured
‘ the place on which thofe fteps were to be
‘ raifed, he took them to the wood, where
‘ they accordingly cut a beam, which they
‘ loaded upon a Cart, and conveyed to the
‘ Convent; but when they attempted to fet-
‘ tle it upon the proper fpot, it was found to
‘ be eighteen inches too fhort. The Prior,
‘ amazed at fuch a grofs miftake, fell into a
‘ paffion, and ordered *difciplines* to be inflicted
‘ upon the Carpenters *.’

* . . . *Tum Præpofitus multum fcandalizans,* &

The other fact I mean to relate, to prove the great ſtrictneſs of certain Eccleſiaſtical Su-

iracundiæ furore ſuccenſus, eiſdem Carpentariis diſci-plinam corporis imponi juſſit.

Aulus Gellius, in his *Noctes Atticæ*, relates a fact which bears much reſemblance to the above; though, indeed, much greater Men were concerned in it, than the Prior of a Convent, and Carpenters : the one was a Roman Conſul, and the other, the Engineer of a Town, allied to the Republick.

The name of the Conſul in queſtion was P. Craſſus, who muſt not, however, be miſtaken for the celebrated M. Craſſus, the partner in power with Pompey and Cæſar ; though both lived in the ſame times. This Conſul P. Craſſus, having been intruſted with the conduct of the war that was then carrying on in Aſia, laid ſiege to the Town of Leucas ; and wanting a ſtrong beam of oak to make a battering-ram, he recollected he had lately ſeen at Elæa, a Town allied to the Romans, juſt ſuch a piece of timber as he wiſhed to have : he therefore wrote to the Magiſtrates of that place, to requeſt them to ſend it to him. The Magiſtrates accordingly directed their Engineer to convey the beam to Craſſus ; but as there was another in the yards belonging to the Town, which, the Engineer thought, would be fitter for the uſe

periors in exerting their power of flagellation,
is contained in the Book written by *Thomas de*

Craffus wanted to put it to, he made choice of the
latter, and conveyed it to the Roman camp. However, the Engineer had been miftaken in his cal-
culations, and the beam unfortunately proved too
fmall, which the Conful did no fooner perceive,
and that his orders had been neglected, than, like
the above-mentioned Prior, he fell into a paffion,
and ordered the Engineer to be ftript, and foundly lafhed.

Some apology, however, may be made in favour of the action of the Roman Conful. As
himfelf obferved upon the fpot, the whole bufinefs of war would be at an end, if thofe whofe
duty it is to obey, were permitted to canvafs
the orders which they receive, and to fet afide
what part they pleafe: befides that an allowance
fhould be made for Men of a military life, and
who are invefted with military command; and
fome little indulgence, I think, ought to be fhewn
them, when they happen to inflict flagellations
fomewhat cavalierly. But as to the above holy
Prior, who had made fo many vows of obedience,
humility, forbearance, and the like, it is not, indeed, quite fo eafy a tafk to excufe him: I fhall
not, therefore, undertake it; and I will content
myfelf with obferving, how advantageous it would

Chantpré. ' There was (that Author says) in
' the Church of Rheims, a very able Dean,
' an Englishman by birth *(genere Anglicano)*,
' who, as I have been informed by several
' persons who knew him, used stoutly to cor-
' rect his brother Canons for their faults. It
' happened in his time, that the venerable Al-
' bert, Bishop of Liege, and Brother to the
' Duke of Brabant, was driven out of Ger-
' many by the Emperor Henry, and treache-
' rously slain by a few Soldiers of that Em-

have been both for the above Engineer and Carpenters, in the perplexing situations in which they
were respectively placed, to have possessed a power
of the same kind as that which the Golden Legend (or perhaps some other Book of equal merit) supposes Jesus Christ to have exerted on a si-
milar occasion. Joseph, as it is related, who had
the care of the infant Jesus trusted to him, tried
to bring him up to his own trade of a Carpenter,
and one day, finding that the Boy had sawed a
piece of wood shorter than the measure he had
prescribed, he ran up to him, full of anger,
with a stick raised in his hand, in order to chastise
him, but the arch apprentice, who was beginning to be conscious of his power of working
miracles, on a sudden exerted it, and lengthened
the piece of wood to its proper size.

' peror, near the City of Rheims. On the
' day appointed to celebrate his funeral, the
' venerable Rothard, who, though he was ftill
' Archdeacon of Rheims, had lately been
' elected Bifhop of Châlons in *Champagne*,
' made his appearance, accompanied by a
' number of noble perfons, without being
' clothed in his Canonical gown. After the
' ceremony was concluded, the Dean called all
' the Canons together, and among them the
' above Bifhop. As foon as they were feated,
' the Dean faid to the Prelate, You have not,
' as far as I know, refigned yet your Canon-
' fhip, or Archdeaconfhip? The latter made
' anfwer, he had not. Well then, faid the
' Dean, come and make fatisfaction to the
' Church, and prepare your back for a difci-
' pline in the prefence of the Brothers, for
' your having been at the choir without the
' nuptial-robe. The Bifhop-elect made no
' objection: he rofe from his feat, ftripped
' himfelf, and received a moft vigorous difci-
' pline from the Dean: this done, he put on
' again his clothes, and, before the whole con-
' gregation, faid to the Dean in a moft grace-
' ful manner, I give thanks to God, and to
' his bleffed Mother, the Patronefs of the

' Church of Rheims, that I leave it under the
' government of fuch a perfon as you *.'

Indeed fo far have a number of Abbots, or
Superiors of Convents, been from fuffering
their power of flagellation to lay dormant and
ufelefs, that they, on the contrary, have abufed
it to a great degree. Ovifiefius cautioned
them, in very early days, againft being guilty
of fuch a fault. Nay, certain Heads of Monafteries have gone fuch lengths in that refpect, that Cefarius, Bifhop of Arles, was obliged to remind them, that, ' if they inflicted
' flagellations continued too long upon Of-
' fenders, fo that they died in confequence
' thereof, they were guilty of homicide.'

Among thofe Abbots who have diftinguifhed themfelves by their feverity, St. Romuald
may be mentioned, who, as we are informed
in his Life written by Cardinal Damianus, was
once expofed to a calumny of the blackeft
kind, from a Monk whom he ufed to fcourge
with great feverity: nay, that holy Man's

* . . . . . . Nec mora, veftes exuit Electus, &
Decani validiffimam difciplinam accepit · quâ acceptâ,
veftibus reindutus, Decano cum maximâ oris gratiâ co-
ram omnibus dixit, gratias ago Deo, & Patronæ
Remenfis Ecclefiæ ejus puiffimæ genitrici, quod te ta-
lim in regimine relinquo. Lib. II. Cap. XXXIX.
Num. 20.

L 4

Monks, as we are alfo informed by Cardinal Damianus, in one inftance rofe againft him, flog ged l im without mercy, and drove him out of the Convent. This Saint, befides, had before been frequently lafhed by the Devil *.

---

* The arbitrary power of inflicting flagella tions, poffeffed by Abbots, ought, one fhould think, to infure them in a high degree the veneration of their Monks, yet, from the manner in which St Remuald is above faid to have been ufed by thofe under his government, we may conclude the cafe is otherwi e

A farther proof of the great freedom with which Monks ufe their Abbet, is to be derived from what Monf Richelet fays, in his well-known Dictionary of the French language, that Monks never trouble their heads about waiting for their Abbot, when he comes too late to dinner. Monf Richelet informs us of this fact under the word *Abbé*, when he explains the origin of the French common faying, *on l'attend comme les Moines font l'Abbé* (they wait for him, as Monks do for their Abbot), which is faid jocularly of a perfon who is not at all waited for this faying is derived, the above Gentleman obferves, from the remarkable

expedition with which Monks fit down to their
dinner, as foon as the bell ftrikes, without caring
whether the Abbot is come or not.

This fingular piece of neglect on the part of
Monks, towards a perfon invefted with fuch formidable prerogatives as thofe abovementioned,
may be accounted for, different ways. In the firft
place, fince Monks are fo celebrated for their love
of good dinners, and even entertain fuch high
notions of the value of a plentiful table, as to
have rated the hardfhip of living upon bread
and water, at that of receiving a hundred lafhes
a day, we may naturally fuppofe, that, when their
mefs is ferved upon the table, their attention is fo
agreeably engaged by the prefence of that object,
that they prefently run to it, wholly regardlefs of
any trifling flagellation that may afterward be the
confequence of fuch expedition.

The fame neglectful conduct of Monks towards their Abbot, though he is poffeffed of fuch
a defpotic power over them, may alfo be explained in another manner · for, the fubject is deep,
and being confidered in a political light, may
admit a number of different interpretations. In
general, it may be obferved. that Monks may eafily form clofe combinations among themfelves
againft their Abbots, that as the latter live together with them, within the walls of the fame Monafteries, they have it in their power to play them

a thoufand tricks; and that thefe confiderations are very apt to induce Abbots to make a mild ufe of their authority, at leaft with refpect to the greater part of their Monks.

Indeed this latter explanation agrees pretty well with feveral facts. It has frequently happened, for inftance, that Abbots who have ufed their Monks with cruelty, have been made away with, in fome way or other, within the walls of their Monafteries. The Abbé Boileau informs us in his Book, that St. Romuald was much maltreated, and at laft expelled by his Monks, which, no doubt, was owing to the flagellations he inflicted upon them, flagellations which the Abbé alfo mentions, though he does not affign the caufes of them, whether it was becaufe they did not wait for him at dinner, or for fome other reafon, but the truth and feverity of which we fhall the more readily believe, if we confider that the Saint, upon a certain occafion, as will be related hereafter, flagellated even his own Father. Nay, it is not quite unlikely that thofe flagellations which the Saint ufed to imagine he received from the hands of the Devil, were the effects of the revenge of his Monks; till at laft they openly revolted againft him, and turned him out of the Monaftery.

Since we are upon the fubject of St. Romuald, it will not be amifs to add, that the flagellations which he received both from the Devil, and from his Monks, were however nothing in compaiifon with the danger to which he was once expofed, on account of his very fanctity.

The Saint, as is related in the Hiftory of his Life, was once fettled in a certain Convent in Catalonia, and was in great reputation for his virtue in the neighbourhood. The report having been fpread that the holy Man was going to leave the Country, the People began to be afraid that they fhould thereby be deprived of the poffeffion of his relicks, to which they thought they had a fair title, on account of the length of time he had refided among them, and they formed the ingenious fcheme of murdering him, in order to fecure to themfelves the poffeffion of his body, but the Saint, having received timely information of the plot, thought proper to decline the honour that was intended for him, and made his efcape.

CHAP. XI.

Difciplines of the fame wholefome kind have been prefcribed for Novices, and fuch perfons as are intended to embrace the Ecclefiaftical Life.

THE framers of Rules and Statutes of religious Orders have alfo extended their attention to the young Men and Novices brought up in Convents; and have ordered flagellations to be inflicted upon them, for the improvement of their morals. In the Rule framed by the holy Fathers Serapion, Macarius, and Paphnutius, which is to be found in the Collection of Holftenius, it is ordered, ‘ That if any Novice is found guilty of theft, ‘ he fhall be lafhed with rods, and never ad- ‘ mitted to the degree of Clerk.’

St. Pacom, in that Rule which was dictated to him by an Angel, expreffes himfelf in the following terms : ‘ Let thofe Boys who are re- ‘ gardlefs of the evil confequences of fin, and ‘ are fo imprudent as not to mind the judg-

' ments of Heaven, in cafe admonitions prove
' ufelefs, be whipped till they have the fear
' of God.'

In the Rule of St. Benedict, Art. LXX.
flagellations are prefcribed as excellent methods of improving the minds of fuch Boys
as are brought up to the Ecclefiaftic life; and
are more particularly recommended to be ufed
till they are fifteen years of age.

St. Ifidorus, archbifhop of Seville, obferves,
that Boys ought not to be excommunicated
for their fins, but that this awful mode of correction ought to be fupplied, with them, by
flagellations.

At the fame time, left thofe who were to
infpect the conduct of the Novices, fhould
fuffer themfelves to be influenced by paffion,
in the flagellations they were directed to inflict, an exprefs provifion was made in the
Rule of St. Benedict, that fuch Teachers as
fhould be guilty of the above fault, fhould
themfelves receive a found flogging *.

---

* A certain modern Latin Author, whofe
name I have forgot, has written a Treatife on the
antiquity of the practice fo much recommended
above, of whipping boys at School. Had I been
fo happy as to have feen his Book, I would have
been enabled to make, in this place, learned re-

marks on the fubject; but as I have not had that advantage, I find myfelf unable to make any, and can only refer the Reader to the difcovery of Uncle Thomas, as well as to the few other critical annotations that are contained in p. 76, 77, 78, of this Work.

I could have likewife wifhed much to be able to add the names of fome of thofe illuftrious Characters who have diftinguifhed themfelves in the practice of flagellating School-boys, to thofe of the refpectable Thwackum, and the *plagofus* Orbilius, mentioned in the above place, but though the Hiftory of great Schools, in this and other Countries, fupplies numbers of fuch names, yet I have not been able to difcover any of fufficient eminence to deferve a place in this Book; except indeed that of the great Doctor *Tempête*, who is mentioned by Rabelais as a celebrated flagellator of School-boys in the *College* of *Montaigu*, in Paris, and which I therefore infert in this place.

Neither fhould we neglect to mention here, the name of Buchanan, his pupil having afterwards been a King, and the more fo, as he ufed, it feems, to make the flagellations beftowed by him on his royal difciple *(the Anointed of the Lord)* the fubject of his jokes with the Ladies at Court *.

---

* King James the Firft.—See Dr. Berkenhout's *Biographia Literaria.*

3

The juſtice which is due to the Reverend Fathers Jeſuits, alſo requires that we ſhould, in a Book like this, give an account of the laudable regularity with which they uſed to inflict flagellations upon the young Men who purſued their ſtudies in their Schools, as well as upon ſuch Strangers as were occaſionally recommended to them for that purpoſe. Among the different facts which may ſerve to prove both the ſpirit of juſtice that has conſtantly directed the actions of the Society, and the punctuality of their flagellations, the following is not the leaſt remarkable.

It was, the Reader ought to know, an eſtabliſhed cuſtom in their Schools, to give prizes every year to ſuch Scholars as had made the beſt Latin verſes upon propoſed ſubjects. One year it happened that the ſubject which had been fixed upon, was the Society of the Jeſuits itſelf; and a Scholar took that opportunity, only by quibbling on the names of the two principal Schools belonging to the Fathers, to give them a ſmart ſtroke of ſatire. The name of the one of theſe two Schools, was the School of the Bow *(le College de l'Arc)*, which was ſituated at Dôle, in Franche-Comté; and the other happened to be called, the School of the Arrow *(la Fléche)*, it being ſituated near the Town of that name in Anjou, and was originally a Royal manſion which was given by the Crown to the Society, in the reign of King

Henry the Fourth   The import of the diftich
made by the School-boy (or perhaps by fomebody
elfe for him) was this . " Dôle gave the Bow to
the Fathers, mother France gave them the Arrow ,
who fhall give them the Sting which they have
deferved?" The following are the Latin verfes
themfelves, which indeed are very beautiful.

Arcum *Dôla dedit Patribus, dedit alma* Sagittam
Gallia , quis funem *quem meruere dabit ?*

The Reverend Fathers, ftruck with the merit
of thefe lines, and, at the fame time, unwilling
to fuffer a bon-mot made at their expence, and
that was fo likely to be circulated, to go unpu-
nifhed, delivered the prize to the boy, and ordered
him to be flagellated immediately after.

The celebrated Fathers of St. *Lazare*, in Paris,
whofe School was otherwife named the " Seminary of the good Boys" (*des bons enfans*) have no
lefs recommended themfelves by the regularity of
the difciplines they inflicted, than the Reverend
Fathers Jefuits. They were even fuperior to the
latter, in regard to thofe *recommendatory* flagellations
mentioned above, which were adminiftered to
fuch perfons as were, by fome means or other,
induced to deliver letters to the Fathers for that
purpofe. Being fituated in the metropolis, the
Seminary carried on, a very extenfive bufinefs in
that way. Fathers or Mothers who had undutiful

Sons, Tutors who had unruly Pupils, Uncles who were intrusted with the education of ungovernable Nephews, Masters who had wickedly-inclined Apprentices, whom they durst not themselves undertake to correct, applied to the Fathers of St. Lazare, and by properly feeing them, had their wishes gratified. Indeed the Fathers had found means to secure their doors with such good bolts, they were so well stocked with the necessary implements or giving disciplines, and had such a numerous crew of stout *Cuistres* to inflict them, that they never failed to execute any job they had engaged to perform, and without minding either age, courage, or strength, were at all times ready to undertake the most difficult flagellations. So regular was the trade carried on, by the good Fathers in that branch of Business, that letters of the above kind directed to them, were literally notes of hand payable on sight; and provided such notes did but come to hand, whoever the bearer might be, the Fathers were sure to have them discharged with punctuality.

This kind of business, as it was carried on, for a number of years, frequently gave rise to accidents, or mistakes, of rather a ludicrous kind. Young men who had letters to carry to the House of St. Lazare, the contents of which they did not mistrust, would often undesignedly charge other persons to carry the same for them, either on ac-

M

count of their going to that part of the town, or for some other reason of a like kind : and the unfortunate bearer, who suspected no harm, had no sooner delivered the dangerous letter with which he had suffered himself to be intrusted, than he was collared, and rewarded for his good-nature by a severe and unexpected flagellation.

Ladies, it is likewise said, who had been forsaken, or otherwise ungenteelly used, by their Admirers, when every other means of revenge failed, would also recur to the ministry of the Fathers of St. Lazare. Either by making interest with other persons, or using some artfully-contrived scheme, the provoked Fair-one endeavoured to have the Gentleman who caused her grief, inveigled into the House of the Seminary. at the same time she took care to have a letter to recommend him, sent there from some unknown quarter, with proper fees in it; for that was a point that must not be neglected: and when the Gentleman came afterwards to speak with the Fathers, he was no sooner found by them, either from the nature of the business he said he came upon, or other marks, to be the person mentioned in the letter they had before received, than they shewed him into an adjoining-room, where this treacherous and deceitful Lover was immediately seized, mastered, and every thing in short was performed that was requifite to procure ample fatisfaction to the fair injured Lady.

It is alfo faid (for a number of ftories are related on that fubject, and the Seminary of St. Lazare was become for a while an object of terror to all Paris) that fchemes of the moft abufive kind were in latter times carried on, through the connivance which the Fathers began to fhew at the knavery of certain perfons: and this indeed feems to be a well-afcertained part of the ftory. Abufes of the fame kind as thofe which once prevailed in the Mad-houfes eftablifhed in this country, were at laft practifed in the Seminary. Men poffeffed of eftates which fome near relations wanted to enjoy, or whom it was the intereft of other perfons to keep for a while out of the way, were inveigled into the Houfe of St. Lazare, where they were detained, and large fums paid monthly for their board. Though they might be full-grown perfons, they were boldly charged with having been naughty, or fuch-like grievous guilt, and the Fathers, in order to fhew that they meant to act a perfectly honeft part in the affair, ordered them to be flagellated with more than common regularity.

Nor was it of any fervice for the unfortunate boarders to expoftulate with the Fathers, to infift that it was unlawful to detain them by force in a ſtrange houſe, and uſe them in the manner they were uſed, that they had important affairs which they muſt go and ſettle, that they were no boys, after all, or to offer other equally pertinent arguments : the Fathers continued to be well paid, they cared for no more, and all the complainants got by raiſing objections like theſe, were cold negative anſwers, and freſh flagellations. Abuſes of the kind we mention, came at laſt to the knowledge of the Government, which interpoſed its authority, and the Seminary was aboliſhed.

C H A P. XII.

The same discretionary power of inflicting disci-
ciplines, has been established in the Convents
of Nuns, and lodged in the hands of the Ab-
besses, and Prioresses.

NOR have the holy Founders of religious
Orders considered flagellations as being
less useful in the Convents of Women, than
in those of Men; and in the Rules they have
framed for them, they have accordingly ordered that kind of correction to be inflicted
upon those whose bad conduct made it necessary.

This chastisement of flagellation, upon Women who make profession of a religious life,
is no new thing in the world. It was the
chastisement appropriated to the Vestals, in antient Rome; and we find in the Historians,
that when faults had been committed by them
in the discharge of their functions, it was
commonly inflicted upon them by the hands
of the Priests, or sometimes of the Great
Priest himself.

M 3

Dionyfius of Halicarnaffus relates, that the Virgin Urbinia was lafhed by the Priefts, and led in proceffion through the Town.

The High-prieft, Publius Licinius, ordered, as we read in Valerius Maximus, ' that a ' certain Veftal who had fuffered the facred ' fire to be extinguifhed, fhould be lafhed and ' difmiffed.'

Julius likewife relates, ' that the fire in the ' Temple of Vefta, having happened to be ' extinguifhed, the Virgin was whipped by ' the High-prieft, M. Æmilius, and promifed ' never to offend again in the fame manner.' And Feftus fays in his Book, that ' whenever ' the fire of Vefta came to be extinguifhed, ' the Virgins were lafhed by the Great Prieft.'

Severities of the like kind have been deemed neceffary to be introduced into the Convents of modern Nuns, by the holy Fathers who have framed religious Rules for them.

In that very antient Rule for the conduct of Nuns, which is contained in Epiftle CIX. of St. Auguftin, the mortification of difcipline is prefcribed to the Priorefs herfelf. ' Let her ' (it is faid in the above Rule) be ever ready ' to receive difcipline, but never impofe it but ' with fear *.'

* Num. XIL " D f p nem dens h bat, me t ens impona:."

Cefarius, Archbifhop of Arles, in the Rule framed by him, which is mentioned with praife by feveral antient Authors, fuch as Gennadius, and Gregory of Tours, prefcribes the difcipline of flagellation to be inflicted upon Nuns who have been guilty of faults; and enters, befides, into feveral particulars about the propriety as well as ufefulnefs of this method of correction. ' It is juft (he fays) that ' fuch as have violated the inftitutions con-' tained in the Rule, fhould receive an ade-' quate difcipline: it is fit that in them fhould ' be accomplifhed what the Holy Ghoft has ' in former times prefcribed through Solomon. ' *He who loves his Child, frequently applies the* ' *rod to it.*'

St. Donat, Archbifhop of Bezancon, in the Rule he has framed for Nuns, has expreffed the fame paternal difpofition towards them, as Archbifhop Cefarius has done: he recommends flagellations as excellent methods of mending the morals of fuch of them as are wickedly inclined, or carelefs in performing their religious duties; and he determines the different kinds of faults for which the above correction ought to be beftowed upon them, as well as the number of the blows that are to be inflicted. The above Rule of St. Donat

M 4

has been mentioned with much praife by the Monk Jonas, in his Account of the Life of St. Columbanus, which the venerable Beda has inferted in the third volume of his Works.

In that Rule, commonly called the *Rule of a Father*, which St. Benedict, Bifhop of Aniana, in his Book *on the Concordance of Rules*, and Smaragdus, in his Commentaries on the Rule of St. Benedict, have both mentioned, provifions of the fame kind as thofe above, are made for the correction of Nuns. ' If a ' Sifter (it is faid in that Rule) that has been ' feveral times admonifhed, will not mend her ' conduct, let her be excommunicated for a ' while, in proportion to the degree of her ' fault: if this kind of correction proves ufe- ' lefs, let her then be chaftifed by ftripes.'

Striking a Sifter, has likewife been looked upon as an offence of a grievous kind; and St. Aurelian, in the Rule he has framed for Nuns, orders a difcipline to be inflicted on fuch as have been guilty of it.

To the above regulations, Archbifhop Cefarius has added another, which is, that the corrections ought, for the fake of example, to be inflicted in the prefence of all the Sifters. ' Let alfo the difcipline be beftowed upon ' them in the prefence of the Congregation,

' conformably to the precept of the Apoftle,
' *Confute Sinners in the prefence of all* *.'

The Abbé Boileau, after the manner of the
Learned of former times, has added to his quotations on the flagellations of Veftals, a ftring of
names of Writers who have alfo occafionally mentioned that cuftom ; fuch as *Rofinus* on the Roman
Antiquities, *Fortunius Licetus* on the Lamps of
the Ancients, *Jofephus Laurens* of Lucca, *Poly-
mathias* in his Differtations, and *Jacobus Ghuterius*
on the rights of the ancient Pontiffs. Thefe
Writers, as far as I can perceive, have neglected
to inform us of an important circumftance, which
is, of what kind thofe *difciplines* were, that were
inflicted upon Veftals, whether *upper* or *lower*
difciplines. However, they have informed us of
a fact about which the Reader, no doubt, particularly wifhes to be fatisfied, which is, that a
great regard was paid to decency in the above flagellations, and that, as the correction was inflicted in an open place, and by the hands of a
Prieft, the guilty Veftal was wrapped in a veil during the ceremony.

The flagellations which perfons who live in
Convents, are upon different occafions made to undergo, the obligation they are under, of receiving

fuch corrections before the whole Brotherhood or
Sifterhood, together with the comparifons which
the holy Founders of religious Orders have made
of them with naughty children, have drawn numerous jefts upon them, but fuch jefts can only
come from perfons who have not paid a fufficient
attention to the fubject.

Politicians inform us, that it is abfolutely neceffary that, in all States, there fhould be Powers
of different kinds, eftablifhed to maintain the general harmony of the whole, and that Legiflative,
Executive, Military, and Judicial Powers, for inftance, fhould be formed, and lodged in different
hands.   Hence we may conclude, that fome power
analogous to thefe, ought to exift in every numerous Society either of Men or Women, for the
prefervation of good Order, and that it is neceffary that, in fuch Societies, a power of flagellation fhould be lodged fomewhere.

Nor are we to think that Convents are the
only Societies in which fome authority of this
kind takes place.   In the Eaftern Seraglios, for
inftance, Societies which are by no means con-
temptible, and may very well bear a comparifon
with Convents, we are not to doubt, a power of
occafionally inflicting flagellations, exifts: nay,
we are exprefsly informed that Empreffes themfelves are not always exempt from them.   Thus
M. de Montefquieu, in the 26th Chapter of the

Book XIX. of his Spirit of Laws, relates, after the Hiſtorian of Juſtinian the Second, that the Empreſs, Wife of the Emperor, ' was threaten- ' ed, by the great Eunuch, with that kind of ' chaſtiſement with which children are puniſhed ' at School :' a treatment certainly very ſevere, and from which one ſhould be tempted to judge that Empreſſes, at leaſt, ought to be exempt, if it were not that the advantages of peace and good order are ſuch, as ought to ſuperſede every other conſideration.

In the Palaces of the Weſtern Sovereigns, though they have conſtantly borne a very different appearance either from Convents or Seraglios, we find that diſciplines like thoſe abovementioned were found extremely uſeful about two centuries ago (a time when Men had notions of decorum much ſuperior to ours) and were in conſequence employed as common methods of preſerving good order, without much diſtinction of rank or ſex.

Of the above fact we have a proof, in the misfortune that befel Mademoiſelle de Limeuil, at the Court of France, where ſhe was a Maid of Honour to the Queen, Wife to King Henry II. as we find in the *Mémoires de Brantôme :* for my reſpect for the Reader induces me to offer him only ſuch anecdotes as are ſupported by good authorities. Mademoiſelle de Limeuil, as Bran- tôme relates, was a very witty handſome young

Lady, extremely ready at her pen, and related to the beſt families in the Kingdom. She was placed at Court in the capacity of Maid of Honour to the Queen; and ſhe had been there but a few months, when ſhe tried her wit at the expence of the Gentlemen and Ladies at Court, and wrote a copy of verſes, or Paſquinade, in which few Characters were ſpared. As theſe verſes were ingeniouſly written, they ſpread very faſt, and people were very curious to know who had compoſed this piece of ſatire: at laſt, it was found out that Mademoiſelle de Limeuil was the Author of it; and as the Queen, beſides being a perſon of a ſerious temper, was grown diſguſted with the great licence of writing that had of late prevailed at Court, and had determined at leaſt to prevent any ſatire, or lampoon, from originating in her own Houſhold, orders were given in conſequence of which Mademoiſelle de Limeuil was rewarded for her verſes by a flagellation, and thoſe young Ladies in the ſuite of the Queen, who had been privy to the compoſition of the Paſquinade, were likewiſe flagellated.

The inſtances of flagellations juſt now related, from which, neither the beauty, nor the birth, nor the rank of the Culprits, nor the brilliancy of their wit, their readineſs at their pen, nor happy turn for Satire, could ſcreen them, clearly ſhew how much flagellations were in eſteem in the times

we fpeak of, and how much efficacy they were
thought to poffefs, for infuring thofe two great advantages, good order and decorum   There is no
doubt therefore, but that they were ftill more
ftrictly ufed for the improvement of the morals of
thofe fwarms of unruly young Men, who then
filled the Houfes of Kings, or of the Great, and
went by the name of Pages.   Indeed we find that
the Gentlemen, or Equerries, whofe care it was
to fuperintend their conduct, were invefted with a
very extenfive power of inflicting flagellations;
and fo frequent were the occafions in which they
found it neceffary to ufe corrections of this kind,
that the words *flagellation*, and *Page*, are become
as it were effentially connected together, and it is
almoft impoffible to mention the one, without
raifing an idea of the other : I fhall therefore for-
bear to relate any inftances of fuch corrections;
and flagellations of Pages, like thofe of School-
boys, are too vulgar flagellations to have a place in
this Book.

Nor were difciplines like thofe we mention,
impofed only upon thofe perfons who exprefsly
made part either of the Royal or Noble Houfholds, for the edification of which they were inflicted ; but wholefome corrections of the fame
kind were alfo occafionally beftowed upon fuch
Strangers as happened to infringe the rules of decorum, or in any other manner, offended againft

6

the refpect that was owing to the Royal or Noble Proprietor of the Houfe.

Of this we have an undeniable proof in the Story of that Reverend Father Jefuit, who wa. flagellated at Vienna, as Brantôme relates, by command of a Princefs of the Auftrian Houfe, whofe difpleafure he had incurred.

The Princefs here alluded to, was daughter to the Emperor Maximilian II. She had been former-ly married to Charles IX. King of France, and after the death of that Prince, by whom fhe had had no children, fhe retired to Vienna in Auftria. Philip II. King of Spain, having about that time loft his wife, fent propofals of marriage to the Princefs we mention, who was at the fame time his Niece, and the Mother of the Princefs, a Sif-ter to Philip II. was very prefling to induce her to accept the above propofals; which the Princefs Elizabeth (fuch was her name) otherwife Queen-Dowager of France, perfevered in refufing. The Emprefs, and the King of Spain, then thought of employing the agency of a Father Jefuit, a learned fmooth-tongued Man, who was to per-fuade the Princefs to accept the offers of Philip; but the endeavours of the Father having proved ineffectual, he at laft defifted from importuning the Princefs any more, and retired. The King of Spain then fent new letters to the Princefs con-cerning the fame fubject, and the Jefuit was fent for a fecond time, and injoined to exert again all his efforts to make the affair fucceed. In confequence of thefe orders, the Jefuit refumed his function ; but the Princefs, whom Brantome reprefents as having been a perfon of much merit, and who certainly muft have had fome, fince fhe refolutely perfevered in refufing to marry that abominable Tyrant, Philip the Second, the Princefs, I fay, grew much difpleafed with the importunities of the Jefuit ; and at laft fpoke very harfhly to him, and plainly threatened him, if he dared to mention a word more to her on the fubject, with an immediate flagellation *(de le faire fouetter en fa cuifine)*.

To the above account Brantôme adds, that fome fay that the Jefuit having been fo imprudent as to renew afterwards his follicitations, actually received the chaftifement he had been threatened with. But though himfelf is rather inclined to difbelieve the fact, yet he does not, we are to obferve, alledge any reafons for fo doing, that are drawn, either from the impropriety of flagellations in general, or from the inability he fuppofes in them to reprefs bold intrufion, to put a ftop to teazing importunities, or to confute captious arguments : by no means ; he only fays that the Princefs in queftion was of too gentle a temper to have made good her threats to the Jefuit, befides that fhe generally bore great refpect to Men of his cloth.

To the above remarkable inftances of flagellations performed in the Palaces of the Great, I
will add another which is not lefs pregnant with
interefting confequences. I mean to fpeak of the
Story of that Court Buffoon, who, upon a certain occafion, was flagellated at the Court of Spain.

The fact is related in the fame Memoirs of
Brantôme, in a Chapter the fubject of which is,
that ' *Ladies ought never to be difrefpectfully fpoken
to, and the ill confequences thereof.*'

· The name of the Buffoon in queftion was *Le-
gat*, and he ventured once to try his wit upon the
Queen herfelf, Wife to Philip II. This Queen,
who was a Princefs of France, and is the fame
whom Philip was afterwards accufed of having
made away with, on account of the love he fuppofed between her and his fon Don Carlos, had
taken a particular fancy for two of the Country
Houfes belonging to the King; and one day, being in converfation with the Ladies at Court, fhe
mentioned her liking to the two feats in queftion,
which were fituated, the one in the neighbourhood of Madrid, and the other of Valladolid,
and expreffed a wifh they were fo near to each
other, that fhe might touch both at once with her
feet: faying which, fhe made a motion with her
legs, which fhe opened pretty wide: the Buffoon
could not hold his tongue, and made rather a
coarfe remark on the fubject, which Brantôme has

related at length in Spanifh : the confequence of
which was, that he was inftantly hurried out of
the room, and entertained with a found flagellation. It may not, however, be improper to add,
that Brantôme tries in fome degree to excufe him,
at leaft for thinking as he did ; and he concludes
with faying, that the Queen (whom he had had feveral occafions of feeing) was fo handfome, and
fo civil to all, that there was no want of Men difpofed to love her, who were an hundred thoufand
times better than the Buffoon *.

All the facts above related, manifeftly fhew that
flagellations have been frequently ufed in the Palaces both of the Eaftern Sovereigns, and of the
Princes of Europe , that they were employed for
the correction of the higheft as well as the loweft
perfonages, and for the prevention of every kind
of fault, from that of meddling in State affairs

---

* Corrections of a flagellatory kind continue, in thefe
days, to be looked upon as excellent expedients for infuring
good order, in the houfes of great people, in Ruffia, in fome
diftricts of Germany, and efpecially in Poland, where moft
of the feudal cuftoms that prevailed two or three hundred
years ago in other parts of Europe, are ftill in full force :
lower difciplines are, in the latter kingdom, the method
commonly employed for mending the manners of Servants of
both fexes. A regulation was made, a few years ago, in
Poland, as it appeared from the foreign new-papers, with a
view to abridge the power affumed by Mafters in regard to
their Servants

N

(which we may suppose was the fault committed by the Empress, though the Historian of Justinian II. says nothing about it) down to wanton language and immodesty: now all these considerations are wonderfully fit to confute the jests which are thrown upon Monks and Nuns, for also making flagellations their usual means of self, or mutual, correction.

It is, however, very important to observe, that though we are fully informed of the different ceremonies with which flagellations are imposed in Convents, we have not the same advantage in regard to those which were inflicted in the Palaces of Princes, or Noble Personages. We are, for instance, told by Authors, by Du Cange among others, in one or two places of his Glossary, of the modesty with which culprits upon whom a correction is to be inflicted in Convents, are to strip off their clothes, and the silence which must be observed by the whole Assembly during the operation; unless the persons invested with the different dignities in the Convent, choose to speak in behalf of the sufferer, and pray the Abbot, or Abbess, to put an end to the flagellation. We are abundantly informed, in different Books, of the various causes for which flagellations are to be employed in Monasteries: and we moreover know that they are to be inflicted in the presence of the whole Congregation, in the Convents of Men, by the hands of a vigorous Brother, and in those of Nuns, by those of an elderly morose Sister.

In regard to the corrections of the same kind that were served in the Palaces of the Great, we have, I repeat it, no such compleat informations as these. Though the instances of such corrections are undeniable, we are much in the dark about the different rites and solemnities that used to accompany them · yet it would be a very interesting thing to be acquainted with these several circumstances, and to know, at least, what particular place, in Palaces, was set apart for the operations we mention. Concerning this latter object, I will try to offer a few conjectures, for I do not think so meanly of my Readers, as to rank them among that class of shallow readers, who only mind the outward superficies of things.

In the first place, I do not think that there was any place so expressly appropriated for flagellations, in the Palaces we speak of, but that others might occasionally be used for the same purpose, according to circumstances. Though Politicians lay it down as assured maxims, that punishments are to be inflicted for the sake of example, and that such examples ought to be public, yet, there were so great differences between the dignities of the personages who were liable to receive corrections of the kind we mention, that they must needs have introduced exceptions in favour of some of them;

at leaft with regard to the places of the ope‑
rations.

Thus, for inftance, though in the Eaftern Se‑
raglios they may be fully fenfible of the truth of
the above maxim, and of the expediency of cor‑
recting Offenders in the prefence of all, yet, we
are not to think, that when the Emprefs herfelf
is to receive a flagellation, fuch correction is ferved
in a place abfolutely public; for inftance, in the
third, otherwife the outmoft, inclofure of the Se‑
raglio, in which a fwarm of *Icoghlans, Boftangis,
Capigi-Bafhis,* and other officers of every kind
are admitted.   Neither is the ceremony performed
in the fecond, or the firft inclofure of the Serag‑
lio, nor even in any common apartment in the in‑
fide of the Palace, in fight of a croud of vulgar
beauties, who have never been admitted to the
honour of the embraces, or even of the prefence
of the Monarch.   A flagellation ferved upon a
perfonage of fo much eminence as an Emprefs, is
an event fufficiently important of itfelf, for the
bare report of it, to produce all the good effects
that are ufually expected from examples of that
kind.   The only effential thing, is to afcertain fuch
fact: this important point being obtained, every
proper regard ought to be fhewn to the delicacy of
the great perfonage who is to receive the correction
we mention; and whenever an Emprefs, in the
Eaftern Seraglios, happens to be ferved with a fla‑

gellation, we are to judge that the operation is performed in the Emprefs's own private Chamber, in the prefence of two or three favourite Sultanas.

Nor were prudential confiderations of the fame kind, lefs attended to in the Palaces of the Weftern Princes. When Maids of Honour had the misfortune to draw upon themfelves the correction of a flagellation, we are not to think that the perfons charged with the fuperintendence of the ceremony, adhered fo blindly to thofe maxims which require that examples of this kind fhould be public, as to have the operation performed in a place literally public and open to all perfons; that they, for inftance, chofe for the fcene of the ceremony, that vaft Yard, or Court, that lay before the Palaces of Kings, and was continually filled with Grooms, Pages, Keepers of Hounds, Huntfmen, and Servants of every denomination, fome of whom blew the French horn, others the trumpet, and others played on other mufical inftruments. No, fuch a place would have been in a high degree improper: nor would any open apartment or office, within the Palace, have been much more fuitable for the occafion. The bare report of a flagellation being ferved upon fo interefting a perfon as a Maid of Honour, was fufficient to produce all the good effects for which fuch examples are commonly intended: there was no neceffity rigidly to adhere either to the above-

N 3

mentioned maxim, or to the rule laid down by
Horace, who fays, that mens' minds are more
ftrongly affected by fuch objects as are laid before
their eyes, than by thofe of which they only receive an hearfay information.   The report well
afcertained, of fuch an event, was fully fufficient
to remind a croud of unlucky Pages, and wanton
Chambermaids, of their refpective duties, and engage them in a ferious examination of their own
conduct.   All that was neceffary, was to put fuch
fact beyond a doubt, to prevent its being afterwards queftioned by fome, and flatly denied by
others . but thefe important ends being attained,
there was no juft reafon to refufe to fhew the
greateft tendernefs for the delicacy of the Lady
who was to receive the above correction . and
whenever one or more Maids of Honour, therefore,
have been fo unfortunate as to make it neceffary
that a flagellation fhould be inflicted upon them,
we are to conclude that the operation was performed in a private apartment of the Palace, in which
only the other Maids of Honour were admitted,
with a few Ladies of the Bedchamber.

In all the above reafonings, I have only meant
to offer my conjectures to the Reader, and have
accordingly fpoken with becoming diffidence. But
with refpect to the flagellations that were inflicted
on perfons of inferior rank, or on thofe Strangers,
fuch as Fathers Jefuits or others, who had given

a juft caufe of difpleafure to the Noble Proprietor of the Houfe, I am able to fpeak with more certainty, and confidently to inform the Reader, that the place appropriated for fuch corrections, was the Kitchen.

Nor do I found fuch an affertion only upon the conveniency of the place in general, upon its being fheltered from both fun and rain, upon its being plentifully ftocked with the neceffary implements for ferving corrections of the kind we mention, or poffeffing other advantages of a like nature, but I ground it upon precife facts. We fee, for inftance, that executions of a fimilar culinary kind, are exprefsly founded upon the law of this Country, and are the means provided by it for avenging the honour of the Sovereign, when infulted in his own houfe. Thus, if a Man dares to ftrike another in the King's *Court*, or within two hundred feet from the Palace Gate (which kind of offence has been always looked upon by Kings as a great piece of infolence) all the different Officers in the Kitchen are to co-operate in the Man's punifhment. The Serjeant of the *Wood-yard* is to bring a block of wood to faften the Culprit's hands to: for the punifhment is no lefs than to have it cut off. The Yeomen of the *Scullery*, and of the *Poultry*, are likewife to concur in the operation in one manner, the Groom of the *Saucery* and the *Mafter Cook* in another; the

N 4

Serjeant of the *Ewry*, again in another : even the concurrence of the Serjeant of the *Larder* has been deemed neceffary, and a proper fhare has been likewife affigned him in the ceremony : nay, the chief Officers of the *Cellar* and *Pantry* are alfo ordered to lend their affiftance , and their allotted function is to folace the fufferer, when the fad operation is over, by offering him a *cup of red wine* and a *manchet*.

Another proof of the reality of the culinary executions we mention, as well as of the great fhare which the people of the Kitchen bore in former times, in fupporting the dignity of Kings, is to be found in the defcription of the manner in which the Knights of the Bath are to be inftalled, according to the Statutes of the Order.   The inftalled Knight is, on that occafion, to receive admonitions, not only from the Dean of the Order, but alfo from the Mafter-Cook of the Sovereign, who repairs purpofely on that day to Weftminfter Church , though the place be rather diftant from his diftrict.   After the different ceremonies of the inftallation, fuch as taking the Oath, hearing the exhortation of the Dean, and the like, are over, the inftalled Knight, invefted with the *infignia* of his dignity, places himfelf on the one fide of the door , the Cook, invefted with the *infignia* of his own, viz. his white linen apron and his chopping-knife, places himfelf on the other, and addreffes the Knight in the following eloquent fpeech : *Sir, you know what great oath you have taken ; which if you keep, it will be great honour to you · but if you break it, I fhall be compelled, by my office, to hack off your fpurs from your heels.*

As the punifhment that has been defcribed above, is in itfelf of a grave nature, the particular ceremony with which it is to be inflicted, together with the refpective fhares allotted in the ceremony to the different Officers of the Royal Kitchen, have been carefully fet down in writing. In regard to thofe flagellations inflicted with a view to avenge any flighter difrefpect fhewn for the prefence or the orders of the Sovereign, as they were corrections of a different, and, we may fay, of a more paternal nature, fuch accuracy has not been ufed , but there is no doubt that they were performed in the fame place in which the punifhment above defcribed was to be executed, and by much the fame hands, whether they were to be beftowed in the Palaces of Englifh, or of foreign Kings, or of the great perfonages who were nearly related to them.

In fact, we are pofitively informed that the abovementioned Reverend Father Jefuit was threatened, and according to others actually ferved, with a flagellation in the *Kitchen.* The above Court Buffoon was chaftifed for his impudence in the fame place, and Brantôme exprefsly fays that he was fmartly flagellated in the Kitchen *(il fut bien fouetté à la Cuifine)*. Nay, when great Men, who have at all times been fond of aping Kings, have affumed in their own Palaces, or Country Seats, the above power of flagellation, the operation has alfo been conftantly performed in their Kitchens. Of this a number of inftances might be produced, but I will content myfelf with mentioning that which is related in the Tales of the Queen of Navarre *(Contes de la Reine de Navarre)* of a \ ton Friar Capuchin, who frequented the Houfe of a Nobleman in the Country, and who wanted once to perfuade a young Chambermaid in it, to wear, by way of mortification, a hair-cloth upon her bare fkin, which he himfelf offered to put upon her · the young Woman mentioned the faft, and the Nobleman who heard of it, grew very angry at the attempt, as he thought, committed by the Friar in his Houfe, and got him to be foundly flagellated *in the Kitchen*. Nor that I mean, however, to offer this faft to the Reader, as a faft for the truth of which I vouch to him, in the fame manner as I have done with refpeft to the preceding ones ; but though the above-quoted Book bears only the title of *Tales*, yet, as it is undoubtedly an old Book, and has been in fo much efteem as to have been fuppofed to have been written by Queen Margaret, Wife to Henry the Fourth, it is at leaft to be

depended upon with refpect to thofe particular cuftoms and manners it alludes to *.

That flagellations were, in not very remote
times, much in ufe in the Palaces of the Great,
and were ferved in the Kitchen, are therefore affured facts. With refpect to our being fo imperfectly informed of the different ceremonies that
ufually accompanied fuch corrections, it is owing
to different caufes, and firft, to a kind of carelefs-
nefs with which, it muft be confeffed, the affair
was commonly tranfacted. The great Perfonages
who gave orders in that refpect, were not fufficiently correct in their manner of giving them,
nor did they take fufficient care to confine themfelves to any fettled forms of words for that purpofe: whence it always proved an impoffible thing
for the Mafters of the Ceremonies to collect and
fet down in writing any thing precife on that head.
For here we are to obferve, that the Princes who
gave fuch orders, did not give them in their capacity of Truftees of the Executive. Legiflative,
Military, or Judicial Powers in the Nation. Neither did the Great Men about them, order corrections of the fame kind in their own houfes, in

---

* The French word *Cuiſſe*, which is the common word
to exprefs a flagellator, in a public School, was the old word
for a Cook . whence we may conclude, that, in large public
Schools alfo, the people of the Kitchen were fuppofed to poffefs peculiar abilities for performing flagellations.

their capacity of Admirals, Generals, or Knights of the Garter, or of the *St. Efprit.* The flagellations in queftion, as hath been above obferved, were corrections of quite a paternal kind : they were commonly ordered on a fudden, according as circumftances arofe, *pro re natâ*, without much ceremony or folemnity, and they may extremely well be compared with thofe boxes on the ears which Queen Elizabeth would fometimes beftow upon her Maids of Honour, or with thofe marks of attention with which fhe honoured thofe who made their appearance in the neighbourhood of her Palaces with high ruffs and long fwords, who had them immediately clipped or broken.

When the above great Perfonages were defirous that a flagellation fhould be inflicted, a word from them, a gefture, an exclamation, commonly proved fufficient. The numerous Servants who furrounded them, through a zeal that cannot be too much praifed, conftantly faved them the trouble of expreffing themfelves more at length on the fubject : they quickly laid hold of the perfon of the culprit, hurried him down into the Kitchen, and without lofs of time proceeded to ferve the prefcribed flagellation, the conduct of which was now intirely left to their difcretion : only they took care to regulate their actions upon what they had formerly feen practifed on fimilar occafions, or in cafes of a more ferious nature : they, for inftance, never forgot, when the flagellation was accomplifhed, to offer the fufferers the abovementioned *cup of wine* and *manchet*; nor are we to think that the latter always refufed to accept them.

And indeed it is no wonder, to conclude on this fubject, that the Kitchen had become the appropriated part of Palaces for ferving flagellations. The Kitchen was the place of the general refort of thofe numerous bodies of Servants, who, in former times, filled the Houfes of the Great : it was the place in which they deliberated upon every important occurrence ; in which they kept their Archives , and where their General Eftates were continually affembled. There Great Men were fure, upon every fudden emergency, to find a fufficient *Poffe* of Servants, ready to do any kind of mifchief under the fanction of their Royal or Noble Mafter, and who were never fo pleafed as when their affiftance was requefted to effect a flagellation. When a Reverend Father Jefuit, or fome faucy Friar Capuchin, was to be the fufferer, the contentment was, no doubt, much increafed ; but when the Buffoon himfelf, who commonly was the moft mifchievous animal of the whole Crew, was to be flagellated, then indeed we may fafely affirm, that an univerfal joy and uproar prevailed over the whole Royal or Noble manfion.

C H A P.   XIII.

The subject of voluntary flagellations among
Christians is at last introduced. That me-
thod of self-mortification appears to have been
practised in very early times; but it does not
seem to have been universaly admitted before
the years 1047 *and* 1056; *which was the*
time Cardinal Damianus wrote *.

VOLUNTARY flagellations were not a
practice that was contrived on a sudden,
and then immediately diffused over the Christian world.

---

* The Reader, no doubt, feels a great pleasure
in seeing the subject of pious flagellations among
Christians again introduced, and a fresh Chapter
begun upon it: indeed the Author had taken a
great liberty, in losing sight of his main subject
for so long a time, and dwelling, through so many
pages, upon the flagellatory corrections which,
after the example of Convents, were, in not very
remote days, practised in the Palaces of the Great:

Long before the period in which their use began to be univerfally adopted, they were

his zeal in the defence of Friars and Nuns has infenfibly carried him thefe lengths.

In the prefent Chapter, the Author has alfo indulged himfelf in a piece of great freedom with the Abbé Boileau, his original, or rather his model · which is no lefs than to have given a direct contradiction to the main doctrine advanced by the Abbé in his Work.

Thus, the principal, or rather fole point, which the Abbé labours to prove in his Book, is, that voluntary flagellations only began to be practifed among Chriftians, in the years 1047 or 1056 ; this is an affertion which he introduces almoft at every page, and which exprefsly conftitutes the title of one of his Chapters (the 7th) : yet he has himfelf quoted (without difputing the truth of them) feveral facts that fhew fuch practice to have been much older : I have therefore taken the liberty, in the prefent Chapter, in which thofe facts are collected, to diffent from the doctrine maintained by him, and have advanced, that voluntary flagellations were practifed in early times among Chriftians, though they began to be univerfally admitted only in the years 1047 and 1056.

And indeed if the Reader now afked my own opinion concerning the antiquity, or novelty, of

I

practised by divers persons, in different times and places, as we may judge from the ac-

the practice in question, a subject which has caused much disputation among Catholic Divines, I would answer, that I do not think it in the least probable, that a practice like this, after having been unknown for so many Centuries, should afterwards have been thought of on a sudden, and then adopted by the whole Christian world, at the same period.

In the first place it is to be observed, that though the strict truth of those early instances of voluntary flagellations, which are to be found in the Abbé's text, might perhaps be controverted, yet, as the reader will see, such instances are related by early and contemporary Writers, as common facts, at which they do not express any surprise.

In the second place, since the opposers of the opinion of the antiquity of self-flagellations admit, that cruel voluntary penances, such as wearing iron cuirasses inwardly armed with points, being continually loaded with enormous weights, dwelling in the bottom of dwells, or on the tops of columns, were practised by the first Christians, it is difficult to understand why they make such objections against flagellations in particular, which they agree to have been employed, from the earliest times, by Ecclesiastical Superiors, as common

counts that have been left us, of feveral early facts; a few of which I here purpofe to relate.

methods of correcting offences of a religious kind, and which were likewife ufed for pious purpofes, before the eftablifhment of Chriftianity

Nay, beating and lafhing one's felf, are means of felf-mortification, which, more readily than any other, occur to the minds either of fuperfti-tious, or hypocritical perfons. Practices of this kind prefently gratify the fudden fits of fanaticifm of the one, and ferve extremely well the purpofes of the other, in that they catch the minds of the vulgar, by the difplay of an apparatus of cruel in-ftruments and a fhow of great feverity, at the fame time that they are in reality much lefs difficult to be borne than the penances above alluded to, and want what conftituted the moft intolerable hard-fhip of thefe latter, diuturnity and uninterruption.

Befides, thofe who make felf-flagellation part of their religious exercifes, always have it in their power to take, like Sancho, their own time for performing them, as well as to choofe what ftation they pleafe for that purpofe. In Summer, they may fettle themfelves in a cool place, in Winter, near a good fire, and have conftantly by them fome excellent liquor, to refrefh themfelves with;

O

One is contained in the Life of St. Peter, the Hermit of the *Pont Euxin*, which was written by Theodoret, Bifhop of Cyrus, who has been mentioned in a former Chapter, and lived about the year 4co. This holy Hermit having found means to refcue a young Woman from the hands of a military Officer, who wanted to feduce her, was much perplexed afterwards how to prevent the effects of both the wrath and luft of that impure man; nor could he, in the iffue, compafs this any other way than by locking himfelf up, as Theodoret relates, and feverely flagellating

during the different paufes they think proper to make.

They may moreover ufe juft what degree of feverity they choofe. They even may, like Sancho, who only lafhed the trees around him, or like the Hermit mentioned by La Fontaine, content themfelves with flagellating the walls of their apartment: nay, they may perform no flagellation at all, and yet make afterwards what boaft they pleafe. Having duly weighed all the above important confiderations, as well as the facts quoted by the Abbe, the truth of which he does not take the trouble to deny, I have ventured to diffent from his inconfiftent affertions, and have made the abovementioned change in his doctrine.

£

himfelf, in company with the Mother of the young Woman *.

Palladius, Bifhop of Hellenopolis, in his Hiftory of the Lives of feveral holy Solitaries, which he wrote in the year 420, and dedicated to Laufus, whence the Book was called *Laufiacum*, relates a fact which inconteftably proves that flagellations voluntarily fubmitted to, by thofe perfons who underwent them, were in ufe fo early as the fourth Century. He fays, in the Life of Abbot Arfifius, that on the mountain of Nitria, in Thebaid,

* The above fact related by Theodoret is very pofitive, and it fupplies an evident proof, that the practice of felf flagellation was not unknown in the times of that early Writer: the filence of the fame Author in other parts of his Wiitings, concerning the practice in queftion, fhews nothing more, except that the fame was not univerfally adopted in his time, as hath been obferved in the Note, pag. 124 of this Work.

The hafty affertions of the Abbé Boileau againft the antiquity of felf-flagellation, which are repeated almoft in every page of his Book, in fpite of the facts which himfelf produces, gives juft caufe to guefs that he ufed to practife but little upon himfelf that falutary kind of mortification.

O 2

there was a very large Church, in the vicinity of which ſtood three Palm-trees, on each of which hung a ſcourge : the one ſerved to chaſtiſe ſuch Monks as proved refractory againſt the Rule ; the other to puniſh Thieves ; and the third ſerved to correct ſuch *accidental comers* as became guilty of ſome fault : the delinquents, according to what claſs they belonged, embraced one of the Palm-trees, and in this ſituation received a certain number of laſhes with one of the above ſcourges.

It is expreſsly ſaid of St. Pardulph, a Benedictine Monk and Abbot, who lived during the time of Charles Martel, about the year 737, that he uſed in Lent-time to ſtrip himſelf ſtark-naked, and order one of his diſciples to laſh him. The fact is related in the life of that Saint, formerly written by an Author who lived about the ſame time ; and it was, two hundred years afterwards, put into more elegant language, by Yvus, Prior of Clugny, at the deſire of the Monks of St. Martial, in the Town of Limoges : Hugh Menard, a Benedictine Father, and a very learned Man in all that relates to Eccleſiaſtical Antiquities, has inſerted part of it in his Book, intitled, *Obſervations on the Benedictine Martyrology*. The following is the Paſſage in St. Pardulph's Life, which is

here alluded to. ' St. Pardulph feldom went
' out of his cell; whenever ficknefs obliged
' him to bathe, he would previoufly make
' incifions in his own fkin. During Lent, he
' ufed to ftrip himfelf intirely naked, and or-
' dered one of his difciples to lafh him with
' rods *.'

St. William, Duke of Aquitain, who lived
in the time of Charlemain, that is, about the
year 800, and many years before Cardinal Damian, is faid to have alfo ufed flagellations,
as a means of voluntary penance. Arduinus,
the Writer of the holy Duke's Life, and a
cotemporary Writer, fays, that ' it was com-
' monly reported that the Duke did frequent-
' ly, for the love of Chrift, caufe himfelf to
' be whipped, and that he then was alone
' with the perfon who affifted him †.' Haeftenus, Superior of the Monaftery of Affligen,
relates the fame fact, and fays that the Duke
of Aquitain ' took a great delight in fleeping
' upon a hard bed, and that he moreover
' lafhed himfelf with a fcourge.' Hugh Menard, the learned Benedictine juft now men-

* . . . . *Tempore quadragefimo, toto corpore nudato, fe à quodam difcipulo virgis cædi præcipiebat*

† Part I. Actor. Ord. S. Benedicti, pag. 208.
*Aiunt nonnulli fe fæpe pro Chrifti amore flagellis cædi,
nullo alio præter eum qui aderat confcio, juffiffe.*

O 3

tioned, has adopted the teftimony of Arduinus, and upon that Writer's authority inferted the above fact in his *Obfervations on the
Benedictine Martyrology.*

Other perfons, who lived before the times
of Cardinal Damian, are alfo mentioned by
different Writers, as having practifed voluntary flagellations. Gualbertus, Abbot of
Pontoife, who lived about the year 900, upon
a certain occafion, ' feverely flagellated him-
' felf (as M. Du Cange relates in his Gloffa-
' ry) with a fcourge made of knotted thongs.'
And the abovementioned Haeftenus, Prior of
Affligen, has advanced that the fame practice
was followed by St. Romuald, who lived
about the fame time as Gualbertus, and by
the Monks of the Camaldolian order, who
were fettled in Sitria.

Another early inftance of voluntary flagellations occurs in the Life of *Guy*, Abbot of
Pompofa. Heribert, it is faid, Archbifhop of
Ravenna, formed the defign of pulling down
the Monaftery of *Pompofa*; and this piece of
news caufed both Abbot *Guy* and his Monks,
' to lock themfelves up in the Capitular
' Houfe, and to lafh themfelves every day, for
' feveral days, with rods *.' Abbot Guy was

* . . . *Quotidiè acriter fe cædendi virgis in domo
Capitulari.*

born in the year 956; and he was made Abbot of Pompofa in the year 998, in which capacity he continued forty-eight years.

All the facts above related were anterior to
the year 1056, the time at which Peter Damian *de Honeftis* was raifed to the Cardinal-
fhip by Pope Stephen IX; and it is evident
from them, that the practice of voluntarily
flagellating one's felf, as a penance for committed fins, had been adopted before the period in queftion; though it cannot be faid to
have been then univerfally prevalent: at leaft,
only a few inftances of it have been left us by
the Writers of thofe times. But at the æra
we mention, this pious mode of felf-correction, owing to the public and zealous patron-
age with which the above Cardinal favoured
it, acquired a vaft degree of credit, and grew
into univerfal efteem; and then it was that
perfons of religious difpofitions were every
where feen to arm themfelves with whips, rods,
thongs, and befoms, and lacerate their own
hides, in order to draw upon themfelves the
favour of Heaven.

We are informed of this fact by the learned Cardinal Baronius, in his Ecclefiaftical An-
nals: ' At that time (he fays) the laudable
' ufage of the faithful, of beating themfelves
' with whips made for that purpofe, though

' Peter Damian may not be faid to have been
' the author of it, was much promoted by
' him in the Chriftian Church; in which he
' followed the example of the bleffed Demi-
' nic the *Cuircffed*, a holy Hermit, who had
' fubjected himfelf to his authority ⁘.'

The fame Cardinal Damian has moreover
left numerous accounts of voluntary flagellations practifed by certain holy Men of his
times; but thefe are furely more apt to create our admiration, than to excite us to imitate them. Indeed, the flagellations he mentions cannot be propofed to the Faithful as examples they ought to follow; and they were
executed with fuch dreadful feverity, as makes
it impoffible for the moft vigorous Men to go
through the like, without a kind of miracle.

In the Life of the Monk St. Rodolph, who
was afterwards made Bifhop of Eugubio,

---

* The Abbé Boileau, in his Book, concludes
the above quotation, with wifhing that Parenius
had been pleafed to inform us of the name of the
real Author of the practice of voluntary flagellation. As he thinks that there has exifted a certain particular period, at which this practice began to be univerfally followed, prior to which it
was utterly unknown, fo he hopes that fome un-
difputed inventor of the fame may be fixed upon

the Cardinal relates, ' That this holy Man
' would often impofe upon himfelf a penance
' of an hundred years, and that he performed
' it in twenty days, by the ftrenuous applica-
' tion of a broom, without neglecting the
' other common methods ufed in doing pe-
' nance. Every day, being fhut up in his
' cell, he recited the whole Pfalter (or Book
' of Pfalms) at leaft one time when he could
' not two, being all the while armed with a
' befom in each hand, with which he inccf-
' fantly lafhed himfelf *.'

The account which the Cardinal has left
of Dominic, firnamed the *Cuiraffid*, is not
lefs wonderful. ' His conftant practice (he
' fays) is, after ftripping himfelf naked, to
' fill both his hands with rods, and then vi-
' goroufly flagellate himfelf: this he does in
' his times of relaxation. But during Lent-
' time, or when he really means to mortify
' himfelf, he frequently undertakes the hun-
' dred years penance; and then he every day

---

* *Sæpè pœnitentiam centum fufcipiebat cruorem,
quam per viginti dies, allifione fcoparum, cateri/que
pœnitentiæ remedias, perfolvebat Pfalt i um quotidiè,
cùm duo non poffit unum faltem, non negligibet im-
plere quod nimirùm cum eff' in cladio, adiutus,
armatâ fcopis utrâque manu, totum cum d f i idia con-
tinuare confueverat.*

‘ recites the Pfalter at leaft three times over,
‘ all the while flogging himfelf with be-
‘ foms *.’

Cardinal Damian then proceeds to relate
the manner in which the fame Dominic informed him he performed the hundred years
penance. ‘ A Man (faid he) may depend he
‘ has accomplifhed it, when he has flagellated
‘ himfelf during the whole time the Pfalter
‘ was fung twenty times over †.’ The fame
Author adds feveral circumftances which make
the penances performed by the holy Man appear in a ftill more admirable light. He, in
the firft place, was fo dextrous as to be able
to ufe both his hands at once, and thus laid
on twice the number of lafhes others could
do, who only ufed their right-hand. In one
inftance, he fuftigated himfelf during the time
the whole Book of Pfalms was fung twice

* *Cap. viii. Hanc autem vitæ confuetudinem in-
differenter habet, ut utrâque manu fcopis armatâ, nudum corpus allidat ; & hoc rem ff-ori tempore. Nem
quadragefimalibus circulis, five cum pœnitentiam pera-
gendam habet, crebro centum cniorum pœnitentiam
jufcipt tunc per dies fingulos, dum fe fcoparum tun-
fionibus afficit, ut minus tria Pfalteria meditando
perfolvit.*

† *Hominem tempore quo viginti Pfalteria recita-
bantur vapulantem, pœnitentiam centenarium ex-
pleviffe.*

over; on another occasion he did the same
while it was sung eight times; and on another,
while it was repeated twelve times over;
' which filled me with terror,' the Cardinal
adds, ' when I heard the fact *.'

Cardinal Damian also relates of the same
Dominic the *Cuirassed*, that he at last changed
his discipline of rods into that of leather-
thongs, which was still harsher; and that he
had been able to accustom himself to that laborious exercise. Nay, so punctual was he in
performing the duties he had imposed upon
himself, that, ' when he happened to go
' abroad (being an Hermit) he carried his
' scourge in his bosom, to the end that, where-
' ver he happened to spend the night, he
' might lose no time, and flog himself with
' the same regularity as usual. If the place
' in which he had taken his refuge for the
' night, did not allow him to strip entirely,
' and fustigate himself from head to foot,
' he at least would severely beat his legs and
' head †.'

---

* Cap. X. *Quod certè quum audivi tremefactus
expavi.*
† *Hoc flagellum, si quando egrederetur, portabat in*

finu, ut ubicunque cum jacere contingeret, à verberibus non vacaret, &c.

Carrying a *difcipline* conftantly about one, like the above Dominic, and making an oftentatious difplay of it, are among the number of thofe characteriftical circumflances which are looked upon, in Catholic Countries, as marking hypocrify to this notion a frequent allufion is made both in Novels and Plays, thus, the firft words of *Tartuffe*, or the Hypocrite, in the Play of Moliere which bears that name, who makes his firft appearance only when the Play is fomewhat advanced, a e to order his Man, with a loud affected voice, to lock up his hair-cloth and *difcipline*. However, we are not to think that all thofe who thus make a difplay of their difcipline, ufe it with fo much earneftnefs and perfeverance as the above-mentioned Dominic the *Cuiraffed*, or Rodolph of Eugubio, though it cannot be denied that feveral perfons of a gloomy fuperftitious temper, ftill practife in thefe days mortifications of that kind with great feverity, and indeed, as hath been obferved in a former Note, the aftonifhing penances practifed by Fakirs in the Eaft Indies, which are undeniable facts, make every account of that fort appear credible to us.

If the evil arifing from the above cruel practices, reached no farther than the ufelefs fufferings which thofe who follow them, bring upon them-

felves, one might fincerely pity their infatuation,
but it is a truth confirmed by experience, that fuperftitious exercifes or mortifications like thefe, are
feldom introduced but at the expence of other really effential obligations, and though the rigour
of fuch mortifications is very wifely abated gradually every day, fo that they are at length reduced to
only fome trifling practices, yet, they are made to
fupply the place of almoft every duty which Men
owe to one another: thus, to quote only one
ftriking inftance on the fubject, Lewis the Eleventh of France, after he had paid a few devo-
tions of his own contrivance to a leaden image of
the Virgin he conftantly wore ftuck to his hat,
thought he had fully atoned beforehand for any
crime he meditated to commit.

I fhall conclude this Note with a ftroke of
ridicule which M. de Voltaire, in one of his
Pieces mêlées, throws upon the dangerous, and at
the fame time arrogant, pretenfions of thofe perfons who voluntarily fubmit to mortifications like
thofe here alluded to. He fuppofes a converfation
to take place with a Fakir, of which a Turk,
then on his travels in India, writes an account to
one of his friends.

‘ I happened to crofs a Fakir, who was reading
‘ in his Book: Ah wretched Infidel! cried he,
‘ thou haft made me lofe a number of vowels that

' I was counting, which will occafion my foul to
' pafs into the body of a hare, inftead of that of
' a parrot, with which I had before the greateft
' reafon to flatter myfelf: I gave him a Rupee to
' comfort him for the accident. In going a few
' paces farther, I had the misfortune to fneeze;
' the noife I made roufed a Fakir who was in a
' trance.—Heavens, cried he, what a dreadful
' noife! where am I! I can no longer fee the
' tip of my nofe! the heavenly light has difap‧
' peared.—If I am the caufe, faid I, of your fee-
' ing farther than the tip of your nofe, here is a
' Rupee to repair the injury: fquint again, and
' refume the heavenly light *.

' Having thus brought myfelf off difcreetly
' enough, I paffed over to the fide of the Gym-
' nofophifts, feveral of whom brought me a par-
' cel of mighty pretty nails to drive into my arms,
' and thighs, in honour of Brahma: I bought
' their nails, and made ufe of them to faften my
' boxes. Others were dancing upon their hands,
' others cut capers on the flack-rope, and others
' went always upon one foot. There were fome
' who dragged about a heavy chain with them,
' and others carried a pack-faddle; fome had al-
' ways their heads in a bufhel, the beft people in

---

* It is needlefs to obferve that all this alludes to real
penances or practices of the Indian Fakirs.

‘ the world to live with. My friend Omri car-
‘ ried me to the cell of one of the moſt famous
‘ of them. His name was Bahabec. He was as
‘ naked as he was born, and had a great chain
‘ about his neck, that weighed upwards of ſixty
‘ pounds. He ſat on a wooden chair, very neat-
‘ ly decorated with little points of nails, that ran
‘ into his poſteriors , and you would have thought
‘ he ſat on a velvet cuſhion. Numbers of Wo-
‘ men flocked to him, to conſult him he was
‘ the Oracle of all the families in the neighbour-
‘ hood , and was, truly ſpeaking, in great repu-
‘ tation. I was witneſs to a long converſation
‘ that Omri had with him.—Do you think, Fa-
‘ ther, ſaid my friend, that, after having gone
‘ through ſeven metempſychoſes, I may at length
‘ arrive at the houſe of Brama.—That is as it may
‘ happen, ſaid the Fakir. What ſort of life ao
‘ you lead ?—I endeavour, anſwered Omri, to be
‘ a good ſubject, a good huſband, a good father,
‘ and a good friend . I lend money without in-
‘ tereſt to the rich who want it, and I give it to
‘ the poor: I preſerve peace among my neigh-
‘ bours.—But have you ever run nails into your
‘ backſide, demanded the Brahmin —Never, re-
‘ verend Father.—I am ſorry for it, replied the
‘ Father , very ſorry for it indeed. It is a thou-
‘ ſand pities , but you will not certainly reach

‘ above the nineteenth Heaven.—No higher? faid
‘ Omri. In troth I am very well fatisfied with
‘ my lot. But pray, what heaven do you think
‘ of going to, good Mr. Bahabec, with your
‘ nails and your chain? Into the thirty-fifth, faid
‘ Bahabec, &c. &c *.’

The above recited feats of Dominic the *Cui-raffed*, and Rodolph of Eugubio, who have had numerous imitators, together with the very ferious endeavours of Men in the ftation of Cardinal Damian, to recommend fuch practices, are very extraordinary facts. It really feems that, in our part of the world, where the Arts and Sciences have been promoted to fo high a degree, and the powers of the human mind carried to their utmoft extent, we have, in regard to the folly and ignorance of our fuperftitious notions and cuftoms, been equal to any Nation upon earth, to any of thofe Nations whom we defpife moft nay, perhaps it might be ftrictly proved that we have been worfe.

* See Voltaire's Works, tranflated by *Smollet, Franklin, and others*, Vol. XIII. pag. 23, &c.

CHAP. XIV.

The practice of self-flagellation meets with some opposition; but this is soon over-ruled by the fondness of the Public.

VOLUNTARY flagellations, notwithstanding the zeal with which Cardinal Damian endeavoured to promote them, were not, however, admitted, in his time, by all persons, without exception. Thus, Odillon, Abbot of Cluny, and Maurus of Cesena, two Saints whose Lives Cardinal Damian himself has written, forbore the use of flagellations; or at least no mention is made of their having practised them, in the Accounts the Cardinal has given of their actions.

Nay, several persons openly blamed the pious ceremonies in question, during the times of Cardinal Damian; for it was too alarming a practice, for Men not to be concerned at its sudden progress; it was an exercise of too ticklish a nature, for them to suffer themselves

P

to fall afleep on its introduction, or too interefting in its confequence, for them not to
be roufed by the rattling of the blows.

Among thofe who thus condemned voluntary flagellations, the moft confpicuous was
Peter Cerebrofus, a Monk who lived in thofe
times, and was moreover a friend to Cardinal
Damian. This brought on, an epiftolary debate on the fubject, between Cerebrofus and
the Cardinal, as we learn from the Works of
the latter. Nor did the Cardinal, it is to be
obferved, advance in his letters, that felf-
flagellations were matter of ftrict duty : he
only proved by the authority of the Scriptures, that it was lawful to flagellate perfons
who were guilty of offences ; and he then
gave it as his opinion, that it was a laudable
act in a Chriftian, voluntarily to inflict upon
himfelf that punifhment which God had awarded againft him, and which he ought to fuffer
from the hands of other perfons.

The oppofition made by Cerebrofus had
efpecially for its object, the manner in which
voluntary flagellations were performed. He
blamed the length of time, and the vehe-
mence, with which certain perfons executed
them; and condemned the extraordinary feverity with which the abovementioned flogging Mafters ufed to lafh themfelves, while

2

they were finging a number of Pfalms over.
This caufed the Cardinal to write a new letter
to him, in order to defire him to explain better his fentiments on that fubject : the following is an extract from the Cardinal's
letter : ' Perhaps you do not blame the
' practice of felf-difcipline, though you con-
' demn it when too long continued, and per-
' formed with cruelty : perhaps you do not
' difapprove that difcipline be performed dur-
' ing the time one Pfalm is finging, but you
' fhudder at the thought of finging the whole
' Pfalter over. Now fpeak, my Brother, I
' befeech you, if I may afk you the queftion,
' do you find fault with thofe difciplines
' which are practifed in the chapters of Con-
' vents ? do you alfo blame the ufe adopted
' in them, of prefcribing to a Father who
' confeffes himfelf guilty of any flight fault,
' to undergo twenty, or at moft fifty lafhes ?'

To the above facts, an obfervation is to be
added, which is, that, though Cerebrofus
maintained a different opinion from that of
Cardinal Damian, yet the latter never charged
him with having fallen, in that refpect, into
any kind of criminal error, or herefy, but on
the contrary, calls him his dear Son, his Brother in Chrift, and his good Friend, as appears from his Epiftles xxvii. and xxviii ; as

well as from his lxiid Epiftle, which he wrote
to the Fathers of the Monaftery of Mount
Caffin, in commendation of flagellations. This
mild and civil manner with which the above
difpute was carried on, between Cardinal Damian, and Peter Cerebrofus, reflects much
honour upon both, and fhews that they were
perfonages of eminent merit. Nor did the
Cardinal ufe the opinions of Cardinal Stephen,
who, when alive, had likewife oppofed felf-
flagellations, with lefs moderation; and he frequently calls him a Man of pious memory:
though it is but juft to add, that this Cardinal
Stephen was commonly fufpected of having
died fuddenly, on account of his having defpifed the exercife in queftion.

However, notwithftanding the doubts of
Peter Cerebrofus, and of Cardinal Stephen,
the practice of voluntary flagellations foon
fpread itfelf far and wide; and we find it to
have been adopted, fince the times we mention, by numbers of perfons, eminent on account either of their dignity, or their merit;
feveral of whom have been mentioned by Father Gretzer. Among them were St. Andrew
Bifhop of Fiefola, Laurence Juftinian, Abbot
Poppo, and efpecially St. Anthelm, Bifhop
of Bellay, who lived about an hundred years
after Dominic the *Cuiraffed* and Rodolph of

Eugubio, and glorioufly trod in the footfteps of thefe two holy Men. 'Every day (it is 'faid in that Saint's Life, which was written 'by one of his intimate friends) every day he 'fcourged himfelf, making lafhes fall thick 'on his back and fides, and by thus heap. 'ing ftripes upon ftripes, he never fuffered 'his fkin to remain whole, or free from marks 'of blows *.'

Even Sovereigns, and Great Men, in the times we fpeak of, adopted for themfelves the practice of voluntary flagellation.

The Emperor Henry, who lived about the year 1070, 'never ventured (if we may cre- dit Reginard's account) to put on his Imperial

---

* The abovementioned Anthelm, I think I have read, lived to a very great age. The famous felf-flagellator Dominic the *Cuiraffed*, lived eigh- ty-four years; St. Romuald, notwithftanding the flagellations he received from himfelf and his Monks, attained, it is faid, the age of an hun- dred and twenty years, and Leon of *Preza*, ano- ther illuftrious felf-flagellator, lived, according to fome accounts, to the age of an hundred and for- ty. If fo, it would thence refult, that felf-fla- gellations, befides the other great advantages they poffefs, are alfo attended with that of being con-. ducive to health.

' robes, before he had obtained the permiffion
' of a Prieft for that purpofe, and had de-
' ferved it by confeffion and difcipline.'

William of Nangis, in the Life of St.
Lewis King of France, which he has written rela es that that Prince, after he had made
his confeffion, conftantly received difcipline
from his Confeffor.   To this the fame Author
adds the following curious account.   ' I ought
' not to omit to fay, concerning the Confeffor
' the King had before Geoffrey *de Bello loco*,
' and who belonged to the Order of the *Pre-*
' *dicant* Friars, that he ufed to inflict upon
' him, hard and immoderate difciplines;
' which the King, whofe fkin was rather ten-
' der, had much ado to endure.   This hard-
' fhip, however, he never would fpeak of
' to this Confeffor; but after his death, he
' mentioned the fact, fomewhat jocularly,
' though not without humility, to the new
' Confeffor *.'

An inftance of much the fame nature with
the facts above recited, is to be found in one
of *Ojbertus's* Books.   A certain Englifh Count
having contracted an unlawful marriage with
one of his near-relations, not only parted af-

---

* . . . . *Jocando ridendo hoc alteri Confiffori fuo
humiliter recognovit.*

terwards with her, but requefted befides to
be difciplined in the prefence of St. Dunftan,
and of the General Affembly of the Clergy.
‘ Terrified (fays *Ofbertus*) by the greatnefs of
‘ his offence, his obftinacy ceafed ; and after
‘ having renounced his unlawful wedlock, he
‘ impofed upon himfelf the tafk of penitence.
‘ As Dunftan was then prefiding over a meet-
‘ ing of the Clergy of the Kingdom, which
‘ was holden according to cuftom, the Count
‘ came into the middle of the Affembly, bare-
‘ footed, clothed with wool, and carrying
‘ rods in his hands ; and threw himfelf, groan-
‘ ing and weeping, at the feet of St. Dunftan.
‘ This inftance of piety moved the whole Af-
‘ fembly, and Dunftan more than the reft.
‘ However, as his wifh was thoroughly to re-
‘ concile the Man with God, he preferved an
‘ appearance of feverity in his looks, fuitable
‘ to the occafion, and for a whole hour per-
‘ fevered in denying his requeft : when, at laft,
‘ all the Prelates having joined in the entrea-
‘ ties of the Count, St. Dunftan granted him
‘ the indulgence he was fuing for.’ From
the above fact, we might conclude that flagellations voluntarily fubmitted to, had become, even before the æra of Cardinal Damian, a fettled method of atoning for paft
fins, fince St. Dunftan lived about an hundred

years before the Cardinal; that is, about the year 950.

Instances of Sovereigns, and Great Men, requesting to undergo flagellations, must have been pretty common in the days we mention, frequent allusions being made to it, in old books: among others, in that old French Romance, intitled, *The History of the Round Table, and the Feats of the Knight, Lancelot du Lac.* King Arthur is supposed in it, to have summoned all the Bishops who were in his army, to his Chapel; and there to have requested of them, a correction of the same kind as that undergone by the Count mentioned by Osbertus [*].

From the times we mention, we find numerous proofs of self-flagellations being used in Convents: and indeed it would have been a very extraordinary circumstance, if, while the persons abovenamed adopted that practice, Monks had rejected it. In the liiid Article of the Statutes of the Abbey of Cluny, which were collected by Peter Maurice, firnamed the Venerable, who was raised to the dignity of Abbot in the year 1122, the fol-

* .... *Après, prist discipline d'eux; moult doucement la recut. Imprimé à Paris, par A. Gerard, le 1. Juillet,* 1494. This must have been one of the first books that were printed.

3

lowing account is given. ' It was ordained
' (it is faid in that Article) that that part of
' the Monaftery which is on the left, beyond
' the left Choir, fhould remain open to no
' ftrange perfons, whether Ecclefiaftical or
' Lay, as it was formerly, and nobody admit-
' ted into it, except the Monks. This was
' thus fettled, becaufe the Brothers had no
' place, except the old Church of St. Peter,
' in which they could practife fuch holy and
' fecret exercifes as are ufual with religious
' perfons; they therefore claimed the ufe of
' the above new part of the Church, both for
' the night and the day, that they might con-
' ftantly therein make offerings of the per-
' fumes of their prayers to God, fupplicate
' their Creator by frequent acts of repentance
' and genuflexions, and mortify their bodies
' by often inflicting upon themfelves three
' flagellations, either as penances for their
' fins, or as *an increafe of their merit* *.'

* . . . . *ubi fancta & fecreta orationum aromata
Deo affiduè accenderent ; frequentibus metas œis vel ge-
nufluxionibus pio conditori fupplicarent ; à tribus fæpè
flagellis, vel ad pœn tentiam, vel ad augendum meritum, corpus attererent.*

I will take this occafion to inform the Reader,
that Monks, or perfons of religious difpofitions,
do not always mean, in the penances they impofe

The practice in question gained so much credit, about those times, in Monasteries, that St. Bruno, who, a few years after the death of Cardinal Damian, founded the Carthusian Order, thought it necessary to restrain his Monks in that respect; not unlikely, perhaps, with the view to check the pride which they used to derive from such exercises. In one of the statutes laid by that Saint, which Prior Guigues has collected, the following regulation is contained. ‘ In regard to such disci-‘ plines, watchings, and other religious exer-‘ cises as are not expressly enjoined by our In-‘ stitution, let nobody among us perform ‘ them, except it be by the Prior's per-‘ mission.’

So much were flagellations grown into fashion in the days we mention, such attrac-

on themselves, to atone for their sins, which they do not by any means consider as being in propor tion to the number of their flagellations. They practise mortifications of this kind, either for the good of other persons, or for delivering souls from Purgatory, or in order (as the Reader may see from the words above quoted) to increase their own merit, and, like the Fakir mentioned in a former place, go of course to the thirty-fifth Heaven.

tions did they even feem to poffefs, that Ladies of high rank would alfo inlift among the
abovementioned Whippers, and almoft vied
with Dominic the *Cuiraffed*, Rodolph *de Eugubio*, St. Anthelm, and Abbot Poppo, in
regard to the regularity with which they performed fuch meritorious exeicifes. Among
thofe Ladies, particular mention is made of
St. Maria of Ognia, of St. Hardwigge, Dut-
chefs of Poland, of St. Hildegarde, and above
all of the Widow Cechald, who lived in the
very times of Cardinal Damian, and performed wonderful feats in the fame career, as we
are informed by St. Antonius, in the fecond
Volume of his Hiftory. The following is the
account given by St. Antonius, upon the authority of Cardinal Damian himfelf. ' Not
' only Men, but alfo Women of noble birth
' eagerly fought after that kind of Purgatory;
' and the Widow of Cechaldus, a Woman of
' great birth and dignity, gave an account,
' that in confequence of an obligation fhe had
' previoufly impofed upon herfelf, fhe had
' gone through the hundred years penance,
' three thoufand lafhes being the number al-
' lotted for every year *.'

---

* Tit. 16. Cap. VIII. fol. 102.—*Ut non folùm
viri fed & mulieres nobiles hoc purgatorii genus inhi-*

anter acciperent ; relictamque Cechald', mulierem mag-
ni generis & magnæ dignitatis, retuliſſe ſe, per præ-
fixam hujus regulæ diſciplinam, pœnitentiam centum
annorum peregiſſe, tribus diſciplinarum millibus pro uno
computatis anno.

The Widow Cechald, in her account of the
wonderful penance ſhe performed after the example of Domiiic the *Cuiraſſed*, has neglected to
inform us in what manner ſhe performed it, and
whether ſhe imitated that holy Man in every reſpect, and uſed, for inſtance, both her hands at
once in the operation. Be it as it may, three
hundred thouſand laſhes, the total amount of the
hundred years penance ſhe went through, were
certainly a very hard penance. However, as we
are not to doubt either the account which the
above Widow gave in that reſpect, or the declaration Cardinal Damian made after her, the wonder
is to be explained another way, and perhaps by
the nature of the inſtruments ſhe made uſe of:
they poſſibly were of much the ſame kind as thoſe
uſed by a certain Lady, who was likewiſe much
celebrated on account of the frequent diſciplines
ſhe beſtowed upon herſelf, and who was at laſt
found out to uſe no other weapons for performing
them, than a bunch of feathers, or, as others
have ſaid, a fox's tail.

CHAP. XV.

Another difficulty. Which is the best plight to be in, for receiving a discipline?

EMINENT persons, in the times we speak of, did not differ from one another only in their opinions concerning the advantages of religious flagellations; but they also dissented with respect to the manner of performing them, as we may likewise conclude from the Writings and Ordinances of those times. Cardinal Damian, the great Patron of Flagellators, prescribed to them to strip themselves naked, and when thus perfectly free from every obstruction and impediment, to flog themselves in company with one another: this we learn from his xliid *Opusculum*, which he wrote to the Fathers of Mount Cassin, who were not intirely reconciled to the thought of those flagellations. On the other hand, an Ordinance which had been framed in the Assembly which was held at Aix-la-Chapelle, so early as the year 817, under the reign of Lewis *le Débonnaire*, forbad the above manner of flagellating Monks, because it did more harm than good. ' Let the ' Monks (it is faid in the 16th Canon) never ' be lafhed naked, in the prefence of the ' other Monks; let them not be whipped ' naked, for every trifling fault, in fight of ' the Brothers.'

Several religious Orders fubmitted to the directions of the above Canon; St. Lanfranc, among others, ordered, in his Statutes, ' That ' Monks, guilty of offences, fhould be beat- ' en with a thick rod, or wand, over their ' growns.' The Monks of Afflıgen, in the Netherlands, adopted the fame Canon; and it was fettled in their Ritual, as Haeftenus informs us, that the Monks fhould have their gowns on, when they were to be cudgelled.

However, the wife precautions we mention were adopted only in a few particular places; and the regard which ought to be paid to decency, as well as to the prudent Ordınance of the Affembly held at Aıx-la-Chapelle, was utterly forgotten in moft Monafteries; the practice recommended by Cardınal Damian being adopted in them, upon the fcore of more complete mortification. Nay, fo cheap did the Framers of regulations, in feveral Monafteries, make their own nakednefs, as well

as that of the Brothers, that in certain cafes they ordered delinquents to be ftript in order to be flagellated, in fight not only of the Congregation, but even of the whole Public. In an Article of the Conftitutions of the Abbey of Cluny, which Udalric has collected together, it is exprefsly fettled that the perfons guilty of the different faults enumerated therein, are ' to be ftripped naked in the mid-
' dle of the next ftreet or public place, fo
' that every perfon who choofes may fee them,
' and there tied up and lafhed *.'

Among the Promoters and Recommenders of nakednefs, we muft not omit to mention Cardinal Pullus, a perfon of no lefs importance than Cardinal Damian, and who, in his life-time, was high Chancellor of the Roman Church : in the Collection of Sentences with which this Cardinal has obliged the World, he gives it as his opinion, that the very nakednefs of the Penitent, is a confiderable increafe of his merit †.

---

* Pars Cap. III. p. 166.——*Cunctis enim qui videre voluerint, videntibus, & maximè in mediâ plateâ, nudatur, ligatur, & verberatur.*

† To the above differtation on the propereft plight for receiving flagellations, another, no lefs

interefting, might be added, viz. which are the fitteft inftruments for inflicting them? Indeed, an infinite variety of inftruments have been ufed for that purpofe, whether they were contrived at leifure by the ingenious perfons who were to ufe them, or were fuddenly found out, from the fpur of fome urgent occafion. Incenfed Pedants, who could not quickly enough find their ufual inftrument of difcipline, have frequently ufed their hat, their towel, or, in general, the firft things they laid their hands upon. I once faw a Gentleman flagellate a faucy young fifh-women, with all the flounders in her bafket. Among Saints, fome, like Dominic the *Cuiraffed*, have ufed befoms: others, like St. Dominic the Founder of the Dominican Order, have ufed iron chains; others, like Gualbert, have employed knotted leather-thongs, others have ufed nettles, and others thiftles. A certain Saint, as I have read in the Golden Legend, had no *difcipline* of his own, but conftantly took, to difcipline himfelf with, the very firft thing that came under his hand, fuch as the tongs for the fire, or the like. St. Bridget, as I have read in the fame book, difciplined herfelf with a bunch of keys; a certain Lady, who hath been mentioned in a former place, ufed a bunch of feathers for the fame purpofe; and laftly, Sancho did things with much more fimplicity, and flagellated himfelf with the palms of his hands.

C H A P. XVI.

*Confeffors at length affume to themfelves a kind
of flagellatory power over their Penitents.
The abufes that arife from it.*

THE fubmiffion of Sovereigns to receive
difciplines from the hands of their Confeffors, together with the accounts of fuch
difciplines, which, though they might not always be true, were induftrioufly circulated in
Public, helped much, without doubt, to increafe the good opinion which people entertained of the merit of flagellations, as well as to
ftrengthen the power of Confeffors in general.
In fact the latter, from prefcribing Difciplines,
foon paffed to inflicting them upon their penitents with their own hands; and, without
lofs of time, converted this newly-affumed
authority into an exprefs kind of privilege, to
which it was a moft meritorious act, on the
part of penitents, readily to fubmit. On this
occafion, I fhall again quote the old French

Q

Book, mentioned in p. 218; which, though it be only a Romance, may ferve to fhew the opinions generally entertained by people, during the times in which it was written. ‘ If ‘ you are eftranged from our Lord's love, you ‘ cannot be reconciled to him, unlefs by the ‘ three following means: Firft, by confeffion ‘ of mouth; fecondly, by a contrition of ‘ heart; thirdly, by works of alms and cha- ‘ rity. Now, go and make a confeffion in that ‘ manner, and receive difcipline from the ‘ hands of thy Confeffors; for it is the fign ‘ of merit.’

The power of Confeffors of *difciplining* their penitents, became in procefs of time fo generally acknowledged, that it obtained even with refpect to perfons who made profeffion of the Ecclefiaftical life, and fuperfeded the laws that had been made againft thofe who fhould ftrike an Ecclefiaftic. To this an allufion is made, in the lines of that Poet of the middle age, who has put the *Summula* of St. Raymund into Latin verfes. ‘ You are ‘ guilty of facrilege if you have violated holy ‘ things, if you have ftruck a perfon in reli- ‘ gious Orders, or of the Clergy; unlefs it ‘ be a holy beating, fuch as is performed by ‘ a Teacher with refpect to his Difciple, or a

' Confeſſor with reſpect to a perſon who con-
' feſſes his ſins *.'

Attempts were, however, made to put a
ſtop to theſe practices of Prieſts and Confeſſors ; and ſo early as under Pope Adrian I.
who was raiſed to the Purple in the year 772
(which by the by ſhews that the power aſſumed by Confeſſors, was pretty ancient) a regulation was made to forbid Confeſſors to beat
their Penitents. ' The Biſhop (it is ſaid in the
' Epitome of Maxims and Canons) the Prieſt,
' and the Deacon, muſt not beat thoſe who
' have ſinned †.' But this regulation proved
uſeleſs : the whole tribe of Prieſts, as well as
the firſt Dignitaries of the Church, neverthe-
leſs continued to preach up the prerogatives
of Confeſſors and the merit of flagellations ;
and Cardinal Pullus, that Chancellor of the
Roman Church who has been mentioned in
the foregoing Chapter, did not ſcruple to declare, that the nakedneſs of the Penitent, and
his ſituation at the feet of his Confeſſor, were

---

* Es vir ſacrilegus ſi res ſacras violaſti,
Si percuſſiſti perſonam religioſam,
Vel quem de Clero ; niſi percuſſio ſancta,
Doctor diſcipulum, Confeſſor prob. a fatentem.

† Cap. XV. Epiſcopus, Presbyter & Diaconus,
peccantes fideles diverberare non debeant.

additional merits in him in the eye of God, as being additional tokens of his humility *.

All thefe different practices of ftripping and flagellating Devotees and Penitents, at length gave rife to abufes of a very ferious nature; inftances of which take place, we may fay, every day. Numbers of Confeffors, in procefs of time, have made fuch religious acts as had been introduced with a view to mortification, ferve to gratify their own luft and wantonnefs. They have tried to inculcate the fame notions, as to the merit of flagellations, into the minds of their Devotees of the other fex, as they had brought even Kings and Princes to entertain; and at laft have made it a practice to inflict fuch corrections on their female Penitents, and under that pretence, to take fuch liberties with them, as the bleffed St. Benedict, St. Francis, St. Dominic, and St. Loyola, had not certainly given them the example of.

Among the many inftances that might be recited of the abufes here alluded to, it will fuffice to produce that of a Man who wore a

---

* *Card. Pulli* fententiarum *L. vii. Cap.* 3. *p.* 220. *Eft ergo fotisfactio quædam, afpera tamen, fed Deo tanto gratior qnanto humilior, cum quilibet facerdotis proftratus ad pedes, fe cædendum virgis exhibet nudum.*

hood, and was girt with a cord (a *Cordelier* or *Francifcan*) who lived about the year 1566. This Man's name was Cornelius Adriafem; he was a native of Dort, and belonged to a Convent in Bruges, and was a moft violent preacher againft the Heretics, called *Gueux.* He had found means to perfuade a certain number of Women, both married and unmarried, to promife him implicit obedience, by certain oaths he made them take for that purpofe, and under the fpecious pretence of greater piety. Thefe Women he did not indeed lafh with harfh and knotted cords, but he ufed gently to rub their bare thighs and pofteriors, with willow or birch rods ✝.

* I have in the courfe of this Work frequently produced the original words of the Authors who are quoted therein, as I thought this precaution would not be difagreeable to the critical part of Readers. In regard to the Abbé Boileau himfelf, no occafion has offered of doing the fame, as he feldom introduces any fact, in his Book, but in the words of the Writer from whom he borrows it: however, as in relating the above ftory, which he has extracted from a much longer account, he fpeaks for himfelf, I fhall take this opportunity of introducing him perfonally to the Reader, and of transcribing his own words, in

In order to fhew how common the above practices were become, as well as to entertain the Reader, I fhall conclude this Chapter with the following ftory, which is to be found in *Scot's* Book, entitled, *Menfa Philofophica.* A Woman, fays Scot, who was gone to make her confeffion, had been fecretly followed by her hufband, who was jealous of her; and he had hid himfelf in fome place in the Church, whence he might fpy her; but as foon as he faw her led behind the altar by the Prieft, in order to be flagellated, he made his appearance, objected that fhe was too tender to bear a flagellation, and offered to receive it in her ftead. This propofal the Wife greatly applauded; and the Man had no fooner placed himfelf upon his knees, than fhe exclaimed,

order to enable the Reader to judge of the goodnefs of his Latin.——' *Inter exempla tam infauftæ* ' *notitiæ non pertimefcam Hiftoriam narrare hominis* ' *cucullati et cordigeri, Conventus Brugenfis, anno* ' *circiter MDLXVI, cui nomen erat Cornelius Adri-* ' *afem, origine Dordracenfis, adverfus hæreticos Gue-* ' *zios ftomachofiffimi concionatoris, qui puellas feu fœ-* ' *minas quafdam facramento fidelitatis & obedientiæ* ' *fibi adftrictas, & fpecie pietatis devotas, non qui-* ' *dem afperatis & nodofis funibus verberabut, fed nu-* ' *data ea um femora & nates, inhoneftis vibicibus ro-* ' *rantes, betuleis aut vimineis virgis, ictibus molliter* ' *inflictis, perfricabat.*'

' Now, my Father, lay on luftily, for I am a
' great Sinner *.'

---

* ' *Domine, tota tenera eft ; ego pro ipfâ recipio
difciplinam · quo flectente genua dixit Mulier, Per..
cute fortiter, Domine, quia magna peccatrix fum.'*—
Men. Phil. Lib. iv. Cap. 18.

The above ftory, related by Scot, together
with the words he fuppofes to have been faid by
the Woman, have fince been turned into a French
epigram, which I have met with in the *Menagiana*,
as well as in two or three different collections of
French Poetry.

> *Une femme fe confeffa,*
> *Le Confeffeur à la fourdine*
> *Derriere l'Autel la trouffa*
> *Pour lui donner la difcipline.*
> *L'époux non loin d'elle caché*
> *De miféricorde touché*
> *Offrit pour elle dos & feffe.*
> *La femme y confentit dabord,*
> *Je fens, dit-elle, ma foibleffe,*
> *Mon mari fans doute eft plus fort ,*
> *Sus donc, mon Pere, touchez fort,*
> *Car je fuis grande pechereffe.*

The abovementioned flagellating practices of
Confeffors, are alluded to in feveral Books ; and
Confeffors are exprefsly charged with them by fe-
veral Writers, befides what is faid above. Among

others, Sanlec, a *bel Efprit* who lived under Lewis the Fourteenth, and wrote feveral Satires, in one of them, which he has intitled *The Directors*, has made the above practices of Confeffors, or Directors, the fubject of his animadverfion. ' This ' zealous Confeffor (fays Sanlec) who, for every ' trifling fault, with a difcipline in his hand, fuf- ' tigated his female Devotees.'

Ce Confcffeur zèlé, qui, pour les moindres faures,
La difcipline en main fuftigeoit fes Dévotes.

Among the number of thofe who have adminiftered difciplines of the kind here alluded to, a few have been fo happy as to acquire much more reputation than the others. Among thefe muft be ranked the abovementioned Cornelius Adriafem, whofe cafe is related at length by Meteren, in his Latin Hiftory of the Netherlands, publifhed in the year 1568, from which the Abbé Boileau has extracted it. This Cornelius Adriafem (or Adrianfen) was a loud declaimer againft the faction called the *Gueux*, whom the Abbé calls Hereticks, but who were, in fact, the fame party who oppofed the Spanifh Government in thofe parts, and afterwards fucceeded in overthrowing it, and founded the Republic of Holland. As the above Reverend Father had thus ftrongly oppofed a powerful, numerous, as well as incenfed party, in the State and the Church, the difcovery that was made of his frailties, afforded matter of much

triumph, as well as made a great noife, and fupplied his enemies with an opportunity of inveigh-
ing afterwards againft him, which they did not
neglect, as we may conclude from Meteren's account of the fact, which he relates at great length,
and with much fpleen and dulnefs. However,
new names were coined to exprefs that particular
kind of difcipline which Cornelius Adrianfen ufed
to ferve upon his female penitents : thofe who
oved to deduce their new appellations of things
from Greek words, called it the *Gynopygian* difcipline ; and others, who, proceeding upon a more
liberal plan, thought that the proper appellation
of any particular practice, ought to be derived from
the name of fome perfon who has eminently
diftinguifhed himfelf by it, called the difcipline in
queftion, from the name of the above Gentleman,
the *Cornelian* difcipline : a name by which it ftill
continues to be expreffed in thofe quarters.

The devifers of the appellation juft now mentioned, did not however mean to fay, that Cornelius Adrianfen was the inventor of the above
kind of difcipline, or even the firft man of note
who had recourfe to it: or, if fuch was their meaning, they were wrong. In fact, Abelard, who
certainly is a well-known character, alfo ufed to
adminifter flagellatory corrections to his pupil Heloifa, whofe name is not lefs illuftrious than that
of her Mafter. The Canon Fulbert, as every one

knows, had intrufted him with the care of her education, and as the Canon was very defirous fhe
fhould become diftinguifhed by her learning, he
had peimitted him to correct her, whenever fhe
fhould fail in performing her duty. Abelard, in
time, made an extenfive ufe of the power that had
thus been conferred upon him, though, to fay
the truth (and as himfelf confeffes in one of thofe
Latin letters he wrote to her after their feparation)
he, at laft, did not fo much ufe it, when fhe had
been guilty of faults, as when fhe too obftinately
refufed to commit any.—*Sed & te nolentem* (fays
he) *fæpiùs minis atque flagellis ad confenfum tra-
hebam.*

As Cornelius Adrianfen was preceded in the
career we mention, by a character as diftinguifhed
as himfelf, fo has he been followed by another
who was no lefs fo, and who made no lefs noife
in the world. The perfon I mean, is the celebrated Jefuit, Father Girard; and among the
number of his pupils or penitents, was Mifs *Ca-
dicre*, who certainly may alfo be looked upon as
an illuftrious character. The Cornelian difciplines which the Father ufed to ferve upon her,
were one of the fubjects of the public complaint fhe afterwards preferred againft him, about
the year 1730, which gave rife to a criminal law-
fuit or profecution that made a prodigious noife,
as it was thought to be a kind of ftroke levelled at

the whole Society of the Jefuits, and was known
to have been ftirred up by Monks belonging to
Orders who were at open enmity with them. The
Demoifelle Cadiere likewife brought againft Father
Girard a charge of forcery, and of having be-
witched her; in order, no doubt, to apologize
for her having peaceably fubmitted to the licentious actions of which fhe accufed the Father,
as well as to thofe difciplines with which fhe reproached him, which fhe circumftantially defcribed in the original complaint, or charge, which
fhe preferred againft him, for Judges are perfons
who will not underftand things by half words;
one muft fpeak plain to them, and call every thing
by its proper name.

Among thofe who have diftinguifhed themfelves
in the fame career of flagellation, Readers (I
mean thofe who poffefs fome patriotifm and love
of their Country) will, no doubt, be much pleafed
to find one who belonged to this Nation, I mean
to fpeak of the Reverend Zachary Crofton, Curate of St. *Botolph's, Aldgate,* who, on a certain
occafion, ferved a Cornelian difcipline upon his
Chambermaid, for which fhe afterwards fued him
at Weftminfter.

The aforefaid Zachary Crofton, as Bifhop Ken-
net relates in his Chronicle, from Dr. Calamy's
notes, was formerly a Curate at Wrenbury, in
Chefhire (it was a little before the Reftoration)

and he ufed to engage with much warmth in the religious and political quarrels of his times : his refufal to take the *engagement*, and endeavours to diffuade others from taking it, caufed him to be difmiffed fiom his place. He was, however, afterwards provided with the Curacy of St. Botolph's, Aldgate , but as his turn for religious and political quarrels ftill prevailed, and he had wiitten feveral pamphlets, both Englifh and Latin, about the affairs of thofe times, he was fent to the Tower, and deprived of his Curacy : he was afterwards caft into piifon likewife in his own County, and when he procured his liberty, fet up a Grocer's fhop. While he was in the above Parifh of St. Botolph, ' he gave,' as Dr. Calamy relates, ' the correction of a fchool-boy to his fervant-maid,' for which fhe piofecuted him in Weftminfter-hall. This fact the Doctor relates as an inftance of the many fcrapes into which Zachary Crofton's warm and zealous temper brought him , and he adds that, on the laft mentioned occafion, ' he was bold to print his defence.'——Indeed this fact of Parfon Crofton's undauntedly appealing to the Public in print concerning the lawfulnefs of the flagellation he had performed, places him, notwithftanding what Dr. Calamy may add as to the mediocrity of his parts, at leaft upon a level with the Geniufes abovementioned, as well as any other of the kind

that may be named, and cannot fail for ever to fecure him a place among the moſt illuſtrious Flagellators.

In fine, to this liſt of the perſons who have
diſtinguiſhed themſelves by the flagellations they
have atchieved, I think I cannot avoid adding that
Lady, mentioned by Brantôme, who (perhaps as
an exerciſe conducive to her health) took great delight in performing correƈtions of this kind, with
her own hands. This Lady, who was moreover
a very great Lady, would often, as Brantôme relates, cauſe the Ladies of her Houſhold to ſtrip
themſelves, and then amuſe herſelf in giving them
ſlaps upon their poſteriors, pretty luſtily laid on :
with reſpeƈt to thoſe Ladies who had committed
faults, ſhe made uſe of good rods ; and in general, ſhe uſed leſs or greater ſeverity, according
(Brantôme ſays) as ſhe propoſed to make them either laugh or cry. The following are Brantôme's
own words.

‘ J'ai ouï parler d'une grande Dame de par le
‘ monde, voire grandiſſime, qui ne ſe contentant pas de
‘ laſciveté naturelle, & étant mariée & étant Veuve,
‘ pour la provoquer & exciter davantage, elle faiſoit
‘ dépouiller ſes Dames & filles, je dis les plus belles,
‘ & ſe deleƈtoit fort à les voir, & puis elle les battoit
‘ du plat de la main ſur les feſſes, avec de grandes
‘ clacquades & blamuſes aſſez rudes ; & les filles qui
‘ avoient delinqué en quelques choſe, avec de bonnes
‘ verges.——Autres fois, ſans les depouiller, les faiſoit trouſſer en robes, car pour lors elles ne portoient

' *point de calecons, & les clacquettoit fur les feffes, fe-*
' *lon le fujet qu'elles lui en donnoient, pour les faire ou*
' *rire, ou pleurer.'*

It is no eafy matter to point out what precife views the Lady in queftion had, when fhe ferved the abovementioned flagellations. Brantôme, who had much travelled, and was grown much acquainted with the wickednefs of the world, infinuates that fhe was actuated by motives of rather a wanton kind, but fince it is extremely difficult to believe that thoughts like thofe Brantôme fuppofes, could be entertained, I fhall not fay by a Lady, but by a perfon of the high rank of the Lady in queftion, I will endeavour to account for her conduct in a different manner, and I fhall confider my time as exceedingly well employed, if I can clear her from the afperfion thrown upon her by the above Gentleman.

In the firft place, it is very poffible, that (as hath been above infinuated) fhe confidered the flagellations in queftion as an exercife advantageous to her health : and Phyficians have often made worfe prefcriptions.

In the fecond place, fhe might, without looking faither, be prompted by a defire of doing juftice, for Brantome makes exprefs mention of Ladies who had committed faults : now, fuch a conduct on the part of the Lady we fpeak of, would

3

reflect much honour upon her, and shew that she did not difdain to superintend her own family.

Perhaps also it might be, that the abovementioned flagellations were of the same jocular kind merely, with those which, as hath been related in the sixth Chapter of this Book, were in ufe in Rome, and were often practised in the presence of the Emperor Claudius, and sometimes upon that Emperor himself. Nor is the circumstance mentioned by Brantome, of the high Lady in question sometimes using pretty great severity, contrary to this suppofition: it is a well-known fact that Great people, when they do their inferiors the honour to play with them, will often carry the joke too far, farther than the latter have a liking to: jokes or tricks of this kind, gave rife to the French common saying, *Jeux de Princes, qui plaifent à ceux qui les font.* ‘ Tricks of Princes, ‘ which pleafe thofe (*only*) by whom they are ‘ played.’

In fine, fince the flagellations in question were often carried on, as appears from the account of Brantome himfelf, in a manner really very jocular, even fo much fo as to make the Ladies laugh, it is natural to fuppofe that they were then executed by the common and perfectly free confent of the whole company. The Ladies poffibly propofed to reprefent among themfelves the feftival of the *Lupercalia,* which has been defcribed in a former Chapter : intending to reprefent it as it was performed in the times of Pope Gelafius, they ftripped themfelves in the manner Brantome has related : the great Lady, in confideration of her high birth and ftation, was permitted to fill the part of the *Lupercus* , the wielding of the *difcipline* was of courfe exclufively left to her : nor was this peculiar advantage which the other Ladies granted her, in that kind of farce they agreed to act among themfelves, materially different from the favour which certain Clergymen ufed to grant to their Bifhop, when they played at Whift with him, who allowed his Lordfhip the privilege of naming the trump.

In regard to the Gentlemen who have been mentioned above, it is however pretty evident that (owing, no doubt, to the good-nature inherent in their fex) they ufed no kind of feverity in thofe difciplines they ufed to beftow , except indeed Parfon Crofton, who, from the circumftance of his writing a pamphlet, and a quarto pamphlet too, in defence of the flagellation he had performed, feems really to have been in earneft, both when he planned, and when he ferved it.

Thus Abelard, in one of the abovementioned Letters he wrote to his Pupil, while fhe lived retired in the Monaftery of *Paraclet*, exprefsly fays that the blows he gave her, were fuch blows as friendfhip alone, not anger, fuggefted : he even adds that their fweetnefs furpaffed that of the fweeteft perfumes,——*virbera quandoque dabat amor, non furor, gratia, non ira, quæ omnium un-guentorum fuavitatem tranfcenderent.*

Father Girard, as is evident from the whole tenor of the declaration of Mifs Cadiere herfelf, had as little intention as Abelard, to do any kind of injury to his pupil or penitent, and Cornelius Adrianfen, as appears from Meteren's account, ufed to proceed with the fame caution and ten-dernefs for his difciples, as the two above-men-tioned gentlemen, and contented himfelf, as the Abbé Boileau obferves, with gently rubbing them with his inftruments of difcipline,——*molliter per-fricabat.*

That Confeffors fhould contract fentiments of friendfhip for their female penitents, like thofe mentioned by Abelard, is however nowife fur-prizing. La Fontaine fays, that

Tout homme eft homme, & les Moines fur tous.

" Every Man is a Man, and Monks above all " others." He might at leaft have faid, " Every " Man is a Man, and Monks as well as others," and to this have added, that their virtue, efpeci-ally that of Confeffors, is expofed to dangers of a peculiar kind. In fact, the obligation which thofe who perform that office are under, to hear, with feeming indifference, the long confeffions of Women of every age, who frequently enter into numerous particulars concerning the fins which they have either committed, or had diftant wifhes to commit, is no very eafy tafk for Men who, as hath juft now been obferved, are after all nothing but Men, and they are, under fuch circumftances, frequently agitated by thoughts not very confonant with the apparent gravity and fanctity of their looks. Nay, raifing fuch thoughts in them, and in general creating fentiments of love in their Confeffors, are defigns which numbers of female penitents, who at no time entirely ceafe being actuated by womanifh views, exprefly entertain, notwithftanding the apparent ingenuity of their confeffions, and in which they but too often fucceed, to their own, and their frail Confeffors, coft. Thus, it appears from Mifs Cadiere's declarations, that fhe had of herfelf aimed at making the conqueft of Father Girard, though a Man paft fifty years of age, being induced to it by his great reputation both as a preacher and a man of parts ; and fhe exprefsly confeffed that fhe had for a long while been making intereft to be admitted into the number of his penitents.

Indeed, thefe dangers to which Confeffors are expofed from their continual and confidential intercourfe with the Sex, (for, to the praife of Women be it fpoken, they are infinitely more exact than Men in making their confeffions) are much

taken notice of in the books in which directions
are given to such priests as are designed for that
employment, and they are warned against nothing
so much as an inclination to hear preferably the
confeffions of the other Sex.————St. Charles
Borrommee, as I have read in one of thofe books.
prefcribed to Confeffors to have all the doors
wide open, when they heard the confeffion of a
Woman, and he had fupplied them with a fet of
paffages from Pfalms, fuch as, *Cor mundum crea
in me Domine,* and the like, which he advifed
them to have pafted on fome confpicuous place
within their fight, and which were to ferve them
as ejaculatory exclamations by which to vent the
wicked thoughts with which they might feel
themfelves agitated, and as kinds of *Abracadabras,*
or *Retrò Satanas,* to apply to, whenever they
fhould find themfelves on the point of being overcome by fome too fudden temptation.

Numbers of Confeffors, however, whether it
was that they had forgotten to fupply themfelves
with the paffages recommended by St. Charles
Borrommee, or that thofe paffages really proved
ineffectual in thofe inftants in which they were
intended to be ufeful, have, at different times,
formed ferious defigns upon the chaftity of their
penitents, and the fingular fituation in which
they were placed, both with refpect to the Public, and to their penitents themfelves, with

whom changing the grave fupercilious Confeffor into the wanton lover, was no eafy tranfition, have led them to ufe expedients of rather fingular kinds, to attain their ends. Some, like Robert d'*Arbriffel*, (and the fame has been faid of Ad-helm, an Englifh Saint who lived before the Con-queft) have induced young Women to lie with. them in the fame beds, giving them to under-ftand, that, if they could prove fuperior to every temptation, and rife from bed as they went to it, it would be in the higheft degree meritorious. Others, Menas for inftance, a Spanifh Monk whofe cafe was quoted in the proceedings againft Father Guaid, perfuaded young Women to live with him in a kind of holy conjugal union which he defcribed to them, but which did not however end, at laft, in that intellectual manner which the Father had promifed. Others have perfuaded Women that the works of matrimony were no lefs liable to pay tithes than the fruits of the earth, and have received thefe tithes accord-ingly. This fcheme was, it is faid, contrived by the Fryars of a certain Convent in a fmall Town in Spain, and La Fontaine has made it the fubject of one of his *Tales*, which is entitled *The Cordeliers of Catalonia*, in which he defcribes with much humour the great punctuality of the Ladies in that Town, in difcharging their debts to the Fathers, and the vaft bufinefs that was, in confequence, carried on in the Convent of the latter.

Laftly, other Confeffors have had recourfe to their power of flagellation, as an excellent expedient for preparing the fuccefs of their fchemes, and preventing the firft fufpicions which their penitents might entertain of their views.

In order the better to remove the fcruples which the modefty of thefe latter caufed them at firft to oppofe, they ufed to reprefent to them, that our firft Parents were naked in the garden of Eden, they moreover afked, whether people muft not be naked, when they are chriftened; and fhall not they likewife be fo, on the day of Refurrection? Nay, others have made fuch a ftate of nakednefs, on the part of their penitents, a matter of exprefs duty, and have fupported this doctrine, as the Author of the *Apologie pour Herodote* relates, by quoting the paffage of Jefus Chrift, in which he fays, *Go, and fhew thyfelf to the Prieft.*

However, inftances of the wantonnefs of Priefts like this latter, in which a ferious ufe was made of paffages from the Books on which Religion is grounded, in order to forward fchemes of a guilty nature, certainly cannot, in whatever light the fubject be confidered, admit of any juftification: though on the other hand, when the national calamities produced by fophifms of this kind and the arts of Men of the fame cloth, are confidered, one cannot help wifhing that they had conftantly employed both thefe fophifms and their artifices in purfuits like thofe above men‚ tioned, and that, enfnaring a few female penitents (who were not perhaps, after all, extremely unwilling to be enfnared) and ferving flagellations, had been the worft exceffes they ever had com‚ mitted.

CHAP.

C H A P. XVII.

The Church at large also claims a power of publicly inflicting the discipline of flagellation. Instances of Kings and Princes who have submitted to it.

AS it was the constant practice of Priests and Confessors, to prescribe flagellation as a part of the *satisfaction* that was owing for committed sins, the opinion became at last to be established, that, receiving this kind of correction, was not only an useful, but even an indispensible act of submission: without it penitence was thought to be a body without a soul; nor could there be any such thing as true repentance. Hence the Church itself at large, became also in time to claim a power of imposing castigations of the kind we mention, upon naked sinners; and a flagellation publicly submitted to, has been made one of the essential ceremonies to be gone through, for obtaining the inestimable advantage of the repeal of a sentence of excommunication:

R 4

the Roman Ritual expreſsly mentioning and requiring this teſt of the culprit's contrition.

Theſe flagellatory claims and practices of the Weſtern Chriſtian Church, are, we may obſerve, one of the objections made againſt it by the Greek, or Eaſtern, Chriſtians, as the learned M. Cotelier, a Doctor of the Sorbonne, obſerves in his *Monuments of the Greek Church:* ' When they abſolve a perſon from ' his excommunication (they ſay) he is ſtrip- ' ped down to the waiſt, and they laſh him ' with a ſcourge on that part which is bare, ' and then abſolve him, as being forgiven his ' his ſin *.'

Among the different inſtances of diſciplines publicly inflicted by the Church, upon independent Princes, we may mention that which was impoſed upon Giles, Count of the *Venaiſſin* County, near Avignon. This Count having cauſed the Curate of a certain Pariſh to be buried alive, who had refuſed to bury the body of a poor Man, till the uſual fees were paid, drew upon himſelf the wrath of the Pope, who fulminated againſt him a ſentence of excommunication. And in order to procure the repeal of it, he found it neceſſary

---

* Ἀφορισμῶ τινὰ λύοντες, γυμνῶσιν αὐτὸν ἕως ὀσφύος, κ̀ μαςίζοντες ἐπὶ γυμνῶ λώροις, ἀπολύεσιν ὡς συγκεχωρημένον ἐνῖευθεν.

to fubmit to a flagellation, which was inflicted upon him before the gate of the Cathedral
Church of Avignon.

But no fact can be mentioned more ftriking, and more capable of having gratified the
pride of the Clergy, at the time, than that
of Henry II. King of England. This Prince
having, by a few hafty angry words he uttered on a certain occafion, been the caufe of the
affaffination of Thomas Becket, Archbifhop
of Canterbury, expreffed afterwards the greateft forrow for his imprudence : but neither
the Priefts nor the Nation would take his
word on that account : they only gave credit
to the reality of his repentance, when he had
fubmitted to the all-purifying trial of a flagellation ; and in order the more completely
to remove all doubts in that refpect, he went
through it publicly. The following is the
account which Matthew Paris, a Writer who
lived about thofe times, has given of the
tranfaction. ' But as the flaughterers of this
' glorious Martyr had taken an opportunity
' to flav him from a few words the King had
' uttered rather imprudently, the King afked
' abfolution from the Bifhops who were pre-
' fent at the ceremony, and fubjecting his bare
' fkin to the difcipline of rods, received four

' or five ftripes from every one of the religi-
' ous perfons, a multitude of whom had af-
' fembled *.'

---

* .... *Carnemque fuam nudam difciplinæ virga-
rum fupponens, à fingulis viris religiofis, quorum
multitudo magna convenerat, ictus ternos vel quinos
accepit.*

Among the inftances of Sovereigns who have
been publickly flagellated, may alfo be reckoned
that of Raymond, Count of Touloufe, whofe
Sovereignty extended over a very confiderable part
of the South of France. Having given protec-
tion in his dominions to the Sect called the *Albi-
genfes*, Innocent III. the moft haughty Pope that
ever filled the Papal Chair, publifhed a Croifade
againft him; his dominions were in confequence
feized, nor could he fucceed to have them reftored
to him, before he had fubmitted to receive difcipline from the hands of the Legate of the Pope,
who ftripped him naked to the waift, at the door
of the Church, and drove him up to the altar in
that fituation, all the while beating him with
rods.

With refpect to the difcipline undergone by
King Henry II. though he may be faid to have
freely fubmitted to it, yet it did not, at bottom,

materially differ from that impofed upon Raymond, Count of Touloufe. This Prince had,
no doubt, too much underftanding to fubmit to a
ceremony of this kind, out of regard for fome
prevailing notion of the vulgar merely, and much
lefs out of any fuperftition of his own, but he
thought it neceffary to perform fome remarkable
religious act of that fort, for filencing at once the
clamours of the Priefts, the whole body of whom,
incenfed by the death of Becket, were every where
endeavouring to fpirit up the people to a revolt;
and he may with truth be faid to have fubmitted
to being flagellated, in order to preferve his kingdom : which may ferve as a proof, among others,
that it is a pleafing thing to be a King.

The laft inftance of a Sovereign who received
a correction from the Church, was that of Henry
IV. of France, when he was abfolved of his excommunication and herefy, and the difcipline undergone by that Prince fupplies the folution for
an interefting queftion, that may be added to thofe
above difcuffed, viz. Which is the moft comfortable manner of receiving a flagellation ?—It is by
Proxy.—This was the manner in which the King
we fpeak of, fuffered the difcipline which the
Church inflicted upon him. His proxies were
Meff. D'Offat, and Du Perron, who were afterwards made Cardinals. During the performing
of the ceremony of the King's abfolution, and

while the Chorifters were finging the Pfalm *Mife-rere mei Deus*, the Pope, at every verfe, beat, with a ród on the fhoulders of each of the two proxies; which fhews how effential a part of the ceremony of an abfolution, flagellations have been thought to be, and alfo, how ftrictly the Church of Rome adheres to fuch forms as are prefcribed by its Ritual, or, by the *Pontifical*, as it is called. Exprefs mention was moreover made of the above beating, in the written procefs that was drawn of the tranfaction. *Dominus Papa verberabat & per-cutiebat humeros Procuratorum, & cujuflibet ipforum, virgâ quam in manibus habebat.*

As a farther indulgence to the King who was thus difciplined by proxy, and very likely alfo out of regard for the age in which the ceremony was performed, the two Gentlemen who reprefented him, were fuffered to keep their coats on, during the operation; and the lafhes feem moreover not to have been laid upon them, with any great degree of vigour. However, fome perfons at the Court of France, either out of envy againft the two above Gentlemen, on account of the com-miffion with which the King had honoured them, or with a view to divert themfelves, had, it feems, circulated a report, that, on the day of the cere-mony, the 17th of September 1595, they had been made actually to ftrip in the Church, and undergo a dreadful flagellation. This report M.

D'Offat contradicts in one of his Letters, and says, that the difcipline in queftion was performed to comply with the rules fet down in the *Pontifical*, but that, ' they felt it no more than if it ' had been a fly that had paffed over them, being ' fo well coated as they were.'

Very exprefs mention of the above difcipline was neverthelefs made, as hath been above obferved, in the written procefs drawn on the occafion, though the French Minifters would not fuffer it to be joined with the *Bull* of abfolution which was fent to the King for his acceptation, and in which no fuch account was contained.

The bufinefs of the King's abfolution, and efpecially the point of the flagellation, was negotiated at Rome for about two years. When the fact was at laft publicly known to have taken place, the Hugonots, who ftill continued to look upon Henry IV. as the friend of their party, were exceedingly mortified · they vented their ill humour by libels and ludicrous prints ; and Daubigné, in his *Catholic Confeffion of Mr. Sancy*, comforts himfelf by comparing the King's two pioxies, lying flat on the ground in St. Peter's Church, to *two mackrels on a gridiron*. Sully, in his Memoirs, has expreffed himfelf with much concern on the fame fubject, and fays that Meffrs. Doffat and Duperron, who belonged to the Clergy, had deferted the honour of their King and Country, in order to get preferment in the Church.

Another inftance of royal flagellation occurs in the Life of Henry IV. Emperor of Germany, which I cannot tell why I have omitted to mention in the firft and fecond Edition of this Book, but is well worth adding to this. This Emperor, having been excommunicated by Pope Gregory, whofe power he had oppofed, was obliged to repair to Rome to the Caftle where the Pope refided: theie he was made to wait three days at the gate, without attendants, cloathed in a coarfe woollen jacket, barefooted, in the month of January, and, according to Malmfbury's account, holding a broom in his hand. At length he was let in. his broom was laid on his imperial back, and he received his abfolution.

From the above three inftances of Henry II. of England, Henry IV. of Germany, and Henry IV. of France (the authenticity of which is beyond any doubt), we find that three crowned Heads, Sovereigns of the three firft States in Europe, all three of the name of Henry, have publicly fubmitted to the difcipline of flagellation, either in their own perfon, or by proxy ' two, in order to preferve their Crown; and the other, in order to qualify himfelf for taking poffeffion of it. I defire the judicious Reader to ponder well all thefe facts, and not to charge me with having chofen too unimportant a fubject to treat in this work.

It may be added, that an inftance of a Sovereign fubmitting to a flagellation, may be feen in

our days, at every vacancy of the See of Wurtz-
burgh; a fovereign Bifhoprick in Germany. It
is an antient cuftom in the Chapter of that
Church, that the perfon who has been elected to
fill the place of the late Bifhop, muft, before he
can obtain his inftallation, run the gantlope, naked to the waift, between the Canons, who are
formed in two rows, and fupplied with rods. Some
fay this cuftom was eftablifhed in order to dif-
courage the German Princes from being Candi-
dates for the above Bifhoprick, but perhaps alfo
the Canons who eftablifhed the fame had no
other defign than procuring the pleafure to themfelves and fucceffors, when they fhould afterwards
fee their equal become their Sovereign, of remembering that they had cudgelled him.

Other facts, befides that of Henry II. fhew that
the power of the Clergy was carried as far in
England, as in any other Country. In the reign
of Edward I. Sir Ofborn Gifford, of Wiltfhire,
having affifted in the efcape of two Nuns from the
Convent of Wilton, John Peckham, who was
then Archbifhop of Canterbury, made him fubmit, before he abfolved him of his excommunication, to be publicly whipped, on three fucceffive Sundays, in the Parifh Church of Wilton,
and in the Market and Church of Shaftfbury *.

* See Dr, Berkenhout's *Biographia Litteraria*, Art. *John
Peckham*.

C H A P. XVIII.

The glory of flagellations completed: they are
made ufe of for curing herefy.

AMONG all the inftances contained in
this Book, of the extenfive advantages
of flagellations, we certainly ought not to
omit mentioning the application that has been
made of them to the information of Heretics;
the holy perfonages, whofe office it was to convert them, having frequently recurred to them
as an excellent expedient, either for opening
the eyes of fuch as abfolutely refufed to believe, or for confirming the faith of thofe
who did as yet believe but imperfectly. As
one inftance of that ufe of flagellations we
fpeak of, we may, mention that of Bonner,
Bifhop of London, who, though he had, under the reign of Henry VIII. confented to the
fchifm which then took place in the Church,
made it his conftant practice, under Queen
Mary, to fuftigate the Proteftants with rods
with his own hands, at leaft if we are to cre-

dit the account given by Bifhop Burnet, in his Hiftory of the Reformation, in England *.

---

* I do not remember to have met with the above fact in Burnet: Mr. Hume, who alfo mentions it, quotes, it feems, another Author. however, Bifhop Burnet relates a fact of much the fame nature, which is that of Mr. James Bainham, a Gentleman of the Temple, who was accufed of favouring the new opinions : Chancellor More caufed him to be fuftigated in his own (More's) houfe, and thence fent him to the Tower. The Abbé Boileau, fiom whofe text I have really borrowed the inftance of Bifhop Bonner, had however no occafion to look out of his own Country, for inftances of Heretics who have been reformed by flagellations : though, to fay the truth, that inftance, together with that of Chancellor More, which is here added to it, are the more interefting, in that they evince the great merit of flagellations, fince the Divines of all Countries have alike reforted to them.

S

C H A P. XIX.

The subject of the merit of flagellations, conti-
nued. Holy perfons, though without any pub-
lic authority, have ufed them occafionally, in
order to give weight to their admonitions.

THE general efteem for flagellations,
which had led people to confider them
as an infallible method of atoning for paft
fins, alfo induced them to think they would
be extremely ufeful to ftrengthen thofe admonitions with which it is the duty of good Chriftians to affift each other. Hence we find that
Saints, who, like other perfons, have been
pretty free with their advices to other men,
have frequently affumed a power to corrobo-
rate them by flagellations.

Among thofe inftances of corrections beftowed by Saints upon perfons who did not
afk them for their advice, none can be quoted
more remarkable than that of St. Romuald,
who, on a certain occafion, feverely flagellated
his very Father, whofe conduct he difapprov-

ed, as Cardinal Damian relates, who, we may
obferve, greatly approves the action of the
Saint. The following is the account given by
the Cardinal. ' After he had received per-
' miffion for that purpofe from his Superiors,
' he fet out upon his intended journey, with-
' out either horfe or cart, but only with a
' ftick in his hand, and with his feet bare ;
' and, from the remoteft borders of France,
' at laft reached Ravenna. There finding his
' Father determined to return to the World,
' he put him in the ftocks ; he tied him with
' heavy chains, dealt hard blows to him, and
' continued ufing him with this pious feverity,
' till, by the favour of God, he had brought
' his foul back to a ftate of falvation '.'

To thofe flagellations beftowed by Saints
upon perfons who did not afk for them, we
may fafely add thofe with which they have, at
different times, ferved fuch Ladies, as, fmit-
ten with their charms (with the Saints charms,
I mean) have ventured to make them propofals totally inconfiftent with their virtue. Thefe
propofals the Saints not only conftantly rejected magnanimoufly, but moreover feldom

* .... " In ligno pedes ejus fortiter ftrinxit, gra-
vibus eum vinculis alligavit, verberibus duris affixit,
& tamdiù corpus ejus piâ feveritate perdomuit, donec
ejus mentem ad falutis ftatum Deo medente reduxit."

S 2

difmiffed the Ladies who attempted them, without making them feel the points of their difciplines. This was the manner in which St. Edmund, who was afterwards Bifhop of Canterbury, behaved on an occafion like thofe we mention, as the learned Claude Defpence, a Parifian Theologian, relates in his Book on *Continence.* St. Edmund, the above Writer fays, during the time he was purfuing his ftudies in Paris, was folicited by a young Woman to commit with her the fin of fornication; he thereupon bade her come to his ftudy, where, after tearing off her clothes, he flagellated her naked, fo feverely, that he covered her whole body with ftripes *.

Brother Mathew, of Avignon, a Capuchin Friar who lived about the year 1540, and fpent many years in Corfica with a reputation of fanctity, gave juft fuch another capital inftance of virtue as that exhibited by St. Edmund. The Saint having been charitably received in a certain Caftle in Piedmont, where he was then begging about the Country, a young Lady, extremely handfome, and of noble birth, came during the night, ftripped

* . . . . " *Eam ad muſæum ſuum excivit, ibique ſpoliatam virgis cæcidit, ac nudatum corpus vibicibus conſcribillavit.*"

to her fhift, to vifit him, in the room that
had been affigned to him, and approaching
the bed in which he was afleep, folicited him
to commit the carnal fin. But the holy Friar,
inftead of anfwering her, 'took up his difci-
' pline, made with found and well-knotted
' Spanifh fmall cords, and flagellated her fo
' brifkly upon her thighs, her pofteriors, and
' back, that he not only made her blufh with
' fhame, but moreover left upon her fkin
' numberlefs vifible marks of the lecture he
' gave her *.'

To thefe inftances of the holy feverity with
which Saints have treated fuch Ladies as ventured to make attempts upon their virtue,
may be added that of Bernardin of Sienna,
according to the account given by Surius;
for the virtue of Saints has been expofed to
more dangers than the vulgar think of. 'One
' day (fays Surius) as Bernardin was gone
' abroad to buy fome bread, a Woman, the

---

* Here an opportunity occurs of giving a fecond fpecimen of the Latin of the Abbe Boileau,
the firft was produced in p. 232.

.... *Eandem flagello nodis afperato, ex funibus
Ibericis compacto, tamd.ù diverberavit, totque vibicibus fulcos fanguinolentos in femoribus, clunibus, ac fca-
pulis diduxit, ut non folùm fuffufo vi pudoris, verum
etiam effufo vi doloris, fanguine, fugaverit.*

' Wife of a Citizen of Sienna, called him to
' her houfe : as foon as he had got into it, fhe
' locked the door, and faid, Unlefs you now
' let me have my wifh, I declare I will cover
' you with fhame, and fay that you have of-
' fered violence to me. Bernardin, finding
' himfelf drawn into fuch a dangerous fitua-
' tion, prayed to God, within himfelf, not to
' forfake him; for he greatly detefted that
' crime. God did not difregard his prayer:
' he prefently fuggefted to him to tell the
' Woman, that fince fhe would abfolutely
' have it fo, fhe muft ftrip off her clothes.
' To this the Woman made no objection;
' and fhe had fcarcely done when Bernardin
' exhibited his whip, which he happened to
' have about him, and laying faft hold of her,
' began to exert it vigoroufly; nor did he
' give up fuftigating her, till her luftful ar-
' dour was extinguifhed. She loved the holy
' Man the better for that afterwards; and fo
' did her Hufband, when he knew how things
' had been tranfacted *.'

---

* . . . Eâ caufâ impenfiùs mulier amavit fanctum
virum, itemque maritus ejus, ubi comperit rem ab eo
geftam.

The accounts of the advances Ladies have made to the above holy perfonages, muft certainly give pleafure to the judicious and fenfible Reader. Confidering the opinion entertained by a number of perfons, that Rakes, Coxcombs, and in general the moft worthlefs part of the male fex, are commonly the moft welcome to the favours of the Ladies, I think it reflects much honour upon them all, that feveral have gone the greateft lengths in favour of Saints, and have fet afide, out of love for them, thofe rules of referve and decency which Ladies are otherwife fo naturally inclined to refpect.

In regard to the manner in which the Saints themfelves ufed the Ladies, it is certainly fomewhat fingular: however, I muft poftpone giving my opinion about it, till a few remarks are made on what more precifely conftitutes the fubject of the foregoing Chapters, which is the great merit and dignity of flagellations. In fact, we find that Great Men, Conquerors, and Kings, have publicly fubmitted to receiving them, and they have moreover occafionally inflicted them with their own hands. The Reader may remember the method mentioned at pag. 54. of this Work, which was adopted by the Grecian Heroes, for conveying to their vanquifhed Opponents, a proper fenfe of their fuperiority and indignation. And the fame magnanimous kind of admonition was alfo commonly made ufe of by the Romans, in regard to thofe Kings or Generals whom they had taken in war.

Caligula, a Roman Emperor, did not difdain, as we read in Suetonius, to ufe the fame kind of correction, for filencing thofe who happened to make a noife near him in the Theatre, and thereby prevented him from attending to the play, and efpecially to his favourite Actor: the culprit was inftantly ftripped, and the Emperor himfelf did the reft *.

Another Emperor we may name here, viz. Peter the Firft, of Ruffia. He frequently condefcended to beftow, with his own imperial hands, that kind of Ruffian flagellation, the *Knout:* at other times, when he could not attend to the bufinefs, he trufted the care of it to his Buffoon Witafki, who was moreover invefted with an unlimited power of cudgelling thofe who came to pay their court to his Czarian Majefty.

The inftances of flagellations above produced, have however been confined to actions of Kings, Conquerors, Emperors, and Saints, or to cafes of great emergency, in which whole Nations were

* He punifhed differently, on a certain occafion, a Roman Knight who had been guilty of the abovementioned fault. He fent him, without delay, to carry a letter to Africa; without allowing the time to call at his houfe, and take leave of his family.

concerned, fuch as the confutations of herefies, and the acquifition of Sovereignties and Kingdoms, but if we defcend into the different fpheres of private life, we fhall find their advantages to have alfo been very extenfive.

Thus, flagellations have been ufeful to feveral perfons, to make their fortunes. Not to mention here the common ftory about thofe who have been flagellated, when Boys, in the room of the Heir to the Crown, we find that the two abovementioned Gentlemen, Meffrs. D'Offat and Du Perron, who had had the honour to be difciplined at Rome, on the account of their Royal Mafter, were afterwards, through his intereft, promoted to the high dignity of Cardinals, befides obtaining confiderable emoluments.

Others, though they have not gained fuch fubftantial advantages as places and penfions, have acquired, which in the opinion of many judicious perfons is not lefs valuable, extenfive reputations. Some have acquired fuch reputations, by the flagellations they have inflicted,—among thefe are to be ranked Cornelius Adrianfen, Zachary Crofton, and the Lady mentioned by Brantome; and others, by the flagellations they have undergone, fuch was Titus Oates, fo well known in the Hiftory of this Country; Bifhop Burnet exprefsly obferving, that *this treatment did rather raife Oates's reputation, than fink it.* (A. 1685.)

In the intercourfe of private life, though among perfons diftinguifhed from the vulgar, flagellations, being employed as corrections, have alfo proved of very great fervice.

Thus *bon-mots*, at the expence of other perfons, fatires, lampoons, have, on numberlefs occafions, been confuted by flagellations. The Reader furely has not forgotten the cafe of Mifs de Limeuil, which has been recited in a former place , nor that of the Court Buffoon which is introduced in the fame Chapter · and to thefe inftances might be added that of the Poet Clopinel, the Continuator of that old and celebrated Romance, the *Roman de la Rofe*, who was once very near being flagellated by the Ladies of the Court of France, for his having tried his wit at the expence of the Sex in general, as will be related in another place.

Indeed, to difcufs the fubject of the ufefulnefs of flagellations in a manner adequate to its importance and extenfivenefs, would lead us into narratives without end : I will therefore, for the fake of fhortnefs, content myfelf with adding a few facts to thofe before recited , as, befides fupplying interefting confequences, they are fufficiently authenticated.

The firft, which is very ufeful to prove that *the fecrets of Ladies ought never to be betrayed*, is that of the flagellation which was inflicted on a certain Surgeon, who gave a loofe to his tongue, at the

expence of a great Lady to whom his affiftance
had been ufeful. The Lady I mean, was Wife
to the Prince who became afterwards King of
France, under the name of Henry IV : fhe was
herfelf much more nearly allied to the Crown than
the Prince her Hufband, and would have mount-
ed the Throne in her own right, if it had not
been for the Salic Law. The Princefs in queftion
was learned, witty, handfome, and fhe had, in
particular, fuch a fine aim, that it was commonly
reported that the Marquis of Canillac, under
whofe guard fhe lived for a while as ftate prifoner,
fell in love with her on the fight of it. With
thefe qualifications fhe united gay, amorous difpofitions, having even been fufpected to love the
great Duke of Guife, who afterwards nearly poffeffed himfelf of the Crown ; and fhe had befides
a turn for political intrigues. During the celebrated civil wars of the *League*, being in the City
of Agen, fhe attempted to make herfelf miftrefs
of the place, but the oppofite party having found
means to raife an infurrection againft her, fhe was
obliged to fly, accompanied by a body of about
80 *Gentlemen* and 40 foldiers : her flight was even
fo precipitate, that fhe was obliged to get on horfeback without having time to procure a pillion,
and in that fituation fhe rode a great number of
miles, behind a gentleman, being continually expofed to the greateft danger, for fhe paffed through

a body of a thoufand *Harquebufiers*, who killed feveral of her followers : having at laft reached a place of fafety, fhe borrowed a dry fhift from a fervant maid, and thence purfued her journey to the next Town, named *Uffon*, in *Auvergne*, where fhe recovered from her fears. However, the great fatigue fhe had undergone, threw her into a fever that lafted feveral days , and moreover, the want of that comfortable accommodation which has been juft mentioned, a pillion, during her long precipitate flight, had caufed that part of her body on which fhe fat, to be in a fad condition. A Surgeon was therefore applied to, to procure her relief ; and fuch was the epulotick, farcotick, cicatrizive, incarnative, healing, confolidant, fanative, nature of the falves he employed, that fhè was cured in a fhort time ; and thus far the Surgeon certainly deferved her thanks : but as he afterwards indulged himfelf in idle ftories concerning the cure he had performed, the Princefs, who heard of it, grew much incenfed againft him, and caufed him to be ferved with that kind of correction which is the fubject of the prefent differtation ; that is to fay, fhe caufed him, as Scaliger affures, to be ferved with a flagellation (*elle lui fit donner les étrivieres.*)

'Nobody certainly will think that the revenge taken by the above Princefs was improper ; on the contrary, all perfons will agree that it was a

very becoming satisfaction, and which she owed
to herself. It is true, every body looks with de-
testation upon the action of the Princefs of *Gon-
zaga*, commonly called *the fair Juliet*, who caufed
a Gentleman to be affaffinated, who had affifted
her in making her efcape from the Town of Fon-
di, which the celebrated Corfair Barbaroffa had
furprifed during the night, with a view, as it is
faid, to feize upon her perfon, in order to make a
prefent of her to the Grand-Signior,—being incenfed at the remembrance of the Gentleman
having feen her run in her fhift, acrofs the fields,
by moon-light. But without making any remark
on the difference of the treatment the above Ladies had recourfe to, it will fuffice to obferve that
no comparifon can be made between the cafe of
the above Gentleman, and that of the Surgeon;
the latter had been guilty of an indifcretion of the
blackeft kind, and which none but a talkative
Frenchman could have committed; a thing with
which we are not told the Gentleman in queftion
had been charged,—and when we reflect on the
enormity of his fault, inftead of judging that he
was too feverely ufed, we find he was treated with
exceffive mildnefs.

Indeed, the more we confider the circumftances
of the whole affair, the more we are affected by
the treacherous conduct of that miferable Surgeon. A wretch whom the Princefs had diftin-

guifhed .in fo flattering a manner from all the other perfons of the fame profeffion to whom fhe might have equally applied,—a fcoundrel, a rafcal, a fellow, whom fhe had with fo much affability acquainted with the difagreeable fituation in which fhe found herfelf, and to whom fhe had, no doubt, afterwards given fuch a bountiful and mag-nificent reward, for fuch a man to betray the fe-cret of the Princefs, and give a loofe to his prat-ing tongue at her expence! He certainly richly de-ferved the flagellation that was beftowed upon him, and I hope thofe whofe duty it was to ferve him with it, were animated with the fame fenfe of his guilt with which this article is written. To this I fhall add nothing, except that it is very likely that, conformably to what has been obferv-ed in a former Chapter, the flagellation inflicted on the above Surgeon, or Barber, was inflicted in the Kitchen.

Flagellations have alfo been of fervice for pu-nifhing iniquitous Judges. I could wifh to have many inftances of that kind to relate : however, I will produce the following one. The ftory made its appearance in a news-paper, fome years ago, at the time of the great paper-war that was waged about the American affairs, before the beginning of actual hoftilities. The Writer who fent it to the *Gazetteer*, had adopted the fignature of *A Bof-ton Saint* , and as it made the whole of his firft

Effay, he had meant it, it feems, as a fort of fpecimen to introduce himfelf by, to the notice of
the Public : he continued to write under that fignature, and proved equal, at leaft, to any of thofe
who drew their pens on the occafion, and even
was decifively fuperior in point of local knowledge
of the Colonies. The Story, which will be inferted in that Writer's own words, gives a curious
infight into the puritanical manners that prevailed
in the New-England Provinces. Now, that they
have the feat of their Government among them,
thefe manners will undergo an alteration : they
cannot be much longer the leading fafhion of the
Country.

" About forty years ago, many of the Chief
Saints, at Bofton, met with a fad mortification :
yea, a mortification in the flefh.

" Captain St. Loe, Commander of a fhip of
war, then in Bofton Harbour, being afhore, on a
Sunday, was apprehended by the Conftables, for
walking on the Lord's day. On Monday he was
carried before a Juftice of the peace : he was
fined, refufed to pay it : and for his contumacy
and contempt of authority, was fentenced to fit
in the Stocks, one hour, during the time of
Change. This fentence was put in execution,
without the leaft mitigation.

" While the Captain fat in durance, grave Magiftrates admonifhed him to refpect in future the

wholefome laws of the Province; and Reverend Divines exhorted him ever after to reverence and keep holy the Sabbath-day. At length the hour expired; and the Captain's legs were fet at liberty.

" As foon as he was freed, he, with great feeming earneftnefs, thanked the Magiftrates for their correction, and the Clergy for their fpiritual advice and confolation; declaring that he was afhamed of his paft life; that he was refolved to put off the old Man of Sin, and to put on the new Man of Righteoufnefs; that he fhould ever pray for them as inftruments in the hands of God, of faving his finful foul.

" This fudden converfion rejoiced the Saints. After clafping their hands, and cafting up their eyes to heaven, they embraced their new Convert, and returned thanks for being made the humble means of fnatching a foul from perdition. Proud of their fuccefs, they fell to exhorting him afrefh; and the moft zealous invited him to dinner, that they might have full time to complete their work.

" The Captain fucked in the milk of exhortation, as a new-born babe does the milk of the breaft. He was as ready to liften as they were to exhort. Never was a Convert more affiduous, while his ftation in Bofton Harbour lafted : he attended every Sabbath-day their moft fanctified Meeting-houfe; never miffed a weekly lecture; at

5

every private Conventicle, he was moſt fervent
and loudeſt in prayer. He flattered, and made
preſents to the Wives and Daughters of the Godly. In ſhort, all the time he could ſpare from the
duties of his ſtation, was ſpent in entertaining
them on board his Ship, or in viſiting and praying at their houſes.

" The Saints were delighted with him beyond
meaſure. They compared their wooden Stocks
to the voice of Heaven, and their Sea-convert to
St. Paul; who, from their enemy, was become
their Doctor.

" Amidſt their mutual happineſs, the mournful time of parting arrived. The Captain received
his recall. On this he went round among the
Godly, and wept and prayed, aſſuring them he
would return, and end his days among his friends
in the Lord.

" Till the day of his departure, the time was
ſpent in regrets, profeſſions, entertainments, and
prayer. On that day, about a dozen of the principal Magiſtrates, including the Select-men, accompanied the Captain to Nantaſket Road, where
the Ship lay, with every thing ready for ſailing.

" An elegant dinner was provided for them on
board, after which many bowls and bottles were
drained. As the blood of the Saints waxed warm,
the cruſt of their hypocriſy melted away: their
moral ſee-ſaws, and Scripture-texts, gave place to

T

double-entendres, and wanton fongs : the Captain
encouraged their gaiety ; and the whole Ship re-
founded with the roar of their merriment.

" Juft at that time, into the Cabin buift a body of Sailors, who, to the inexpreffible horror
and amazement of the Saints, pinioned them faft.
Heedlefs of cries and intreaties, they dragged them
upon deck, where they were tied up, ftripped to
the buff, and their breeches let down, and the
Boatfwain with his Affiftants, armed with dreadful cat-o'-nine-tails provided for the occafion, adminiftered unto them the law of Mofes in the
moft energetic manner.   Vain were all their prayers, roarings, ftampings, and curfes : the Captain
in the mean time affuring them, that it was confonant to their own doctrine and to Scripture, that
the mortification of the flefh tended towards the
faving of the Soul, and therefore it would be criminal in him to abate them a fingle lafh.

" When they had fuffered the whole of their
difcipline, which had flayed them from the nape
of the neck to the hams, the Captain took a polite leave, earneftly begging them to remember
him in their prayers.   They were then let down
into the boat that was waiting for them : the Crew
faluted them with three cheers, and Captain
St. Loe made fail.   The Bofton Select-men, to
this day, when they hear of the above, grin like

infernal Dæmons, out of ſympathy to their pre-
deceſſois *."

Anothei uſe that has been made of flagellitions
among polite people, and diſtinguiſhed fiom the
vulgar, has been to ieprefs the aſpiring vie¼s of
rivals who pretended (unjuſtly, as the otheis
thought) to an equality in point of biith, ¼it,
beauty, or other accompliſhments. On this occaſion we might relate the treatment that was in-
fliēted by two Ladies of noble family, near the
Town of Saumur, in France, on the daughter of
a wealthy Farmer, whoſe beauty had caiſed her to
be invited to an entertainment that was given in a
neighbouring Caſtle, or Manor · an affair which
attiaēted the notice of the Public, at the time (A.
1730) as we may judge from the account of it being contained in the collēction of *Celebrated Caiſes*
decided in the French Courts of Law. But our
attention is called off by another much more intereſting inſtance of the ſame kiid, which happened in the ieign of Lewis the Fourteenth, and
made a very great noiſe. I mean to ſpeak of the
flagellation that was ſerved by the Marchioneſs of
Trefnel, on the *Dime*, or Lady, of Liancourt
a faēt which by all means deſerves a place in this

---

* *Gazetteer—Tueſday,* Dec 20, 1774. The main cir-
cumſtancis of the ſame faēt are alſo to be found in Di.
Burnaby's *Travels through the middle Settlements of North
America,* publiſhed in the year 1775.

Chapter, as being in itſelf an extremely illuſtrious inſtance of flagellation. Indeed, one advantage the Author is proud of, which is, that he has inſerted nothing vulgar in this Book, nothing but what is worthy the attention of perſons of taſte and ſentiment.

The Story is as follows. The Lady of Liancourt was originally born of Parents in middling circumſtances. Having had the good luck to marry a rich Merchant, ſhe had addreſs enough to prevail upon him to leave her, at his death, which happened a few years after their marriage, the bulk of his fortune; and, being now a rich, handſome Widow, ſhe married the *Sieur*, or Lord, of Liancourt; a man of birth, whoſe fortune was ſomewhat impaired by his former expenſive way of living. The Lady of Liancourt uſed to reſide, during the ſummer, at the Caſtle, or Eſtate, of her Huſband, near the town of Chaumont: and in the ſame neighbourhood was ſituated the Eſtate of the Marquis of Treſnel. The manner of living of the Lady of Liancourt, together with the reputation of her wit and beauty, excited the jealouſy of the Marchioneſs of Treſnel, who, on account of her birth, conſidered herſelf as being greatly ſuperior to the other: and a ſtrong competition ſoon took place between the two Ladies, which became manifeſted in ſeveral places in a remarkable manner, eſpecially at Church, where the

Marchionefs went once fo far as violently to pufh the other Lady from her feat : the Lady of Lian-court, on the other hand, was faid to have writ-ten a copy of verfes againft the Marchionefs , and in fhort, matters were carried to fuch lengths be-tween them, that the Marchionefs refolved to damp at once the pretenfions of her rival, and for that purpofe applied to that effectual mode of cor-rection which, as hath been feen in the courfe of this Book, fo many great and celebrated perfon-ages have undergone, namely, a flagellation. Having well laid her fcheme in that refpect, and refolved that her rival fhould undergo the correc-tion, not by proxy, like King Henry the Fourth, but in her own perfon, the Marchionefs, one day fhe knew the Lady of Liancourt was to vifit at a Caftle a few miles diftant from her own, got into her coach and fix, accompanied by four Men behind, and three armed Servants on horfeback ; and care had been previoufly taken to lay in a ftock of good difciplines, which were placed in the coach-box. Having arrived too late at the place on the highway at which fhe propofed to meet her antagonift, the Marchionefs alighted at the houfe of the Curate of the Parifh, in order to wait for her return, and ftaid there, under fome pretence, feveral hours, till at laft a Servant who had been left on the watch, came in hafte, and brought tidings that the Lady Liancourt's coach was in

fight : the Marchionefs thereupon got into her
coach with the utmoft fpeed, and arrived juft in
time to throw herfelf acrofs the way, and ftop the
other Lady, when the Servants, who had been
properly directed beforehand, without lofs of
time took the latter out of her coach, immediately proceeding to execute the orders they had received . and, from the complaint afterwards preferred by the fuffering Lady, it really feems that
they endeavoured to difcharge their duty in fuch a
manner as might convince their Miftrefs of their
zeal in ferving her.

The affair foon made a great noife, and the
King, who heard of it, immediately fent exprefs
orders to the Hufbands of the Ladies to take no
fhare in the quarrel. The Lady of Liancourt applied to the ordinary courfe of law, and brought
a criminal action againft the Marchionefs, before
the Parliament of Paris, the confequence of
which was, that the latter was condemned to
afk her pardon in open Court upon her knees,
and to pay her about two thoufand pounds da-
mages, befides being banifhed from the whole extent of the jurifdiction of the Parliament. The
Servants, who are generally very feverely dealt
with in France, when they fuffer themfelves to
become the inftruments of the violence of their
Mafters, were fent to the Gallies. And Mifs De
Villemartin, who had been co-fpectatrefs of the

flagellation, in the fame coach with the Marchionefs, and had fhared her triumph, was fummon-
ed to appear perfonally in Court, there to be *admonifhed*, and condemned to pay a fine of twenty
livres, ' for the bread of the prifoners *.'

That part of the bodies of their enemies, to
which Captain St. Loe, and the above-named
Marchionefs, directed the corrections and infults
by which they propofed to humble them, naturally leads us to remark the oppofite lights in
which that part has been confidered by Mankind,
and to notice the fantaftical and contradictory difpofition of the human mind.

The part we mention, which, to follow the
common definition that is given of it, is that part
on which Man fits, is, of itfelf, extremely de-
ferving of our efteem. It is, in the firft place, a
characteriftic part and appendage of Mankind :
it is formed by the expanfion of mufcles which,
as Anatomifts inform us, exift in no other animal, and are intirely proper to the human
fpecies.

Nor does that part confer upon Man a diftinction from animals, that is of an honorific kind
merely, like the faculty of walking in an erect fituation, which, as Ovid remarks, enables him to
behold the Sun or the Stars, as he goes forward :

* *Caufes célébres*, Vol. IV.

but, by allowing him to fit, it enables him to cal‚ culate the motions, whether real or apparent, of thofe fame Stars, to afcertain their revolutions, and foreknow their peiiodical returns. It puts him in a condition to promote the liberal Arts and Sciences, Mufic, Painting, Algebra, Geometry, &c. not to mention the whole tribe of mechanic Arts and manufactures. It even is, by that power of *affiduity* (or of being *feated*) it confers upon Man, fo ufeful to the ftudy of the Law, that it has been looked upon as being no lefs conducive to it than the head itfelf, with which it has, in that refpect, been exprefsly put upon a par, and it is a common faying in the Univerfities abroad, that, in order to fucceed in that ftudy, a Man muft have an *iron head*, and *leaden pofteriors*; to which they add, a *golden purfe*, to buy books with:—*caput ferreum, aurea crumena, nates plumbeæ.*

Nor does the part of the human body we men‚ tion, only ferve to make Man a learned and induftrious animal; but it moreover contributes much to the beauty of the fpecies, being itfelf capable of a great degree of beauty.

Without mentioning the opinion of different favage Nations on that account, who take great pains to paint and adorn that part, we fee that the Greeks, who certainly were a well-cultivated and polite People, entertained high notions of its beautifulnefs. They even feem to have thought that it had the advantage, in that refpect, of all the other parts of the human body; for, though we do not find that they ever erected altars to fine arms, fine legs, fine eyes, or even to a handfome face, yet, they had done that honour to the part we mention, and had exprefsly erected a Temple to Venus, under the appellation of Venus *with fair pofteriors* ('Αφροδίτη Καλλίπυγη) : the above Temple was built, as fome fay, on occafion of a quarrel that arofe between two Sifters, who contended which of the two was moft elegantly fhaped in the part we mention; a quarrel that happened to make a great noife. To this we may add, by the by, that fo little did the Greeks in general think that the part we allude to, was undeferving of attention, that they fometimes drew from it indications of the different tempers of people; and they, for inftance, gave the appellation of a *Man with white pofteriors* (Πύγαργοι) to a Man whom they meant to charge with having too much foftnefs and nicety.

The Latins entertained the fame notions with the Greeks, as to the beauty of that part, or thofe parts, on which Man fits. Horace more than once beftows upon them the appellation of *fair* (*pulchræ*) : he even in one place exprefsly declares it as his opinion, that, for a Miftrefs to be defective in thofe parts (*depygis*) is one of the greateft blemifhes fhe can have,—is a defect equal to that of being with a flat noffe *(nafuta)* or a long foot, and is in fhort capable of fpoiling, where it exifts, all other bodily accomplifhments. (*Hor. Sat.* 2. *Lib. I.*)

Among the Moderns, notions of the fame kind have prevailed. Rabelais, a well-known Writer, places one of his beft ftories to the account of a certain Nun, whom he calls *Sifter*, or *Sœur Fiffue*, which he would not certainly have done, if he had not been of opinion that the fize and exact fhape of thofe parts of the Nun's body from which he denominated her, were in the number of her greateft perfections.

In times pofterior to Rabelais, other Writers among the French, have expreffed opinions exactly alike. La Fontaine, if I miftake not, fpeaking in one of his Tales, of a certain Beauty whofe charms he means to extoll, exclaims, • Breafts, Heaven knows, and a rump fit for a Canon !'

Tetins, Dieu fait, & croupe de Chanoine !

And the celebrated Poet Rouffeau, happening, in one of his Epigrams, to fpeak of the abovementioned Temple which the Greeks had erected to Venus, declares that it would have been that Temple of Greece which he would have frequented with the greateft devotion.

Nay, other perfons have thought, that, befides the above advantages, the part we mention was moreover capable of dignity, and partaking of the importance of its owners. This is an opinion which the Poet Scarron (to continue to draw our examples from French Authors) clearly expreffed, in a copy of verfes he wrote to a certain Lady, whofe Hufband having lately been made a Duke, fhe had thereby acquired a right to be feated in the Queen's Affembly, or, as they exprefs it, had been given the *Tabouret* (a ftool.) ' To the no fmall pleafure of all (faid Scarron, ' who, we may obferve, had affumed a right to ' fay every thing he pleafed) and of your own ' legs, your Backfide, which is without doubt ' one of the handfomeft Backfides in France, ' like a Backfide of importance, has at laft, at ' the Queen's, received the *Tabouret*.'

Au grand plaifir de tous & de vôtre jarret,
Vôtre cû, qui doit être un des beaux cûs de France,
Comme un cû d'importance,
A recu chez la Reine enfin le tabouret.

Favourable fentiments of the kind juft mentioned, feem alfo to have been entertained by the celebrated Lord Bolingbroke, whofe diftinguifhed character as a Statefman, a Politician, and a Philofopher, render him extremely fit to be quoted in this place: it was on that part of his Miftrefs's body we are alluding to, his Lordfhip, then a Secretary of State, chofe to write, and to fign, one of the moft important difpatches of his Mi niftry, and on which the repofe of Europe depended at that time*.

In fine, others have carried their notions ftill farther, and have thought that the part in queftion was capable, not only of beauty and dignity, but even of fplendor. Thus, Monf. Pavillon, a French *Bel Efprit* under the reign of Lewis XIV. who filled the office of King's General Advocate at Metz, who was one of the forty Members of the French Academy, and Nephew to a Bifhop, wrote a copy of verfes that is inferted in the Collection of his *Works*, which he intitled, *Métamorphofe du Cû d'Iris en Aftre.* ' The Metamor- ' phofe of Iris's Bum, into a Star.' By a Star of that kind, the Duke of York, afterwards King James II, was dazzled, when he became enamoured with Mifs Arabella Churchill, a Maid of Honour to the Duchefs, at the time that Lady had a fall from her horfe, in a party of hunting : and to his Royal Highnefs being fo dazzled, the firft advancement of the great Duke of Marlborough, then Mr. Churchill, the Lady's Brother, became owing ; together with the capital advantages that accrued to this Nation, from his getting afterwards into great employments.

* Mifs Gumley.—She became a few years afterwards, Countefs of Bath. His Lordfhip, no doubt, boafted of the fact, as it feems to have made fome noife at the time.

Yet, on the other hand, we find that that fame part, which has been thought by fome to pof-fefs fo many accomplifhments, and has accord-ingly become the fubject of their refpect and their admiration, has been made by others, the object of their fcoffs, and exprefly chofen as a mark to direct their infults to.

The facts that have been recited a few pages before this, might be produced as confirmations of this remark. The prevailing vulgar practice, in cafes of provocation, of threatening, or even ferving, the part in queftion with kicks, might alfo be mentioned on this occafion. But it will be better to obferve in general, that, among all Nations, the part we are fpeaking of, has been deemed a moft proper place for beatings, lafhings, and flappings.

That this notion prevailed among the Romans, we are informed by the paffages of Plautus, and of St. Jerom, that are recited in the fixth Chap-ter of this Book (p. 94, 95.) The fame practice was alfo adopted by the Greeks, as may be proved by the inftance of the Philofopher Peregrinus, which has been mentioned in the fame Chapter. And under the reign of the Emperors, when the two Nations (the Greek and Roman) had, as it were, coalefced into one, the fame notions con-cerning the fitnefs of the fame part, to bear ver-berations and infults, continued to prevail. Of

this we have a fingular inftance in the manner in
which the ftatue of the Empeior Conftantine was
treated, at the time of the revolt of the Town of
Edeffa : the inhabitants, not fatisfied with pulling
that ftatue down, in order to aggravate the infult
flagellated it on the part we mention. Libanius
the *Rhetor* infoims us of this fact, in the Ha-
rangue he addreffed to the Emperor Theodofius,
after the great revolt of the City of Antioch , in
which he mentions the pardon granted by Conftantine for the above indignity, as an argument
to induce the Emperor to forgive the inhabitants
of the laft-mentioned City : a requeft, however,
which Libanius was not fo happy as to obtain.

Among the French, notions of the fame kind
likewife prevail. Of this, not to confine ourfelves to particular facts, we may derive proofs
from their language itfelf; in which the verb that
is derived from the word by which the part here
alluded to, is expieffed, fignifies of itfelf, and
without the addition of any other word, to beat
or verberate it : thus, Monf. de Voltaire fuppofes
his Princefs Cunegonde to fay to Candide,—*Tan-
dis qu'on vous feffoit, mon cher Candide* , by which,
however, that Author does not mean exprefsly to
fay that Candide was flagellated upon the part we
fpeak of, by order of the Inquifition ; he only ufes
the above word to render his ftory more jocular.
From the above French word *feffer*, has been again

derived the noun *feſſade*, ſignifying a verberation on the ſame part; the ſame as the word *claque* (or *clack*, as they pronounce it) which originally meant a ſlap in general, but, by a kind of *antonoma-tia* (a particular figure of ſpeech) is now come ex-preſly to ſignify a ſlap on the part in queſtion. Among the Italians, the practice of verberating the ſame part, alſo obtains, if we are to truſt to proofs likewiſe derived from their language; and from the word *chiappa*, they have made that of *chiappata*, the meaning of which is the ſame with that of the French word *claque*.

If we turn our eyes to remote Nations, we find they entertain notions of the ſame ſort. Among the Turks, a verberation on the part we ſpeak of, is the common puniſhment that is in-flicted either on the Janiſſaries, or Spahis; I do not remember which of the two. Among the Per-ſians, puniſhments of the ſame kind are alſo eſta-bliſhed; and we find in Chardin, an inſtance of a Captain of the outward gate of the King's Serag-lio, who was ſerved with it, for having ſuffered a ſtranger to ſtop before that gate, and look through it. And the Chineſe alſo uſe a like method of chaſtiſement, and inflict it, as Travellers inform us, with a wooden inſtrument, ſhaped like a large ſolid rounded ſpoon.

Among the Arabians, the part here alluded to, is likewiſe conſidered as a fit mark for blows and

flaps. We find an inftance of this, in one of the
Arabian Tales, called *The one thoufand and one
Nights:* an original Book, and which contains true
pictures of the manners of that Nation. The ftory
I mean, which is well worth reminding the reader
of, is that of a certain Cobler, whofe name, if I
miftake not, was Shak-Abak. This Cobler having fallen in love with a beautiful Lady belonging
to fome wealthy Man, or Man of power, of whom
he had had a glance through the window of her
houfe, would afterwards keep for whole hours every
day, ftaring at that window. The Lady, who
propofed to make game of him, one day fent one
of her female flaves to introduce him to her, and
then gave him to underftand, that if he could over-
take her, by running after her through the apartments of her houfe, he would have the enjoyment
of her favours : he was befides told, that in order
to run more nimbly, he muft ftrip to his fhirt. To
all this Shak-Abak agreed ; and after a number of
turns, up and down the houfe, he was at laft en-
ticed into a long, dark, and narrow paffage, at the
fartheft extremity of which an open door was to be
perceived ; he made to it as faft as he could, and
when he had reached it, rufhed headlong through
it ; when, to his no fmall aftonifhment, the door
inftantly fhut upon him, and he found himfelf in
the middle of a public ftreet of Bagdat, which was
chiefly inhabited by fhoemakers. A number of

thefe latter, ftruck at the fudden and ftrange appearance of the unfortunate Shak-Abak, who, befides
ftripping to his fhirt, had fuffered his eye-brows
to be fhaved, laid hold of him, and, as the Arabian
Author relates, foundly lafhed his pofteriors with
their ftraps.

If we turn again to European Nations, we fhall
meet with farther inftances of the fame kind of
correction. It was certainly adopted in Denmark,
and even in the Court of that Country, towaids
the latter end of the laft Century, as we are informed by Loid Molefworth, in his *Account of
Denmark*. It was the cuftom, his Lordfhip fays,
at the end of every hunting-match at Court, that,
in order to conclude the entertainment with as
much feftivity as it had begun, a proclamation was
made,—if any could inform againft any perfon
who had infringed the known laws of hunting,
let him ftand forth and accufe. As foon as the
contravention was afcertained, the culprit was made
to kneel down between the horns of the ftag that
had been hunted, two of the Gentlemen removed
the fkirts of his coat, when the King, taking a
fmall long wand in his hand, laid a certain number of blows, which was proportioned to the
greatnefs of the offence, on the culprit's breech;
whilft, in the mean time (the Noble Author adds)
the Huntfmen with their brafs horns, and the
dogs with their loud openings, proclaimed the

U

King's Juftice, and the Criminal's punifhment :
the fcene affoiding diverfion to the Queen, and
the whole Court, who ftood in a circle about the
place of execution *.

Among the Dutch, verberations on the pofteriors aie equally in ufe; and a ferious flagellation
on that part, is the punifhment which is eftablifhed at the Cape of Good Hope, one of their Colonies, as Kolben informs us in his *Defcription* of
it, for thofe who are found fmoaking tobacco in
the ftreets : a practice which has frequently been
there the caufe of houfes being fet in fire.

In Poland, a *lower* difcipline is the penance
conftantly inflicted upon fornicators, in Convents,
previoufly to tying them together by the bond of
matrimony; or fometimes afterwards.

In England, caftigations of the fame kind, not
to quote other inftances, are adopted among that
refpectable part of the Nation, the Seamen, as we
find in Falconer's Marine Dictionary; and a
Cobbing-board is looked upon as a neceffaiy part of
the rigging of his Majefty's fhips.

Among the Spaniards, they fo generally confider the part of the human body of which we are
treating here, as the propereft to bear ill ufage
and mortification, that in every place there is
commonly fome good Friar who makes his pof-

* See Lord Molefworth's *Account of Denmark*, IVth
Edit. p. 108, 109.

teriors anfwerable for the fins of the whole Parifh, and who, according as he has been fee'd for
that purpofe, flogs himfelf, or at leaft tells his
Cuftomers he has done fo: hence the common
Spanifh faying, which is mentioned in the Hiftory
of Friar Gerundio de Campazas, *Yo foi el culo del
Frayle*,—' I am as badly off as the Friar's backfide,' which is faid by perfons who think that they
are made to pay, or fuffer, for advantages they
are not admitted to fhare.

Nor is the above method of felf-correction confined to Spanifh Friars only : it is likewife adopted by a number of religious Orders of Men, eftablifhed in the other Countries of Europe. It is
alfo by corrections directed to the fame part, that
is to fay, by Cornelian difciplines, that numbers
of pious Confeffors, zealous for the purity of the
morals of their female penitents, endeavour to
procure their improvement. Nay, it is upon the
fame part we fpeak of, upon that part to which the
Greeks had erected a Temple, that the whole
tribe of Nuns and female Devotees conftantly
choofe to practice thofe mortifications and *lower
difciplines* by which they feek to atone for their
fins ; and feveral among them really treat that
part, by which they perhaps have the beft chance
to create themfelves admirers, with wonderful
feverity.

U 2

The above Differtation, which, before I engaged in it, I did not think would prove fo long,
or fo interefting, has till now kept me from delivering my opinion concerning thofe flagellations
with which certain holy Men have ferved thofe
Ladies who ventured to make amorous applications
to them : a fatisfaction which, before I conclude,
I muft give the Reader, as having pledged my
word for it.   Now, to fulfill my engagement in
that refpect, I declare that I totally difapprove
fuch flagellations, and I am firmly of opinion
that this kind of treatment ought to be ranked
among thofe actions of Saints, which, as hath
been obferved in a former place, are not fit for all
perfons to imitate.

In fact, we find that feveral Authors, among
thofe who beft knew the world, and were excellent Judges of propriety, who had occafion to defcribe fituations like thofe in which the above
Saints were placed, have made their perfonages act
in quite a different manner from that in which the
Saints behaved, and on this occafion we may mention the conduct of Parfon Adams, one of the
Heroes of *Fielding*, in that celebrated night he
fpent at Lady Booby's.   If, in the firft inftance,
he, as muft be confeffed, gave Mis. Slipflop that
remembrance in her guts mentioned by the Author, it was not till fhe had herfelf given him a

dreadful cuff on his chops, befides that he did not know yet her fex, nor what fhe meant. But when he afterwards found himfelf in the fame bed with Fanny, which, as he thought, was his own bed, he fhrunk, as it were, and retired to the fartheft extremity of it, where he lay quiet, and above all manifefted no thought whatever of flagellating her; which if he had done, Jofeph would not certainly have thanked him for it.

Don Quixote, in *Cervantes*, when the lovely Maritornes came during the night to his bed, and threw herfelf into his arms, had no thought of employing either whips or ftraps for difmiffing the amorous Fair-one; and certainly if he had applied to an expedient of this kind, he would have had no right to complain of the boxes and kicks with which the Muleteer prefently after belaboured him in the dark. But, like a gallant and exceedingly well-bred Knight, he excufed himfelf from the nature of the anterior engagements he was under, and above all did not forget to pay proper compliments to the Lady's beauty and great perfections. Indeed, the fpeech which the Knight addreffed to the fair Maritornes, may be propofed as a pattern of compliment for occafions of the kind. ' Oh ! thou moft lovely tempta-
' tion ! Oh that I now might but pay a warm ac-
' knowledgment for the mighty bleffing which

U 3

' your great goodnefs would lavifh on me ! Yes,
' moft beautiful Charmer, I would give an em-
' pire to purchafe your more defirable embraces,
' but Fate has put to it an invincible obftacle ; I
' mean my plighted faith to Dulcinea *del Tobofo*,
' the fole miftrefs of my wifhes, and abfolute fo-
' vereign of my heart. Oh ! did not this oppofe
' my prefent happinefs, I could never be fo in-
' fenfible a Knight as to lofe the benefit of this
' extraordinary favour you now condefcend to of-
' fer me.'

Nor ought the Gentleman, after delivering the
above fpeech, or fome other equally refpectful, to
ftop there, it would be moreover extremely proper for him to defire the Lady to do him the honour to fit upon his bed, and then enter into a
fuller explanation of his conduct, and of the nature of thofe prior engagements by which he is fo
fatally tied.

This done, and the Lady being perfectly convinced of the propriety of his conduct, he fhould
rife from his bed, and offer to attend her, I do
not fay to the bottom of the ftairs, and fo far as
the ftreet door, for that might be the means of
difcovering the fecret of the affair to other perfons and endangering the Lady's reputation, but
to the remoteft door of his own apartment. I
would moreover have him, in his paffage to that

door, keep the Lady's hand tenderly, fqueezed in his own, and all the while manifeft, by the nature of his geftures and exclamations, the grief under which he labours. And laftly, when he had reached the furtheft place to which he may fafely conduct her, he ought to take leave of her by a low and moft refpectful bow, in order completely to convince her, that the kindnefs fhe had ventured to fhew him, has not, in the leaft, lowered her in his efteem.

Such, dear Reader, is the manner in which, for my own part, I have always acted on thofe delicate occafions we are fpeaking of. However, I do not pretend to dictate to others the manner in which they ought to behave, nor infift upon any of the above circumftances in particular. All I intreat of you, is, by all means to forbear to ufe thofe fudden and harfh flagellations that were recurred to, by St. Edmund, St. Bernardin of Sienna, and Brother Mathew. Such a treatment favours too much of ingratitude: nay, to have recourfe to it, is cruel in the extreme, it is heaping diftrefs upon the diftreffed. Nor are you to expect that the Lady will love you the better for it afterwards, as was the cafe with St. Bernardin of Sienna: on the contrary, fuch a proceeding on your part, if it were once known, would irreparably deftroy your reputation with the whole

U 4

Sex, and you may depend, no propofal or application of the like kind would be made to you
ever after.   Now, though you may be ever fo
firmly determined to reject all propofals like thefe;
yet, as every Lady will tell you, it is no unpleaf-
fing thing to have them made to you : befides that
you do not know but you may afterwards alter
your refolution.

C H A P. XX.

The fondnefs of people for flagellations, gives rife to a number of incredible ftories on that fubject.

THE fupporters of the practice of flagellation did not confine their endeavours in recommending it, to fetting the example of it, like Rodolph of Eugubio, or Dominic the Cuiraffed, or to fupporting it by arguments and voluminous writings, like Cardinal Damian; but they mixed their accounts with numbers of ftories of an extravagant kind; whether their enthufiafm in favour of the practice in queftion, induced them to believe fuch ftories to be true, or they thought that their very incredibility would be extremely fit to bring into credit with the vulgar, a doctrine in favour of which they were themfelves fo prepoffeffed.

Thus, flagellations were given out by fome, as having the power of refcuing fouls from Hell itfelf; a thing which even Maffes, though

conftantly ufed to draw them out of Purgatory, were not thought to be able to perform.
As an inftance of the ftories that were circulated on that account, may be produced the
following, related by one *Vincent*, who lived
in the year 1256.

 ‘ Archbifhop Umbert (fays Vincent) re-
‘ cited, that in the Monaftery of St. Sylvef-
‘ ter, in the duchy of Urbino, in Italy, a
‘ certain Monk died; and the Brothers con-
‘ tinued finging Pfalms by his body, from the
‘ firft evening crowing of the Cock, till two
‘ o’clock in the morning; and as foon as they
‘ began, in the Mafs they celebrated for his
‘ fake, to fing the *Agnus Dei*, behold! the
‘ dead Man fuddenly rofe. The Brothers,
‘ greatly aftonifhed, came near him, to hear
‘ what he had to fay; when he began to throw
‘ forth abufes and curfes againft God; he fpit
‘ on the Crofs that was offered him to kifs;
‘ he uttered the moft opprobrious expreffions
‘ againft the immaculate Mother of God, and
‘ faid, Of what fervice to me is your finging
‘ pfalms, and offering facrifices? I have been
‘ in the flames of Hell, where my Lord and
‘ Mafter Lucifer placed a brafs crown, glow-
‘ ing with inextinguifhable heat, on my head,
‘ and laid a coat of the fame metal, with
‘ which himfelf was covered, on my fhoul-

7

‘ ders : this coat was not long enough to
‘ reach down to my heels, but it was so vio-
‘ lently heated, that drops seemed to fall from
‘ it to the ground. The Brothers having then
‘ continued to exhort him to repent of his
‘ sins, he anathemised them, and denied, in a
‘ sacrilegious manner, all the mysteries of our
‘ Redeemer. The Monks thereupon prayed
‘ for him heartily, and after stripping off their
‘ clothes, flagellated themselves, uttering eve-
‘ ry manner of supplication in his behalf;
‘ when behold! that desperate Man recovered
‘ the use of his reason ; he comfessed the om-
‘ nipotence of our Saviour; he renounced the
‘ errors of Satan, adored the Cross, and in-
‘ treated to be admitted to the Sacrament of
‘ Confession and Penitence. Now, the crime
‘ of which he accused himself was that of
‘ having committed fornication, after he had
‘ renounced the world; a thing which he had
‘ kept secret to his death. He thus conti-
‘ nued to live, praising and blessing God, to
‘ the next day, when he again gave up the
‘ ghost.’

Besides stories of the same kind with that
above, which were contrived to heighten the
merit of flagellations, the admirers of that
practice have excogitated others, in order to
terrify those who declined adopting it, or at-

tempted to confute it by arguments. As a fpecimen of this, we may quote the report that
was circulated concerning Cardinal Stephen,
which hath been mentioned in a former place
(p. 214) that he had died fuddenly, for having defpifed the exercife in queftion.

Another ftory, contrived in the fame view
we fpeak of, is to be found in Thomas *de
Chantpré's* Book, in which it is related of a
certain Hugh, a Canon of St. Victor, that,
having on account of his weak ftate of health,
conftantly forbore, during his life-time, the
ufe of flagellations, he paid dearly afterwards
for this tender care he had taken of his fkin;
for at his paffage into Purgatory, the whole
tribe of Devils lafhed him with fcourges.
‘ Hugh (fays Thomas de Chantpré) was one
‘ of the Regular Monks in the Monaftery of
‘ St. Victor, in Paris. He was called the fe-
‘ cond St. Auftin, that is to fay, the fecond
‘ Man in point of learning fince St. Auftin;
‘ but though he deferved much praife in that
‘ refpect, yet, the fame cannot be faid of his
‘ conftant refufal to practife flagellations and
‘ difciplines, for his quotidian mifdeeds, ei-
‘ ther in private, or in the Chapter, in com-
‘ pany with the Brothers: he was, as I have
‘ been informed, of a tender frame of body,
‘ and had, befides, been too much indulged

' in his childhood. Now, becaufe he took no
' pains to overcome by exercife the defect of
' his nature, or rather his bad habit, very fa-
' tal confequences enfued to him, as I am go-
' ing to relate. Being near his death, a bro-
' ther Canon, who was his intimate friend,
' intreated him to fhew himfelf again to him,
' after he was dead. I will, fays he, if the
' Mafter of life and death confents to it. As
' Hugh was making this promife, he died ;
' nor was it long before he returned to his
' friend, who was ftill in expectation of him,
' and faid, Here I am ; make hafte to afk
' what queftion you intend to afk, for I can-
' not ftay. The other, who, though he was
' exceedingly pleafed, yet was not a little.
' frighted, faid, How is it with you, my dear
' friend? It is well with me, faid Hugh ; but
' becaufe I have refufed, while I was alive,
' to receive difcipline, there has hardly been a
' fingle Devil in the whole infernal empire,
' but who gave me a fmart lafh, as I was in
' my way to Purgatory.'

Others, in order to bring flagellations into
ftill greater credit, have fuppofed that the Devils themfelves were fo fenfible of the merit
that was in them, that they would occafionally
practife them upon each other. Thus, St. Al-
len relates that the Holy Virgin Mary having

refolved to refcue a certain James Hall, an Ufurer, from the claws of the Dæmons, thefe unclean fpirits, a great number of whom were prefent, no fooner faw her make her appearance, than they took to blafpheming, flagellated each other, and ran away.

The Devil himfelf has alfo, on certain occafions, prefcribed flagellations, as an atonement for fins; which is certainly wonderful enough. It is related in the Life of St. Virgil, that a Man poffeffed by the Devil, was fuftigated with four rods, by the Devil's prefcription, for having ftolen four wax candles from the Saint's altar. ' I am not come (faid ' the poffeffed Man) of my own accord; but ' I have been compelled to it: I have carried ' off the wax-candles and offerings that were ' on the tomb of the Man of God; and if ' they are not fpeedily returned, my Mafter ' will come with feven fpirits worfe than him- ' felf, and will for ever continue in me. How- ' ever, when the candles, of which they had ' been a long while in fearch, were found ' again, by the Devil's affiftance, and brought ' back, the Devil directed them to fuftigate ' the unhappy Man with as many befoms as ' there were candles.'

To thefe inftances of flagellations voluntarily practifed among Devils, we ought not to

omit to add one, in which the Devil was
fmartly flagellated in fpite of his teeth, by a
Saint, and a female Saint too ; a fact which
cannot fail to give the greateft pleafure to the
Reader, who remembers the deplorable accounts that have been given in a former Chapter, of the wanton flagellations he has himfelf
inflicted upon Saints. The name of the female Saint who thus gave the Devil his due,
was *Cornelia Juliana,* as the Reverend Father
Jefuit, Bartholomew Fifen, relates, in his book
on the *Ancient Origin of the Feftival of the
body of Chrift.* ' One day (fays he) the other
' Nuns heard a prodigious noife in the room
' of Cornelia Juliana, which turned out to be
' a ftrife fhe had with the Devil, whom, after
' having laid hold of him, fhe fuftigated un-
' mercifully ; then, having thrown him upon
' the ground, fhe trampled him under her
' foot, and continued ridiculing him in the
' moft bitter manner *.' The above Reverend Father has neglected to inform us, how
the Devil came to be in Juliana's room ; but
it is moft likely he was come upon his ufual

---

* *Corneliæ fodales ingentem aliquando audeiunt
ftrepitum ex ejus cubiculo, & contentionem Julianæ
adverfus dæmonem, quem manibus comprehenfum
quanti poterat cædebat, in terram deindè proftratim
pedibus obterebat, lacerabat fareifmii.*

antic errand of flagellating Saints, and meant
to ferve Juliana in the fame manner: fortu-
nately fhe was upon the watch, and proved
too many for him. As for the dreadful noife
that was to be heard in the Saint's room, it
was the natural confequence of the hard ftrug-
gle that took place between her and the Devil, while they were thus ftriving who fhould
flog the other.

The Saints who inhabit Paradife have alfo
been fuppofed to have occafionally recourfe to
flagellations; not, to be fure, to inflict them
any longer upon themfelves; but to chaftife,
at the requeft of their friends, thofe who perfecuted them. This misfortune happened to
a certain Servant of the Emperor Nicephorus,
who, not fatisfied with exacting unjuft tributes
from the common people with great rigour,
offered afterwards to ufe Monafteries in the
fame manner. ' The Emperor (fays the Au-
' thor from whom this fact is extracted) fent
' one of the Grooms of his bed-chamber to
' receive the ufual tribute. As he was a Man
' exceedingly eager after money and unlawful
' gain, he committed great oppreffions both
' on the common citizens, and the inhabi-
' tants of the Monaftery of St. Nicon; for
' the government of cities, and the care of
' levying duties, are ufually intrufted, not to

' the juſt and mild, but to hard-hearted and
' inhuman perſons. The Monks, who were
' poſſeſſed of no money, endeavoured to ſooth
' the above cruel unmerciful Man by their
' diſcourſes; but he, thirſty after gold, was
' as deaf to their prayers, as the aſp to con-
' jurations, and made no more account of
' their remonſtrances, than, to uſe the words
' of the Scripture, of *the crackling of thorns
' under a pot.* On the contrary, his wrath
' and inſolence increaſing farther, he cauſed
' ſeveral of them to be thrown into a jail, and
' prepared to plunder the Monaſtery. The
' remaining Monks then applied to their Saint
' for aſſiſtance, who preſently made them ex-
' perience the happy effects of it; for during
' the following night, he appeared to the
' Groom, with a threatening indignant aſpect,
' and laſhed him ſeverely; then ſpeaking to
' him, told him, for his words ought to be
' recorded, *Thou haſt thrown the Heads of the
' Monaſtery into chains; if thou doſt not releaſe
' them inſtantly, thy death ſhall be the con-
' ſequence.*'

The Virgin Mary herſelf, has alſo been
ſaid to have applied to corrections of the ſame
kind as thoſe here alluded to, in order to
avenge the injuſtices done to thoſe whom ſhe
protected; and ſhe, for inſtance, cauſed a cer-

X

tain Bifhop to be flagellated in her prefence, who had taken his prebend from a Canon, who was indeed, but an indifferent perfon to fill his office, but who paid much devotion to her, and with his eyes caft down, fung every day before her Altar certain words contained in the *Angelic falutation.* The illuftrious Cardinal Damian informs us of this fact, in his *Opufc.* xxxiii. *Cap.* iii. which is entitled, *The bleffed Virgin directs that his prebend fhould be returned to a Clergyman who ufed to pay devotion to her.* ‘ The fame Stephanus (fays Cardinal Damian) related to me another fact of ‘ much the fame kind. I remember, he faid, ‘ that there was a certain Clergyman, who ‘ was a dunce, an idle man, a dullard ; to ‘ this add that he was endowed with no reli- ‘ gious gift, and poffeffed no canonical gra. ‘ vity. Yet, amidft the dead afhes of his ‘ ufelefs life, fome fmall particles of pious ‘ fire continued to fubfift, fo that he would ‘ every day approach the altar of the holy ‘ Mother, and, inclining his head with reve- ‘ rence, fing the following both *angelic* and ‘ *euangelic* line, *Hail, Mary, full of grace, the* ‘ *Lord is with thee ; bleffed art thou among* ‘ *Women.* The new Bifhop, however, who ‘ foon difcovered the incapacity of the Man, ‘ thought it wrong that an ufeful office fhould

‘ be left to an ufelefs perfon, and he took from
‘ him the prebend he had obtained from the
‘ preceding Bifhop. But as the Canon was
‘ thereby reduced to great poverty, having
‘ no other means of fupporting himfelf, the
‘ bleffed Virgin interfered in his behalf. Dur-
‘ ing the dead of night fhe appeared to the
‘ Bifhop, preceded by a Man who carried a
‘ difcipline in one of his hands, and a burn-
‘ ing torch in the other, and ordered him to
‘ chaftife the Bifhop by fome lafhes of it ;
‘ then addreffing this latter,—Why, faid fhe,
‘ did you take from a Man who ufed to pay
‘ daily homages to me, a clerical advantage
‘ it was not you who had conferred on him ?
‘ The Bifhop, filled with terror, and foon
‘ awaking from his fleep, prefently returned
‘ the prebend to the Clergyman, and after-
‘ wards greatly honoured as a Man whom Gcd
‘ loved, a perfon who, he thought, was un-
‘ known to him.’

C H A P. XXI.

*A remarkable instance of a flagellation perform-
ed in honour of the Virgin Mary.*

SO well established was the opinion that
Saints, and especially the Virgin Mary,
were to be appeased by flagellations, and such
was, in general, the fondness of people during a certain period of time, for that pious
mode of correction, that a Franciscan Monk,
who wore a hood, and was girt with a cord,
did not scruple, under the Pontificate of Six-
tus IV, to expose to the open day, in the public market-place, the bare rump of a Professor in Divinity, and lashed him with his
hand, in sight of a croud of astonished spectators, because he had preached against the
immaculate conception of the blessed Virgin.
The fact is related in a Sermon written by
Bernardinus *de Bustis*, which, together with
his whole Work in honour of the Virgin
(Opus Mariale) he dedicated to Pope Alexander VI, and seems therefore to be a fact well

enough authenticated: the following is the
manner in which Bernardinus gives the account.

‘ He laid hold of him, and threw him up-
‘ on his knees; for he was very strong. Hav-
‘ ing then taken up his gown; becaufe this
‘ Minifter had fpoken againft the holy *Taber-*
‘ *nacle* of God, he began to lafh him with
‘ the palm of his hand upon his huge breech,
‘ (the Author’s expreffion is, upon his *fquare*
‘ *tabernacles*) which was bare; for he wore
‘ neither drawers nor breeches: and becaufe
‘ he had attempted to flander the bleffed Vir-
‘ gin, by quoting perhaps Ariftotle in the
‘ book of *Priors*, this Preacher confuted him
‘ by reading in the book of his Pofteriors;
‘ which greatly diverted the Byftanders. Then
‘ a certain female Devotee exclaimed, faying,
‘ Mr. Preacher, give him four more flaps for
‘ my fake: another prefently after faid, Give
‘ him alfo four more for me; and fo did a
‘ number of others: fo that if he had at-
‘ tempted to grant all their requefts, he would
‘ have had nothing elfe to do for the whole
‘ day *.’

* * *Apprehendens ipfum, revolvit fuper ejus genua;
erat enim valdè fortis. Elevatis itaque pannis, quia
ille Minifter contrà fanctum Dei tabernaculum locutus*

Nay, so proper did Bernardinus de Buſtis think the above correction to have been, ſo well calculated did he judge it, to appeaſe the holy Virgin's wrath, that he did not ſcruple to declare, in the ſequel of his Sermon, that the Monk who inflicted it, had poſſibly been actuated by an inſpiration from the Virgin herſelf. ' Perhaps (ſays he) was it the Virgin ' herſelf, who induced him ſo to do, moreover ' granting him an exemption from the cen ' ſures incurred, according to the Laws of the ' Church, by thoſe who ſtrike an Eccleſiaſtic, ' and relaxing the rigour of theſe laws in his ' favour +.'

---

fuerat, cœpit cum palmis percutere ſuper quadrata ta-bernacula, quæ erant nuda, non enim habebat femo-ralia vel antiphonam, & quia ipſe infamare voluerat beatam Virginem, allegando forſitan Ariſtotelem in Libro Priorum, iſte Prædicator illum confutavit le-gendo in libro ejus Poſteriorum · de hoc autem omnes qui aderant, gaudeb nt. Tunc exclamavit quædam devota mulier, dicens, Domine Prædicator, detis ei clas quatuor palmatas pro me, & alia poſtmodum dixit, detis ei etiam quatuor; ſicque multæ aliæ roga-bant; itâ quòd ſi illarum petitionibus ſatisfacere vo-luiſſet, per totum diem aliud facere non potuiſſet.——In Opere Mariali, Serm. viii. de Conceptione Beatæ Virginis, circ. fin.

* There prevails, as may have been perceived,

a kind of competition between the Abbé Boileau and me, who shall find out the best story, which is extremely for the benefit of the Reader. However, the story above quoted from Bernardinus *de Bustis*, with which we are supplied by the Abbé's book, is so good in itself, so full of Attic salt, so well in the true Monkish style, that I despair of producing any thing that can match it. I will try, therefore, to make up in number what I may want in point of intrinsic merit; and, instead of one story, I will relate two, which, that I may keep as near to my model as may be (for here it inspires me with uncommon emulation) will both have Friars for their object, and be of the same turn with the above.

The first is contained in the book of the *Apologie pour Hérodote*, the Author of which says he heard it from a Gentlewoman of Lorrain, who had been an eye-witness to it. A Monk, one day, preached in a Country Church, upon the subject of Hell. He took much pains to inspire his Congregation with a great aversion for the place, and made as frightful a description of it as he could, but now and then, pretending that proper expressions failed him, he stopped suddenly, and then exclaimed,—In short, Hell is as horrid as the breech of the Bell-ringer of the Parish, which saying, he uncovered the posteriors of the latter, who had placed himself there for that purpofe, and had agreed with the Friar to act that farce with him.

The fecond ftory I propofe to relate, which I do not remember where I have read, perhaps in the fame book above quoted, is that of another jolly Predicant Friar, who laid a wager he would make one half of his Congregation laugh, and the other cry. As for making his hearers cry, it was what he had often fucceeded in doing, being a very good preacher. On the appointed day, he accordingly came to Church, provided with an excellent Sermon, with that, of his ftock, which he knew was moft likely to produce the defired effect, and he prefently after began reciting it; for they never read their Sermons. But, before I proceed farther, I muft inform the Reader that the pulpit in which he preached, ftood in the middle of the Church; and, befides leaving the door behind him open, he had found means to adjuft his gown and breeches in fuch a manner, that he might let the latter fall down whenever he pleafed. When he had gone through the greater part of his preaching, and his hearers were very near being in the neceffary difpofition to make him win one half of the wager, he, on a fudden, let his breeches drop upon his heels, and exhibited, to ufe the expreffion of Bernardinus *de Buſtis*, his fquare tabernacles to the full view of that part of the Congregation who were feated behind the pulpit. With refpect to him, however, pretending to perceive nothing of the matter, and to be wholly taken up with his Sermon, he went on with it as before : and as he had now reached the latter part of it, confequently that which contain- ed his moft interefting defcriptions as well as ftrongeft arguments, he exerted fo much elo- quence in it; and fuch a power of declamation, that that part of the Congregation who were placed in front of the pulpit, were really melting in tears, while thofe who fat behind, minding lefs what they heard than what they faw, were in a fituation of mind quite different ; and it is need- lefs to fay that the Friar won the wager.

To the above ftories a number of others of the fame kind might be added, which, though it might be a hard matter to vouch for their truth, yet are related by different Authors in a very feri- ous manner, and fuch as fhews that they hoped their accounts would be believed. Thus, the Author of the *Apologie pour Hérodote*, fays he had heard the ftory he mentions, from a perfon who had been an eye-witnefs to it. And Bernardinus *de Buftis*, not only pretends he greatly approves the fact he relates, which he reprefents as hav- ing been peculiarly agreeable to the Virgin, but has moreover inferted it in a Sermon which he publifhed, and dedicated to a Pope.

From the above ftories, as well as from many othels related in the fame manner, we are therefore at leaft to conclude, that they bear great refemblance to a number of facts which commonly happened in the times of the Authors who relate them; and we may thence admire the fingular licence of manners which prevailed among Monks and the Clergy in general, during a certain period of time : a licence which we find to have efpecially obtained when, being the dominant, or rather the fole Chriftian Church that exifted, they were without rivals or competitors; and it may really be faid, that the event of the Reformation proved, in feveral refpects, as much a reformation for them, as for thofe who exprefsly adopted it.

C H A P. XXII.

Another Story of a female Saint appeafed by a flagellation.

AND not only the Virgin Mary, but other female Saints, inhabitants of Paradife, have alfo been thought to be extremely well difpofed to be appeafed, when they had received offence, by flagellatory corrections. The following Story is to be found in the Book intitled, *Itinerarium Cambriæ*, wrote by Sylvefter Geraldus, a native of the Country of Wales, who wrote about the year 1188.

' In the Northern borders of England, and
' on the other fide of the river Humber, in
' the Parifh of Hooëden, lived the Rector of
' that Church, with his Concubine. This
' Concubine, one day fat rather imprudent-
' ly, on the tomb of St. Ofanna, fifter to
' King Ofred, which was made of wood,
' and raifed above the ground in the fhape of
' a feat. When fhe attempted to rife from
' the place, her pofteriors ftuck to the wood
' in fuch a manner, that fhe never could be

' parted from it, till, in the prefence of the
' people who ran to fee her, fhe had fuffered
' her clothes to be torn from her, and had
' received a fevere difcipline on her naked
' body, and that, to a great effufion of blood,
' and with many tears and devout fupplica-
' tions on her part: which done, and after
' fhe had engaged to fubmit to farther peni-
' tence, fhe was divinely releafed *.'

---

*. . . . . *Quæ cum recedere vellet, fixis ligno na-
tibus, evelli non potuit, &c.—Itinerarii Cambriæ,
Lib. I.*

This opinion of Catholic Divines concerning
the great power of flagellations to appeafe the
wrath of female Saints, and the content which
they have fuppofed the latter to receive from fuch
ceremonies, after the example of the antient God-
deffes, might furnifh a new fubject of comparifon
between the Catholic Religion, and that of the
antient Heathens; and if Dr. Middleton had
thought of it, he might have added a new article
on that head, to his *Letter from Rome.*

In fact, the Reader may remember the account
that has been given in the fifth Chapter of this
Book, of the fingular ceremonies that were exhibited at Lacedæmon, before the altar of Diana.

(*See* p. 71, &c.) The fame was done fome-times before the altar of Juno. Rites of much the fame flagellatory kind were practifed in the Temple of the Goddefs of Syria. And fimilar ceremonies alfo ufed to be performed in honour of the *great Goddefs*, in Egypt. (*See* p. 76, 77.)

So prevalent was become the opinion that God-deffes delighted in feeing fuch corrections inflicted before their altars, that feveral of them, among whom was Venus herfelf, were fuppofed to be fupplied with the neceffary implements to inflict them with their own hands, occafionally (p. 55). Nay, the Mufes themfelves had been provided with inftruments of the fame kind: Lucian, in his Letter or Addrefs " to an ignorant Man who was taking much pains in collecting a Library," fays to him, that the Mufes will drive him from Parnaffus, with their *whips of myrtle*. And Bel-lona, the Goddefs of war, has alfo been armed by Virgil, in the 8th Book of his Æneid, with an enormous whip.

Quem cum fanguineo fequitur Bellona flagello.

Thefe notions of the Ancients, concerning the inclination they attributed to Goddeffes, for cor-rections of the kind here alluded to, may be ex-plained in different ways.

In the firft place, they perhaps thought it was owing to the greater irafcibility of temper of the Sex, which prompts them to give effectual marks of their refentment, when they have good reafon to think that no refiftance will be attempted. In the fecond place, they poffibly afcribed that inclination they fuppofed in the female Sex, to their love of juftice ; which is certainly a very laudable difpofition. And, thirdly, they perhaps alfo confidered that propenfity of Women, to ufe inftruments which were, in thofe times, deemed to be characteriftic emblems of power, as the effect of that love of dominion with which the Sex has at all times been charged, and the confequence of fome ambitious wifh they fuppofed in them, of having the uncontrouled fway of the terrible *flagellum*.

However, if I am allowed to deliver my opinion concerning the above inclination of the fair Sex, about which the Antients feem to have entertained fo great a prepoffeffion, I will fay that I think it owing to the fecond of the caufes abovementioned, that is to fay, to their laudable love of juftice, and at the fame time, to the peculiar nature of the Sex, which makes them feel a great reluctance in ufing any inftruments, either of a cruel, or an unwieldly and ungraceful kind, for inftance fire-arms or javelins, fwords or clubs, but prompts them to employ, when they mean to give effectual tokens of their refentment, inftruments fuitable to the mercifulnefs of their tempers, and the elegance of their manners.

3

Of this love of juftice inherent in Women, a fingular inftance occurs in the Greek Hiftory. I mean to fpeak of the flagellations which Ladies, in Lacedæmon, who had reached a certain age without finding hufbands, ufed to beftow, before the altar of Juno, upon fuch Men as continued paft a certain time of life, to live in an unmarried ftate. Thefe flagellations the unmarried Lacedæmonian Ladies (no doubt through the long ufe they had made of them) had at laft converted into an exprefs right, and the ceremony was performed every year, during a certain folemnity eftablifhed for that purpofe. Whether they flagellated all the unmarried Men without exception, who came within the words of the regulation on that fubject, Hiftorians have neglected to inform us : perhaps they ferved in that manner only a certain number, in order to fhew the right they had of flagellating all the reft.

Nor have Women of modern times lefs diftinguifhed themfelves than the Greek Ladies, by their love of juftice, or paid lefs regard to elegance in their choice of the means they have employed to avenge the infults they may have received.

In fact, we have feen in the prefent Chapter, that the perfons who have raifed the fabric of the Catholick Church, or rather Creed, perfons who certainly were good obfervers of the manners of Mankind, have given the fame inclination

and the fame attributes, to their female inhabitants of Paradife, as the Ancients had given
to their Goddeffes. And conclufions to the
fame effect may be derived from the works of
Imagination of a number of refpectable modern Authors, who have all given to the Ladies of whom they had occafion to fpeak, the
fame elegant difpofitions we mention, and made
them act, when offended, upon the fame principles as the Ladies in Lacedæmon : thefe works I
do not fcruple to mention as weighty authorities,
for though they may be, as I faid, works in appearance of imagination merely, yet it is well
known that fuch great Authors, when they relate
any ftories, always allude to certain facts of which
they have either been eye-witneffes, or received
affured information.

And to quote one or two on the fubject, we
find that the celebrated La Fontaine, in one of
his Tales which he has entitled *The Pair of Spectacles*, makes certain Nuns, who, as they thought,
had had a great affront put upon their Monaftery,
have immediate recourfe to the elegant method of
revenge here alluded to. The ftory is as follows.

Several Nuns, in a certain Convent, were
found to be in a fituation which, though pretty
natural for Women to be in, yet was not quite
fo with Women who were fuppofed to have
conftantly lived inclofed in the fame walls with

5

other Women, and made the Abbefs judicioufly conclude that fome *male* Nun was harboured among them, or, as it was expreffed, that fome wolf lay hidden among the fheep · a fufpicion which, by the by, was well grounded, for a young Man, who had as yet no beard, had found means to introduce himfelf into the Convent, where he lived, dreffed like the Sifters, and was reckoned one among them. In order both to afcertain fuch fufpicion, and difcover fo dangerous a perfon, all the Nuns were ordered into one room, and there made to ftrip themfelves ftark naked; when the Abbefs, with her fpectacles on her nofe (whence the Tale has received its name) infpected them all, one after another, carefully. To relate how the young Man, notwithftanding the ingenious precautions he had taken, came to be found out, and how the Abbefs's fpectacles were thrown from her nofe and broken, is foreign to our fubject: let it here fuffice to fay that the young Man was really found out; and that the Nuns, except thofe who had been concerned with him, who were previoufly locked up in a fafe place,—that the Nuns, I fay, laid hold of him, led him into a wood that flood clofe to their Convent, and there tied him to a tree, naked as he was, in order to make him atone for his audacioufnefs by a fmart flagellation. Having forgotten to fupply themfelves with the neceffary inftru-

ments of correction, they ran back to the Convent to fetch them, and whether from the miflay-
ing of a key, or fome other accident, were detained a little time. In the mean time a Miller,
riding upon his Afs, went through the wood;
and feeing the young Man in the abovementioned
plight, ftopped, and afked him the reafon of it:
to which the latter made anfwer, that it was thofe
wicked Nuns who had put him in that fituation,
becaufe he would not gratify their wanton requefts;
that he had rather die than be guilty of fuch
thing. The Miller then caft upon him a look of
the utmoft contempt . . . . but it will be better to
refer the Reader to the abovementioned Author
himfelf, for the inimitable Dialogue that paffed
between the young Man and the Miller: here it
will be enough to fay, that this latter propofed to
the other to put himfelf in his place, and war-
ranted him he would behave in quite a different
manner, and much more to the fatisfaction of the
Nuns than he had done. The young Man had
no need of much encouragement to accept the
propofal: after the Miller had releafed him, and
ftripped himfelf, he tied him faft to the fame tree,
and had juft time enough to fteal away, and hide
himfelf behind fome neighbouring bufh, when
the Nuns rufhed again out of the fame door at
which they had got in, armed with all the difciplines and befoms they had been able to find in

7

the Convent. They immediately marched up to the perfon who was tied to the tree, and without minding the broad fhoulders and brawny limbs which were now offered to their view, began to ufe their difciplines with great agility. In vain did the Miller expoftulate with them on their ufing him fo ill: in vain did he remonftrate that he was not the Man whom they took him to be, that he was not that beardlefs ftrippling, that milk-fop fimpleton, with whom they had formerly had to do, that woman-hater who had given them fo juft a caufe of diffatisfaction; that they ought to try him before they entertained fo bad an opinion of him:—in vain did he even at laft, in the extremity of pain, apply to the utmoft powers of his native language, to convey to them the cleareft ideas he could, both to thofe wifhes he fuppofed in them, and of his great abilities to gratify them: the more loudly and clearly he fpoke, the more unmercifully they laid on, and only left him when they had worn out their difciplines.

Cervantes likewife, whofe authority is equal to that of any Author, and who has moreover thrown a great light upon the fubject of flagellations, has introduced a fact which greatly ferves to confirm the obfervations we are difcuffing here. I mean to fpeak of what happened in that memorable night in which the Senora Rodriguez paid a vifit to the valorous Don Quixote, in his bed.

That Gentlewoman having, in the course of the conversation she had with the Knight, dropped several reflections of a very bad kind on the Duchess and the fair Altisidora, who were at that very instant listening at the door, these two Ladies, though justly and greatly offended at the liberty that was thus taken with their character, recurred to no expedient of a coarse and rough kind to avenge the insult, but they immediately applied to the summary, yet smart,—genteel, yet effectual, mode of correction here alluded to, namely, a flagellation. And here the Author we mention has taken an opportunity of giving a singular instance of the readiness of wit of the fair Sex, and of the quickness with which they usually extricate themselves out of the seemingly most perplexing difficulties. The Duchess and Altisidora were entirely destitute of the necessary instruments to inflict the chastisement they had resolved upon, but they had the great presence of mind to think of using their slippers for that purpose: they presently pulled them off their feet, bounced the door open, ran to the Senora Rodriguez, in the twinkling of an eye made her ready for flagellation, and immediately began to exert their new weapons with great dexterity. Thence, still in the dark, they passed to the astonished Knight, who lay snug in his bed, and who, by his listening to the stories of the Senora, and also by his

queftions, had encouraged her to procced in her
reflections (a thing which he might full as well
have avoided doing) and beftowed upon him a few
of thofe favours they had fo plentifully heaped
upon the above Gentlewoman.

At this place might alfo be mentioned, as being
extremely well in point to the fubject we are treating, the kind of fatisfaction required by Dulcinea, from Sancho, and that which the Lady introduced by Butler, prefcribed to the renowned
Hudibras, while he was in the ftocks; though, I
confefs, it might be faid that the corrections here
alluded to, were only advifed, not inflicted, by
the above Ladies. But it will fuffice to mention,
as a conclufion of thefe quotations from great
Authors, the manner in which *Lazarillo de Tor-
mes*, the notorious Spanifh Cheat, was ferved by
his four Wives. Having found out the place of
his abode, they immediately agreed among themfelves to ferve him with the elegant kind of chaftifement here mentioned; and having all together
furprized him one morning, while he was afleep,
they tied him faft to his bed, and ferved upon him
one of the moft dreadful flagellations that ever
were inflicted, fince the ufe of them has been
contrived, as we are told in the Hiftory of the
Life of the faid *Lazarillo*, a Book which is ftill
in repute in Spain, it being written with humour,
and containing true pictures of the manners of

that Country, and being even, as some say, founded on real facts.

Nor are true and well-authenticated instances
wanting, to confirm the same obfervations.
None, however, can be mentioned, that sets
in a stronger light the love of justice inherent in
the female Sex, and their constant attention to
make choice of expedients of an elegant kind to
exprefs their refentment, than the custom that
prevails in France and Italy, and perhaps in other
Countries, according to which, Ladies use to flagellate their acquaintances, while they are yet in
bed, on the morning of the day of the festival of
the Innocents , whence this flagellatory custom is
called " giving the Innocents" *(dar gli Innocenti)* ·
the word *Innocent*, we may obferve, has, in both
the Italian and French languages, befides the Englifh fignification of it, that of fool, or fimpleton ;
hence the words, *the Day of the Innocents*, feem
alfo to fignify in thofe two languages, the *Fools*
day, or the day of the *Unwary*.

Nay, fo well eftablifhed is the custom we mention, that Women, in thofe parts, look upon that
day, as a day of general juftice and retribution,
or an Affize or Seffions day, to which they refer
taking fatisfaction for the flight offences they may
receive in the courfe of the year, efpecially from
their male friends. They even will fometimes,
when the latter hefitate too much in granting
their requefts, or mifbehave in any manner,

hint to them the fatal confequences that may en-
fue from fuch a conduct, and plainly intimate to
them, that a certain day in the year is to come
on which every thing is to be atoned for.

When this important day is arrived, thofe Ladies who have agreed to join together in the fame
party, or (to continue the comparifon drawn from
the law that has been above employed) who have
agreed to go together upon the circuit, repair early in the morning to the appointed place of rendezvous, for inftance the apartment of one of
them, fufficiently provided with difciplines from
their refpective kitchens, and after laying the
plan of their operations, they fally out, to take
a round to the apartments of their different acquaintances.

The prudent and cautious, on fuch an important day, take great care to fecure well the bolts
and locks of their doors, or rather, fearing that
fleep fhould overcome them, and knowing how
fatal neglect might prove, they take that precaution on the evening before, when going to bed,
and as an additional fecurity, they heap all the
chairs and tables againft the door. Others, who
are of a bold and daring fpirit, on the contrary
affect on that day, to leave the doors of their
rooms wide open, and ftay in bed, refolved to
wait the event, and undauntedly to face the ftorm.
However, as fuch an affectation of bravery feems
to indicate that fome prefent trick, or at leaft fome

Y 4

future retaliation of fome kind or other is intended, the Ladies commonly keep clear from a place they judge fo ominous, unlefs there happens to be one among them of an uncommonly courageous turn of mind, who places herfelf in the van, encourages the whole party, and they all together rufh into the room and fall upon the adventurous Hero, who is then made to pay dearly for his temerity. When this does not happen to be the cafe, and at the fame time they find the doors of all thofe perfons whom they had exprefsly marked out for chaftifement, to be proof againft either a coup-de-main or a regular fiege, as they muft not part without fome effectual bufinefs has been tran'acted, the cloud commonly breaks upon fome unfortunate Simpleton, who has left his door open for no other reafon than becaufe he had forgot what day of the month it was, they lay faft hold of him, and feldom leave him before their difciplines are worn out to the ftumps. The ftory is foon circulated in whifpers in the neighbourhood, and if any perfon who has not yet heard of it, obferves that the Gentleman appears that day uncommonly grave and fulky, his wonder prefently ceafes, when he is told that, on the morning, they have given him the *Innocents*.

The cuftom we mention, feems to be of pretty ancient date, it is alluded to in that old Book formerly quoted, *The Tales of the Queen of Na-*

varre. A Man, an Upholfterer by trade, as it is faid in one of thefe Tales (for Men will fome-times avail themfelves of the practice in queftion when it may ferve their turn) a Man was in love with his fervant Maid ; and as he did not know how to find an opportunity to efcape the vigilance of his Wife, and be alone with her, he pre-tended, in a converfation he brought about on the fubject, on the eve of *Innocent's* day, to find much fault with the Maid , complained that fhe was a lazy Wench, and fo on ; and added, that, in order to teach her better, he propofed, on the .... to give her the *Innocents.* The .... .lauded his refolution : at break ....dingly rofe from his bed, took .... fuch a monftrous fize, that his ....d to think what correction the Maid was about to undergo, and ran up ftairs with a difpofition of feemingly very great feverity : however, I am happy to inform the Reader, that, after he had bounced the door open, and at firft frighted the Maid very much, every thing was concluded in an amicable manner.

If from Ladies of a middling ftation in life, and in the clafs of Upholfteiers, we turn our eyes towards Ladies of rank, and Couit Ladies, we fhall meet with inftances no lefs inftructive and inteiefting.

We may, in the firft place, mention the cafe of the Poet Clopinel, which has been alluded to in a former Chapter. This Poet, who was alfo called *John of Mehun* (a fmall Town on the river Loire) lived about the year 1300, under the reign of Philip the Fair, King of France, at whofe Court he was well received. He wrote feveral Books, and among others tranflated into French the Letters of Abelard to Heloifa. but that of his works which gave him moft reputation, was his conclufion of the celebrated *Roman de la Rofe*, a Poem of much the fame turn with Ovid's *Art of Love*, which had been begun by William *de Lorris*, and met with prodigious fuccefs in thofe times, and was afterwards imitated by Chaucer. However, Clopinel gave great offence to the whole Sex, by four lines he had inferted in that Poem, the meaning of which is as follows :—All of you are, " will be, or were, either in deed, or intention, " wh-res ; and whoever would well fearch into " your conduct, wh-res would find you all " to be."

> *Toutes êtes, ferez, ou futes*
> *De fait ou de volonté, putes ;*
> *Et qui bien vous chercheroit*
> *Toutes putes vous trouveroit,*

The meaning of thefe verfes, if we take from them the coarfenefs of the expreffions, which did not perhaps found fo harfh in thofe times as they

would in our days, did not at bottom differ from
the well-known line of Pope,

" — Every Woman is at heart a Rake."

Yet we do not hear that this Poet fuffered any
flagellation on that account, from the Court Ladies, or any other Ladies, whether it was that he
prudently took care, after writing the above line,
to keep for fome time out of the way, or that the
Ladies felt no refentment at the accufation. With
refpect to Clopinel, however, the cafe proved
otherwife : and whether his expreffions really had,
notwithftanding what has been above fuggefted,
much the fame coarfe meaning as now, or Ladies
had, in thofe days, a nicer fenfibility to any thing
that might touch their honour, the Ladies at
Court were much offended at the harfh charge that
was thus brought againft the whole Sex without
diftinction : they refolved to make the infolent
Poet properly feel the effects of their refentment:
and as they were at the fame time firmly determined, efpecially being Court Ladies, not to ufe any
expedient but of an elegant and refined kind, they
refolved upon a flagellation. One day, accordingly, as Clopinel was coming to Court, entirely
ignorant of the fate that awaited him, the Ladies,
who had previoufly fupplied themfelves with por-
per inftruments, laid hold of him, and immediately proceeded to make him ready for correction.
No poffible affiftance could refcue Clopinel from

having that chaſtiſement ſerved upon him which
he ſo juſtly deſerved, except his wit, which happily did not fail him in ſo imminent a danger,
and ſuggeſted to him to aſk leave to ſpeak a few
words. The favour was granted him, with expreſs injunction, however, to make his ſtory
ſhort: when, after acknowledging the juſtice of
the ſentence that had been paſſed upon him, he
requeſted it, as an act of mercy, that that Lady
who thought herſelf moſt affronted by his lines,
ſhould give the firſt blow: this requeſt ſtruck
the Ladies with ſo much ſurpriſe (owing no doubt
to the fear every one of them immediately conceived, of giving an advantage againſt herſelf for
which ſhe might afterwards repent) that, to uſe
the expreſſion of the Author of Moreri's Dictionary, from which this fact is extracted, the rods
-fell from their hands, and Clopinel eſcaped un-
puniſhed.

Court Ladies of more modern times, have
given ſimilar inſtances of refinement and elegance
in their method of revenging the affronts they
had received. On this occaſion the Reader may
be reminded of the caſe of the Marchioneſs of
Treſnel, which has been related at length in a
former place. Another inſtance of the juſtice of
Ladies, ſtill more intereſting by far, occurred at
the Court of Ruſſia about the year 1740. The
object of the Ladies reſentment, was a Fop of

quality, lately returned from his Travels ; nor will the Reader queftion the propriety of the flagellation that was ferved upon him, when he fhall be informed that this prefumptuous Spark had been guilty of no lefs an offence than having publicly boafted of having received favours which had never been fhewn him. The fact is related in a Book intitled, *Letters from Ruffia*, which was publifhed by a Lady whofe hufband refided at that Court in a public capacity, between the years 1730 and 1740 : the book is written in a pleafing ftyle, and contains a deal of interefting information concerning the Ruffian Court at that time. The Author, it is faid, lived a few years ago at Windfor : her Letters from Ruffia were addreffed to a female friend in England.

In the eleventh letter, the following account is contained. ' I long to tell you a ftory ; but your ' prudery (I beg pardon, your prudence) fright ' ens me : however, I cannot refift, fo pop your ' fan before your face, for I am going to begin. ' We have here a young fellow of fafhion, who ' has made the tour of France, &c. &c. At his ' return he fell in company with three or four ' pretty Women at a friend's houfe, where he ' fung, danced, laughed, was very free with the ' Ladies, and behaved quite *a-la-mode de* Paris. ' As he had given the gazing audience a fpecimen ' of his airs, fo he did not fail afterwards to brag

' of the fondnefs of the Ladies for him, and of
' the proofs they had given him of it. This he
' repeated in all companies, till it reached the
' ears of the hufbands, who looked glum in fi-
' lence, and at laft, in plain terms, expreffed the
' caufe of their ill-humour.' To abridge the account, it will fuffice to fay that the Ladies refolved
to punifh the vain-boafting fop as he deferved : a
letter was written to him by one of them, ap-
pointing a place where fhe was to meet him : " he
flew on the wings of love to the rendezvous," perfumed, we are to fuppofe, and in his fmarteft
drefs. Though he expected to meet only one of
the Ladies, he found them all four waiting for
him, and inftead of that delightful afternoon he
had prepared himfelf to fpend, he was entertained with a moft ferious flagellation. ' Some fay
' (continues the Author who relates this fact)
' that the Ladies actually whipped him ; others,
' they ordered their maids to do it : that the pu-
' nifhment was inflicted with fo much rigour as
' to oblige him to keep his bed fome time, is cer-
' tain, but whether the Ladies were executioners
' or fpectators only, is a doubt.'

For my own part, I fhall be bolder than the fair
Author who gives this account; and I will take
upon myfelf to decide that the Ladies were *fpectators only*. Had this young fellow of fafhion we
are fpeaking of, committed an offence of no very

grievous kind ; had he, for inftance, been guilty of fome word, or even action, moderately inde- cent in the prefence of the Ladies, or affronted them by fome ill-timed jokes, or had he, like Clopinel, indulged himfelf in a bon-mot, or even a whole fong, againft the honour of the Sex, then we might fuppofe the Ladies arms, to have poffeffed fufficient vigour to have ferved him with a correc- tion proportioned to the degree of his guilt. Not that I confider, however, as fome Readers will per- haps do, the falfhood of the facts he had boafted of, as being any aggravation of his offence : very far from it : it is when fuch facts are true, that the boafting of them is really a fault of a black na- ture : it is fuch, in my humble opinion, that no poffible flagellation can atone for it ; the ungrate- ful *Tell-tale* ought to be ftitched in a bag, and thrown into the river. However, as the vain fpeeches of the young fellow were in themfelves highly wicked, we are to fuppofe that the Ladies trufted the care of chaftifing him to more robufti- ous hands than their own ; and we muft fide with that part of the Public, who thought that they or- *dered their Maids* to perform for them ; that is to fay, a fet of Maid-flaves felected among the ftout- eft of thofe who compofed their houfholds, Maids imported from the banks of the *Palus-meotis,* or the Black Sea, and who thought it a glorious opportu- nity for fhewing their miftreffes their zeal in ferving

them.   This fuppofition agrees extremely well
with the enfuing part of the account, viz. that this
vain-boafting Coxcomb *was obliged to keep his bed
fome time:* who knows? perhaps five or fix weeks.

The only perfonal fhare, we are to think, the
Ladies took in the affair, was, when the execution
was concluded, to admonifh the culprit as to his
future conduct.   Milton makes the obfervation,
which is quoted by the Author of the Spectator,
that the Devil feemed once to be fenfible of fhame;
it was when he received a cenfure (unexpected for
him, we may fuppofe) from a young Angel of remarkable beauty.   In like manner, what muft
have been the fhame of that young Coxcomb, who
perhaps had never blufhed in his life, when he
heard himfelf addreffed by the Ladies who had
caufed him to be ferved with fo juft a chaftifement!
what muft have been his remorfe for his naughty
behaviour! his grief in confidering, that, had
he perhaps waited patiently a little time longer,
they would have willingly honoured him with
their moft valuable favours! The Lady who poffeffed the eafieft and moft elegant delivery, advanced towards him a few fteps; and, accompany-
ing her fhort fpeech with the action of an arm of
an exquifite form and hand as white as fnow,
and with a frown on her face, which, without
leffening its beauty, gave a true expreffion of her
juft refentment, fhe made him fenfible, in few

words, of the greatnefs of his fault, and the juftice of the chaftifement that had been adminiftered
to him : then turning towards the Calmouk and
Tartarian Maids who had fo well executed her
former orders, fhe directed them to fhew him
the way to the ftreet door.

To thefe inftances of the juftice of Ladies, we
may add thofe of the corrections they have beftowed upon their hufbands ; as they have an undoubted right. A very remarkable cafe of that fort
is alluded to, in the I. Canto P. II. of Hudibras.

Did not a certain Lady whip
Of late her hufband's own Lordfhip?
And, though a Grandee of the Houfe,
Clawed him with fundamental blows.
Tied him ftark-naked to a bed-poft,
And fiiked his hide, as if fh' had rid poft ;
And after, in the Seffions Court,
Where whipping's judged, had honour for't.

The noble perfon here mentioned, was Lord
Munfon : fimilar acts of authority on their huf-
bands, were performed, about the fame time, by
Sir William Waller's Lady, Mrs. May, and Sir
Henry Mildmay's Lady. From thefe inftances
we find, that, amidft the general wreck of the
Monarchical, Ariftocratical, and Clerical, powers
in the Nation, and while the King, Lords, and
High Clergy, had their prerogatives wrefted from
them and annihilated, Wives knew how to affert

Z

their jurifdiction over their Hufbands, and preferve their juft authority. The fubject however
is too deep to be difcuffed at large here . I intend
to offer more facts to the Public in a feparate
Work, which will be a compleat Treatife, and a
kind of *Matrimonial Code* in which the true principles fhall be laid concerning the rights of Wives,
and the fubmiffion of Hufbands *.

---

* The abovementioned Lord Munfon had fat as one of the
Judges at the King's Trial: he lived at St. Edmundfbury,
when his Wife, with the affiftance of her Maids, ferved him
with a flagellation. An allufion to the fame fact is alfo made
in a fong which is to be found in the Collection of *Loyal
Songs.* The thanks her Ladyfhip received from the Seffions
Court, were owing to its being generally fufpected the Noble
Lord had altered his political principles, for which his Wife
had chaftifed him.

It really feems that a kind of flagellating fanaticifm had
taken place, in thofe days, in this Country, fimilar in many
refpects to that which arofe in the times of Cardinal Damian
and Dominic *the Cuiraffed :* there was this difference however,
that it had for its object to flagellate, not one's-felf, but
others, which was the wifer folly of the two. The thanks
publicly decreed to Lady Munfon (not to mention feveral puritanical publications of thofe days) are proofs of that flagellating fpirit I mention; as well as the correction inflicted
by Zachary Crofton upon his fervant maid (fee p 238), and
the pamphlet he wrote in defence of it, which was very
likely grounded on certain religious tenets concerning the
mortification of the flefh, &c. that were current in thofe
times.

Thofe Authors who have treated of the manner in which Men ought to behave in their intercourfe with the fair Sex, have been fo fenfible
that the latter muft unavoidably, at one time or
other, have occafion to beftow lectures and corrections on their Suitors or Lovers (and alfo their
Hufbands) that they have made it a point to thefe,
to bear thofe momentary mortifications with patience and humility, and not to think that fuch
fubmiffion reflects any difhonour upon them.
This is the piecept exprefsly given by Ovid, in
his *Art of Love*,—' Do not think it in any de-
' gree fhameful for you, to fubmit to the harfh
' words, and the blows, of the young Woman
' you court.'

> *Nec maledicta puta, nec verbera ferre puellæ*
> *Turpe*——

And indeed we find that thofe Loveis who have
beft underftood their bufinefs, have not only conftantly followed the advice of Ovid, and chearfully
fubmitted to receive fuch corrections as their Miftreffes were pleafed to impofe upon them; but
when they have happened to have been involun-
tarily guilty of offences of a fomewhat grievous
kind, they have done more; they have, of themfelves, offered freely to fubmit to them. Thus
Polyenos, in the Satyr of Petronius, who had
been guilty with Circe of one of thofe faults

which Ladies fo difficultly prevail upon themfelves
to forgive, who had in fhort committed that offence which the abovementioned Miller boafted
he never happened to be guilty of, wrote afterwards to her,—" If you want to kill me, I will
come to you with an iron weapon, or if you are
fatisfied with ftripes, I run naked to my Miftrefs."
(*Polyaënos Circæ falutem . . . . . . Sive occidere pla-
cet, cum ferro venio ; five verberibus contenta es, curre
nudus ad dominam. Id tantum memento, non me, fed
infrumenta, peccaffe, &c. Cap.* 130.)

The illuftrious Count of Guiche, as we find
in the Count of Buffi's *Amorous Hiftory of Gauls*,
a Book which caufed the difgrace of its Author,
on account of the liberties he had taken in it with
the charaƈter of King Lewis the Fourteenth, and
his Miftrefs, *Madame de la Valiere*, the Count of
Guiche, I fay, one of the firft-rate Beaux of the
Court of the King juft mentioned, behaved in the
fame manner that Polyenos had done. Having
committed a fault with the well-known Countefs
of Olonne, of the fame kind with that of Polyenos, he wrote the next day to the Countefs
in much the fame terms as the latter had done
to Circe. ' If you want me to die, I will
' bring you my fword, if you think I only de-
' ferve to be flagellated, I will come to you in my
" fhirt.' *(Si vous voulez ma mort, j'irai vous porter*

mon épée; si vous jugez que je ne mérite que le fouet, j'irai vous trouver en chemise.)

The celebrated Earl of Effex, in one of the misunderstandings between him, and Queen Elizabeth, having given her a more than common cause of offence, and wishing in a particular manner to soothe her resentment, wrote to her in much the same terms as those abovementioned. He gave the Queen, as we find in Camden, explicit thanks for the corrections she had inflicted upon him, and kissed (to use his words, as recited by the above Author) and ' kissed her ' Majesty's Royal Hand, and the rod which had ' chastised him.' Not that I propose, however, by quoting the above expressions of the Earl, positively to affirm that they were meant to allude to any express corrections of the kind mentioned in this Book, which his Royal Mistress had at any time used to inflict upon him, or the other persons in her service, but yet, when we, on the one hand, attend to the invariable corruption, profligacy, shamelessness, wickedness, and perverseness of Ministers, ever since the beginning of the world, and on the other, consider to what degree those employed by the Princess we speak of, proved just, and zealous for the public good, we cannot help thinking that that great and magnanimous Queen had found

out fome very peculiar method of rendering them
fuch *.

* It came out, in a certain late debate in the Houfe of
Commons (June 1783) that, among the expences in the office
of a prime Minifter, about a year before out of place, there
was an article (introduced among the Stationary ware) of three
hundred and forty pounds for *whip-cord*, for one year. It
is very probably fince the days of Queen Elizabeth, that this
kind of commodity has been made part of the national ex-
penditure.

C H A P. XXIII.

Formation of the public Proceſſions of Flagel-
lants. Different ſucceſs they meet with, in
different Countries.

THE example which ſo many illuſtrious
perſonages had given of voluntarily
ſubmitting to flagellation, and the pains which
Monks had been at, to promote that method
of mortification by their example likewiſe, as
well as by the ſtories they related on that ſubject, had, as we have ſeen, induced the generality of people to adopt the fondeſt notions
of its efficacy. But about the year 1260, the
intoxication became as it were complete. People, no longer ſatisfied to practiſe mortifications of this kind in private, began to perform them in ſight of the Public, under pretence of greater humiliation : regular aſſocia-
tions and fraternities were formed for that
purpoſe; and numerous bodies of half-naked
Men began to make their appearance in the
public ſtreets, who after performing a few re-

ligious ceremonies contrived for the occafion, flagellated themfelves with aftonifhing fanaticifm and cruelty.

The firft inftitution of public Affociations and Solemnities of this kind, muft needs have filled with furprife all moderate perfons in thofe days; and in fact we fee that Hiftorians of different Countries, who lived in the times when thefe ceremonies were firft introduced, have taken much notice of them, and recorded them at length in their Hiftories or Chronicles. I will lay extracts from a few of thefe different Books, before the Reader; it being the beft manner, I think, of acquainting him with the origin of thefe fingular flagellating folemnities and proceffions, which continue in ufe in feveral Countries.

The firft Author from whom we have a circumftantial account on that fubject, is that Monk of St. Juftina, in Padua, whofe Chronicle Wechelius printed afterwards at Bafil. He relates how the public fuperftitious ceremonies we mention, madè their firft appearance in the Country in the neighbourhood of Bologna; which is the fpot where, it feems, they took their firft origin, and whence they were afterwards communicated to other Countries. The following is the above Author's own account.

" When all Italy was fullied with crimes of
every kind, a certain fudden fuperftition, hitherto unknown to the world, firft feized the
inhabitants of Perufa, afterwards the Romans, and then almoft all the Nations of Italy. To fuch a degree were they affected with
the fear of God, that noble as well as ignoble
perfons, young and old, even children five
years of age, would go naked about the
ftreets, with only their private parts covered,
and, without any fenfe of fhame, thus walked in public, two and two, in the manner
of a folemn proceffion. Every one of them
held in his hand a fcourge made of leather
thongs, and with tears and groans they lafhed
themfelves on their backs, till the blood
ran; all the while weeping and giving tokens
of the fame bitter affliction as if they had really been fpectators of the paffion of our Saviour, imploring the forgivenefs of God and
his Mother, and praying that He who had
been appeafed by the repentance of fo many
Sinners, would not difdain theirs.

" And not only in the day time, but likewife during the nights, hundreds, thoufands,
and ten thoufands of thefe Penitents, ran,
notwithftanding the rigour of winter, about
the ftreets, and in churches, with lighted wax-
candles in their hands, and preceded by Priefts

who carried croffes and banners along with them, and with humility proftrated themfelves before the altars: the fame fcenes were to be feen in fmall Towns and Villages; fo that the mountains and the fields feemed to refound alike the voice of Men who were crying to God.

"All mufical inftruments and love fongs then ceafed to be heard. The only Mufic that prevailed, both in Town and Country, was that of the lugubrious voice of the Penitent, whofe mournful accents might have moved hearts of flint; and even the eyes of the obdurate Sinner could not refrain from tears *.'

"Nor were Women exempt from the general fpirit of devotion we mention: for not only thofe among the common people, but alfo Matrons and young Maidens of noble families, would perform the fame mortifications with modefty, in their own rooms. Then

---

* *Siluerunt tunc tempore omnia mufica inftrumenta & amatoriæ cantilenæ. Sola cantio pœnitentis lugubris audiebatur ubique, tam in civitatibus quam in villis, ad cujus flebilem modulationem corda faxea movebantur, & obftinatorum oculi lacrymis non poterant continere.*———This Monk of St. Juftina, whofe account is here tranflated at length, was certainly no mean Writer: he was quite another Man than the *Abbé Boileau.*

thofe who were at enmity with one another, became again friends. Ufurers and Robbers haftened to reftore their ill gotten riches to their right owners. Others, who were contaminated with different crimes, confeffed them with humility, and renounced their vanities. Gaols were opened; prifoners were delivered; and banifhed perfons permitted to return to their native habitations. So many and fo great works of fanctity and chriftian charity, in fhort, were then performed by both Men and Women, that it feemed as if an univerfal apprehenfion had feized Mankind, that the divine Power was preparing either to confume them by fire, or deftroy them by fhaking the earth, or fome other of thofe means which divine Juftice knows how to employ for avenging crimes.

" Such a fudden repentance, which had thus diffufed itfelf all over Italy, and had even reached other Countries, not only the unlearned, but wife perfons alfo admired. They wondered whence fuch a vehement fervour of piety could have proceeded; efpecially fince fuch public penances and ceremonies had been unheard of in former times, had not been approved by the fovereign Pontiff, who was then refiding at Anagni, nor recommended by any Preacher or perfon of eminence, but had

6

taken their origin among fimple perfons, whofe example both learned and unlearned had alike followed."

The Ceremonies we mention were foon imitated, as the fame Author remarks, by the other Nations of Italy: though they, at firft, met with oppofition in feveral places, from divers Princes, or Governments, in that Country. Pope Alexander the Fourth, for inftance, who had fixed his See at Anagni, refufed at firft, as hath been above faid, to give his fanction to them; and Clement VI. who had been Archbifhop of Sens, in France, in fubfequent times condemned thofe public flagellations by a Bull for that purpofe (A. 1349). Manfredus, likewife, who was Mafter of Sicily and Apulia, and Palavicinus, Marquis of Cremona, Brefcia, and Milan, prohibited the fame proceffions in the Countries under their dominion; though, on the other hand, many Princes as well as Popes countenanced them, either in the fame times, or afterwards.

This fpirit of public penance and devotion was in time communicated to other Countries; it even reached fo far as Greece, as we are informed by Nicephorus Gregoras, who wrote in the year 1361. Attempts were likewife made to introduce ceremonies of the fame kind into Poland, as Baronius fays in his An-nals; but they were at firft prohibited: nor did they meet, at the fame period, with more encouragement in Bohemia, as Dubravius relates in his Hiftory of that Country.

In Germany, however, the Sect, or Fraternity, of the Flagellants proved more fuccefsful. We find a very full account of the firft flagellating proceffions that were made in that Country, in the year 1349 (a time during which the plague was raging there) in the Chronicle of Albert of Strafbourg, who lived during that period.

" As the plague (fays the above Author) was beginning to make its appearance, People then began in Germany to flagellate themfelves in public proceffions. Two hundred came, at one time, from the Country of Schwaben to Spira, having a principal Leader at their head, befides two fubordinate ones, to whofe commands they paid implicit obedience. When they had paffed the Rhine, at one o'clock in the afternoon, crouds of people ran to fee them. They then drew a circular line on the ground, within which they placed themfelves. There they ftripped off their clothes, and only kept upon themfelves a kind of fhort fhirt, which ferved them inftead of breeches, and reached from the waift down to their heels: this done, they placed

themselves on the above circular line, and began to walk one after another around it, with
their arms stretched in the shape of a Cross,
thus forming among themselves a kind of procession. Having continued this procession a
little while, they prostrated themselves on the
ground, and afterwards rose one after another,
in a regular manner, every one of them, as
he got up, giving a stroke with his scourge to
the next, who in his turn likewise rose, and
served the following one in the same manner.
They then began disciplining themselves with
their scourges, which were armed with knots
and four iron points, all the while singing the
usual Psalm of the invocation of our Lord,
and other Psalms : three of them were placed
in the middle of the ring, who, with a sonor-
ous voice, regulated the chaunt of the others,
and disciplined themselves in the same manner. This having continued for some time,
they ceased their discipline ; and then, at a
certain signal that was given them, prostrated
themselves on their knees, with their arms
stretched, and threw themselves flat on the
ground, groaning and sobbing. They then
rose, and heard an admonition from their
Leader, who exhorted them to implore the
mercy of God on the people, on both their
benefactors and enemies, and on the souls in

Purgatory: then they placed themfelves again upon their knees, with their hands lifted towards heaven, performed the fame ceremonies as before, and difciplined themfelves anew, as they walked round. This done, they put on their clothes again; and thofe who had been left to take care of the clothes and the luggage, came forwards, and went through the fame ceremonies as the former had done. They had among them Priefts, and noble as well as ignoble perfons, and men converfant with letters.

" When the difciplines were concluded, one of the brotherhood rofe, and with a loud voice, read a letter, which he pretended had been brought by an Angel to St. Peter's Church, in Jerufalem: the Angel declared in it, that Jefus Chrift was offended at the wickednefs of the age, feveral inftances of which were mentioned, fuch as the violation of the Lord's day, blafphemy, ufury, adultery, and neglect with refpect to fafting on Fridays. To this the Man who read the letter added, that Jefus Chrift's forgivenefs having been implored by the Holy Virgin and the Angels, he had made anfwer, that in order to obtain mercy, finners ought to live exiled from their Country for thirty-four days, difciplining themfelves during that time.

" The inhabitants of the Town of Spira were moved with fo much compaffion for thefe Penitents, that they invited every one of them to their houfes: they however refufed to receive alms feverally, and only accepted what was given to their Society in general, in order to buy twifted wax-candles, and banners. Thefe banners were of filk, painted of a purple colour: they carried them in their proceffions, which they performed twice every day. They never fpoke to Women, and refufed to fleep upon feather-beds. They wore croffes upon their coats and hats, behind and before, and had their fcourges hanging at their waift.

" About an hundred Men, in the Town of Spira, inlifted in their Society, and about a thoufand at Strafburgh, who promifed obedience to the Superiors, for the time abovementioned. They admitted nobody but who engaged to obferve all the above rules during that time, who could fpend at leaft four-pence a day, left he fhould be obliged to beg, and who declared that he had confeffed his fins, forgiven his enemies, and obtained the confent of his Wife. They divided at Strafburgh: one part went up, and another part down, the Country; their Superiors having likewife divided. The latter directed the new

I

brothers from Strasburgh, not to discipline
themselves too harshly in the beginning; and
multitudes of people flocked from the Country up and down the Rhine, as well as the in-
land Country, in order to see them. After
they had left Spira, about two hundred Boys
twelve years old, entered into an Association
together, and disciplined themselves in public."

Flagellating processions and Solemnities of
the same kind, were likewise introduced into
France, where they met, at first, with but indifferent success; and even several Divines opposed them. The most remarkable among
them was John Gerson, a celebrated Theologian, and Chancellor of the University of Paris, who purposely wrote a Treatise against the
ceremonies in question, in which he particularly condemned the cruelty and great effusion
of blood with which these disciplines were
performed. ' It is equally unlawful (Gerson
' asserted) for a Man to draw so much blood
' from his own body, unless it be for medical
' reasons, as it would be for him to castrate
' or otherwise mutilate himself. Else it might
' upon the same principle be advanced, that
' a Man may brand himself with red-hot
' irons; a thing which nobody hath, as yet,
' either pretended to say, or granted, unless it
' be false Christians and Idolaters, such as are

' to be found in India, who think it a matter
' of duty for one to be baptized through fire.'

Under King Henry the Third, however,
the proceffions of Difciplinants found much
favour in France; and the King we mention,
a weak and bigoted Prince, not only encouraged thefe ceremonies by his words, but
even went fo far as to inlift himfelf in a Fraternity of Flagellants. The example thus
given by the King, procured a great number
of Aſlociates to the Brotherhood; and feveral Fraternities were formed at Court, which
were diftinguifhed by different colours, and
compofed of a number of Men of the firft families in the Kingdom. Thefe proceffions,
thus formed of the King and his noble train
of Difciplinants, all equipped like Flagellants,
frequently made their appearance in the public Streets of Paris, going from one Church
to another; and in one of thofe naked proceffions, the Cardinal of Lorrain, who had
joined in it, caught fuch a cold, it being about
Chriftmas time, that he died a few days afterwards. The following is the account to be
found on that fubject, in the *Prefident J. A.
de Thou's* Hiftory of his own times.

" While the civil war was thus carrying
on, on both fides, fcenes of quite a different
kind were to be feen at Court; where the

King, who was naturally of a religious temper, and fond of ceremonies unknown to Antiquity, and who had formerly had an opportunity to indulge this fancy in a Country subjected to the Pope's dominion, would frequently join in the proceffions which mafked Men ufed to perform, on the days before Chriftmas.

"For more than an hundred years paft, a fondnefs for introducing new modes of worfhip into the eftablifhed Religion, had prevailed; and a fect of Men had rifen, who, thinking it meritorious to manifeft the compunction they felt for their offences, by outward figns, would put on a fack-cloth, in the fame manner it it was ordered by the antient Law; and from a ftrained interpretation they gave of the paffage in the Pfalmift, *ad flagella paratus fum*, flagellated themfelves in public; whence they were called by the name of *Flagellants*. John Gerfon, the Chancellor of the Univerfity of Paris, and the pureft Theologian of that age, wrote a Book againft them. Yet the holy Pontiffs, confidering then that Sect with more indulgence than former ones had done, fhewed much countenance to it; fo that multitudes of Men, all over Italy, in thefe days inlift in it, as in a kind of a religious militia, thinking to obtain by that means forgivenefs of their fins. Diftinguifhed by different colours, blue, white, and black, in the fame manner as the Green and Blue factions, though propofing to themfelves different objects, were formerly in Rome, they likewife engroffed the attention of the public, and in feveral places gave rife to the warmeft contentions.

" The introduction which was made of thefe ceremonies into France, where they had till then been almoft unknown, forwarded the defigns of certain ambitious perfons; the contempt they brought on the perfon of the King, having weakened much the regal authority. While the King mixed thus with proceffions of Flagellants, and the moft diftinguifhed among his Courtiers followed his example, Charles, Cardinal of Lorrain, who was one of the party, was, by the coldnefs of the evening, thrown into a violent fever, attended with a moft intenfe pain in his head; and a delirium as well as continual watchfulnefs having followed, he expired two days before Chriftmas."

The Hiftorian we have juft quoted fays, in another place, that the King was principally induced to perform the above fuperftitious proceffions, by the folicitations of his Confeffor, Father Edmund Auger, who wrote a

Book on that subject, and of John Castelli, the Apostolic Nuntio in France; and that the weak complaisance shewn to him on that occasion, by the Chancellor Birague, and the Keeper of the Seals, Chiverny, encouraged him much to pursue his plan in that respect, notwithstanding the strong advices to the contrary, that were given him by Christopher de Thou, President of the Parliament, and Pierre Brulart, President of the *Chambre des Enquêtes.*

As there was, in those times, a powerful party in France, that opposed the Court, and even was frequently at open war with it, there was no want of Men, in Paris, who found fault with the disciplining processions of the King. When they first made their appearance, some, as the above Historian relates, laughed at them, while others exclaimed that they were an insult both to God and Man. Even Preachers joined in the party, and pointed their sarcasms from the pulpit against those ceremonies.

The most petulant among these popular Preachers, was one Maurice Poncet, of the Abbey of Melun, who, using expressions borrowed from a Psalm, compared the King and his brother Disciplinants, to Men who would cover themselves with a wet sack-cloth, to

A a 3

keep off the rain : he was at laft banifhed to his Monaftery. The example which the Court, and the Metropolis, had fet, was followed in a number of Country Towns, where fraternities of Flagellants were inftituted ; and among them particular mention is made of the Brotherhood of the *Blue Penitents,* in the City of Bourges, on account of the Sentence paffed in the year 1601, by the Parliament of Paris, in confequence of a motion of Nicolas Servin, the King's Advocate General, which exprefsly abolifhed it *.

---

* It has no doubt been perceived, that, in the courfe of this Work, I have commonly taken care to conclude the different Chapters into which it is divided, with a Note or Commentary of a certain length, upon the fame fubject with the Chapter itfelf, though of a lefs grave and ferious turn. This precaution I thought neceffary for the relief of the Reader, after the great exertion of his mind, occafioned by the weighty objects that had juft been offered to his confideration. Such final Note I confidered as a farce, after a ferious and moral Drama, and as a kind of *petite piece,* or if you pleafe, of interlude, calculated to revive the exhaufted fpirits of the Rea-

der, and enable him to begin a frefh Chapter with alacrity.

On this occafion, however, I find great difficulty in purfuing the fame plan. The proceffions of Difciplinants that have juft been defcribed, are fuch a difmal and gloomy fubject, that it fuggefts no ideas but what are of a ferious kind, it precludes all thoughts of mirth and jocularity, and I defpair, in this Note, of being able to entertain the Reader fo well as I flatter myfelf I have fucceeded in doing in the former ones.

The flagellating practices and ceremonies alluded to in this Chapter, are certainly moft aftonifhing facts in the Hiftory of Man. and if any thing renders our furprife lefs than it otherwife would be, it is the confideration that fuch practices have not been imagined on a fudden, and at once, but have been the refult of a long feries of flow innovations, introduced by different perfons, at different times, and in places remote from one another.

Befides, it really feems that there is a fecret propenfity in Mankind, for arduous modes of worfhip of all kinds. The obfervation has been made, that in the Science of Moral, fpeculatively confidered, Men, whatever may be their private conduct, are moft pleafed with fuch maxims as are moft rigid; and fo, with refpect to religious rites, do they feem to be moft taken with, and

moſt ſtrongly to adhere to, ſuch as are moſt laborious, and even painful.

We ſee, in faɛt, that bodily auſterities of a
cruel kind, performed with religious intentions,
have obtained among almoſt all the Nations in the
World, and ſelf-ſcourgings, in particular, were
praɛtiſed with views of this kind among almoſt
all the Nations of antiquity of whom accounts
have been left us: on which the Reader is refer-
red to the ſixth Chapter of this Book.

The ſame praɛtice we mention, beſides the advantage of its obviouſneſs to recommend it, had
in its favour, with Chriſtians, the farther circumſtance of its being in a manner ſanɛtified by the
Hiſtory itſelf of the faɛts on which their religion
is grounded. As a puniſhment of that kind made
expreſs part of the ill treatment which our Saviour
underwent, the thoughts of pious perſons were
naturally direɛted to a mode of mortification of
which ſo frequent mention was made in books,
hymns, ſermons, and religious converſations:
hence has it happened, that the praɛtices here alluded to, have been much more conſtantly and
univerſally adopted by Chriſtians, than by the
profeſſors of any other Religion.

A difference, however, took place in the above
reſpeɛt, between the Eaſtern and the Weſtern
Chriſtians. As the Chriſtians who were ſettled in
the Eaſt, lived almoſt always in the midſt of hoſ-.

tile Nations, and befides, never formed among
themfelves any very numerous fect, they never
went fuch lengths in their opinions, nor gave into
fuch extravagant practices, as the Chriftians in
the Weft. They had not, for inftance, adopted
the fond notions fince entertained by the latter,
on the efficacioufnefs of felf-flagellations to atone
for paft fins. Their religious notions had taken
a different turn. They generally confidered a
certain deep fenfe of paft offences, a ftate of unbounded contrition for the fame, as the competent
means of atonement. They confidered tears as
the laft ftage of fuch contrition, and in a manner
a neceffary token of it. Shedding tears was, therefore, the thing they aimed at, in all their devo-
tional acts felf-fcourging was thought by them
to be an excellent expedient for obtaining fo happy an effect, and they hence reforted to it, not
(as hath been done in the Weft) as to a direct and
immediate method of compenfating paft fins, but
only as to a fubfidiary operation, and a means
which, they fagacioufly thought, would foon bring
them to the requifite ftate of tears and falutary
compunction.

Of this turn of the devotion of the Eaftern
Chriftians, as well as of the ends they propofed
to themfelves in their acts of felf-flagellation, we
find proofs in the few inftances that have been left
us in Books, of their having performed acts of

that fort: I fhall relate the following one, which is to be found in the work of Gabriel, Archbi-fhop of Philadelphia, intitled Πατεριχὸν, or Collection of actions of Fathers, or Saints.

A certain Saint had come to a refolution of renouncing the World, and had fixed his habitation on the celebrated Mountain of Nitria, in Thebaid; and next to the cell to which he had retired, was that of another Saint, whom he heard every day bitterly weep for his fins. Finding himfelf unable to weep in the fame manner, and heartily envying the happinefs of the other Saint, he one day fpoke to himfelf in the following terms. ‘ You do not cry, you wretch, you do ‘ not weep for your fins. I will make you cry; ‘ I will make you weep by force, fince you will ‘ not do it of your ówn accord; I will make you ‘ grieve for your fins, as you ought:’ faying which, he took up in a paffion a large fcourge that lay by him, and laid lafhes upon himfelf fo thick and in fo effectual a manner, that he foon brought himfelf to that happy ftate which was the object of his ambition.

Another inftance of the manner of the devotion of the Eaftern Chriftians, is fupplied by the paffage in St. John Climax, that has been recited at pag. 121. Both the Oppofers, and the Promoters, of the practice of felf-flagellation, have gone too far in their interpretations of that paf-

fage. The latter have afferted that it exprefsly alluded to religious difciplines, performed in the
fame manner, and with the fame views, as they
now are in modern Monafteries, while the former
have been as pofitive that it meant no fuch thing
as *beating* or *fcourging*, and is only to be underftood of the lamentations of the Monks in the
Monaftery in queftion, that is, in a bare figurative
manner. The paffage in St. John Climax is this:
' Some among the Monks watered the pavement
' with their tears, while others, who could not
' fhed any, beat themfelves.' The expreffion
ufed in this paffage, to fay that fome among the
Monks beat themfelves, is certainly as precife as
any the Greek language can fupply; yet neither
does it fupply a fufficient proof that they performed, in the above Monaftery, regular and periodical flagellations of the fame kind with thofe that
have been fince ufed in the Weftern Monafteries,
in the times of Cardinal Damian, and the Widow Cechald: the felf-flagellations alluded to, in
the paffage we fpeak of, appear to have been of the
fame kind with thofe performed by the Saint of
the Mountain of Nitria who has been abovementioned, and were calculated to enable thofe who
could not weep, to weep plentifully.

But among the Weftern Chriftians, as the extenfive Country over which they became in time
to be fpread, without any intervening opponents,

afforded a vaſt field for innovations of every kind, they, as hath been above ſaid, went the greateſt lengths in their opinions concerning the uſefulneſs of the practices we mention, to which the Hiſtory of their Religion had at firſt given riſe.

In the firſt place, mortifications of the kind here alluded to, were uſed among them from notions of much the ſame ſort with thoſe entertained by the Eaſtern Chriſtians, that is, with a view of ſanctifying themſelves by their repentance, and aſſiſting their compunction.

In the ſecond place, they were actuated by a ſenſe of love for Jeſus Chriſt, and a deſire of uniting themſelves to him in his ſufferings. The intention we ſpeak of, is particularly recommended in the Statutes of different religious Orders; and the Brothers are exhorted in them, ' when ' they inflict diſcipline upon themſelves, to call to ' their mind Jeſus Chriſt, their moſt amiable ' Lord, faſtened to the column, and to endeavour ' to experience a few of thoſe exceſſive pains he ' was made to endure.' This notion of religious perſons, which proceeds from an unbounded ſenſe of gratitude towards their Divine Saviour, from a wiſh of repaying in any manner the immenſe ſervice he had conferred upon them in ſaving them from deſtruction, and of at leaſt ſharing his ſufferings, ſince they cannot alleviate them, has certainly ſomething intereſting in its principle.

But the moſt univerſal uſe, by far, that has been made of flagellatory diſciplines among Chriſtians, in theſe parts of the world, has been to atone for paſt ſins. And indeed it is no wonder that a practice of ſo convenient a kind, which enabled every one, by means of an operation of the duration and ſeverity of which he was the ſole judge, to pay, as he thought, an adequate price for every offence he might have committed, and ſilence a troubleſome conſcience whenever he pleaſed, ſhould ſo eaſily gain ground, and meet with ſo much favour, not only from the vulgar, but alſo from great Men, and even Kings, to whom we may no doubt add their Miniſters.

Among the ſuperſtitious notions that may be hurtful to Society, it is difficult to imagine one of a woiſe tendency than that here mentioned, the immediate conſequence of which is to render uſeleſs all the diſtinctions implanted in the human mind between evil and good, and, by making offenders eaſy with themſelves, to take off the only puniſhment that is left for the greater number of crimes. When notions like theſe were adopted by Kings, with reſpect to whom human laws are ſilent, the conſequences were pernicious in the extreme, practices of this ſort became as dangerous to the peace and happineſs of their ſubjects, as they would have been conducive to them, if the diſciplines we ſpeak of, inſtead of being in flicted upon fuch high Offenders, every time they were confcious they deferved them, by the hands of Confeffors aiming at Bifhopricks, or under fear of dungeons, had been dealt them to the full fatisfaction of a Jury compofed of impartial perfons, and nowife afraid to fpeak their minds.

Thefe notions of the ufefulnefs of felf-flagella-tions, were carried to a moft extravagant pitch by a Sect formed of thofe itinerant Difciplinants, accounts of whom have been above given. Proud of the cruel difciplines they inflicted upon themfelves, they looked upon them as being of far greater merit than the practice of any Chriftian virtue; and they at laft formed among themfelves a particular Sect of Heretics, who were called *Flagellants.* The title of *Hiftory of the Flagellants,* which the Abbé Boileau has given to his Work, might feem to indicate that he intended to write an Hiftory of that Sect, and of thofe public proceffions of Difciplinants which have fucceeded it: yet, he only mentions that Sect and thofe Proceffions in his ufual loofe manner, in his ninth Chapter, without even diftinguifhing the one from the other. The proper title of his book (and of this, which is imitated from it) fhould be, *The Hiftory of religious Flagellations among different Nations, and efpecially among Chriftians.*

Among the different tenets of the Hereticks we fpeak of, were the following. They pretended

that the blood they fhed, during their flagellations,
was mixed with that of Jefus Chrift;—that felf-
flagellations made confeffion ufelefs,—that they
were more meritorious than martyrdom, for they
were voluntary, which martyrdom was not;—
that baptifm by water was of no ufe, as every
true Chriftian muft be baptized in his own blood;
—that flagellation could atone for all paft and future offences, and fupplied the want of all other
good works. To thefe tenets, and to feveral
others of the fame fort, they added Stories of different kinds; fuch as that of the abovementioned
letter brought from Heaven by an Angel, to order
felf-flagellations, they gave out that a certain Brother of their Sect, who lived at Erford in Thu-
ringe, was Elias, and that another, whofe name
was Conrad Smith, was Enoch, &c. &c.

As the principles maintained by thefe Hereticks,
were deftructive of moft of the effential tenets received by the Church, this reafon, together with
the cruelties they practifed upon themfelves, and
in general their fanaticifm, which really was of a
defpicable kind, caufed Pope Clement IV. to iffue
a Bull againft them, in the year 1350, and feveral
Princes exprefsly prohibited that Sect, in the
places under their dominion.

From thofe Hereticks, muft therefore be diftinguifhed the common Fraternities of Difciplinants,
which continue in thefe days to be eftablifhed in

feveral Countries. Thefe Fraternities are compofed of good orthodox Chriftians, who do not in any degree pretend that their difciplines fuperfede the neceffity of Baptifm or Confeffion, or of any other Sacrament, who tell no ftories about Elias, or Enoch, who dutifully fubfcribe to all the tenets, without exception, recommended by the Church, and above all pay implicit obedience to the authority of the Heads of it. They are Affociations of much the fame kind with common Clubs, or if you pleafe, like Lodges of Free-mafons they have a ftock of effects and furniture belonging to the Fraternity, fuch as banners, cru-cifixes, ornaments for altars, and fo on, and each contributes a certain fmall fum annually, for keeping the above effects in repair, and defraying the expences of paying the mufic, feeing Priefts, and others of a like kind: they have, befides, peculiar Statutes, not unlike the Articles of a common Club.

The principal engagement of thefe Fraternities is to difcipline themfelves in times of great Solemnities, fuch as the Sundays in the Advent, the Sundays before Palm-Sunday, on Maunday Thurfday, and certain days during the Carnival. On thefe days they walk about Towns in regular proceffions. They carry along with them banners, painted with the appropriated colour of the Brotherhood: the Brothers are equipped in a peculiar kind of drefs for the occafion, all wearing, befides, mafks over their faces. With this appa- ratus they vifit different Churches, exhibiting an appearance which, when feen from fome dif- tance, is not unlike that of the trading Com- panies, in London, on a Lord Mayor's Day; and their banners, together with the other orna- ments they difplay, cut a figure not very fhort of the *paraphernalia* of the City.

In the principal Church whence they fet off, and perhaps alfo in thofe which they vifit, they hear a fhort fermon from a Prieft, on the Paffion of our Saviour; and as foon as the Prieft has faid the words, " let us mend and grow better" *(emen- demus in melius)* the difciplines begin with the fing- ing of the *Miferere*, and are continued in the ftreets, as they walk in proceffion. By one Arti- cle of their Statutes, it is ordered that no Brother fhall put a Man to difcipline himfelf in his ftead. Plenty of Indulgences are granted to thofe who difcharge their duty on thofe occafions. And moreover, Bifhops are ordered to infpect, in their refpective Diocefes, the Fraternities there efta- blifhed, and examine their Statutes, in order to ftrike out fuch articles as may contain feeds of Herefy.

Fraternities of this kind obtain in moft of the Catholic Countries in Europe, though with dif-

B b

ferent encouragement from their different Governments.

In France they were, as hath been above faid,
in the greateft favour at Court, under Henry the
Third · this Prince, who, before he was called to
the Throne on the death of his Brother, had given
every hope of an able warrior, and a great King,
having inlifted in one of thefe Fraternities. As
a powerful party was at that time fet up, in France,
againft the authority of the Crown, and moft of
the people in Paris favoured that party, the King
had attempted to overaw them by a difplay of Majefty, and being conftantly accompanied when he
made his appearance in public, by a numerous
body of Halberdiers ; but this not having fucceeded, he tried to amufe the People by public fhews ;
and in that view, as a Writer of thofe times fays,
inftituted in Paris Fraternities of Penitents, in
which he made himfelf a Brother. This expedient, however, did not fucceed : thefe difciplining
proceffions only ferved to bring farcafms upon the
Court, and the King himfelf; and among them
that of Maurice Poncet has been recorded, who,
befides other invectives he delivered from the pulpit, compared the difciplining Penitents, as hath
been abovementioned, to men who fhould cover
themfelves with a wet cloth to keep off the rain.
This reflection of Poncet was thought to be the
more pointed, as, the very day before, the King

had walked in a proceffion of Penitents, during which a moft heavy fhower of rain had fallen, and the King with his Chancellor, and the whole train of Difciplinants, had been thoroughly foaked. The King was informed, the next day, of the jeft of Poncet; and this, together no doubt with the remembrance of the rain of the day before, caufed him to be much incenfed againft the Preacher : however, as notwithftanding his vices and weaknefs, he was a Man of the mildeft temper, as well as of unbounded liberality, he contented himfelf with having the Monk fent back to his Convent.

In fubfequent times, that is in the year 1601, under the reign of Henry IV. a Sentence was paffed, as hath been abovementioned, by the Parliament of Paris, to abolifh the Fraternity of the *Blue Penitents*, in the City of Bourges. The motive of the Parliament was not, however, their tender care for the fkin of thefe Blue Penitents : but that Fraternity had been rendered a kind of political Affociation againft the reigning King, who was during his whole life perfecuted by bigotry, till he fell a victim to it at laft; and they had joined feveral treafonable declarations and engagements, to their Statutes : for this reafon the Fraternity was forbidden to meet again, under pain of being profecuted as guilty of High Treafon. From that time Brotherhoods of Penitents have been conftantly difcountenanced in France; and they are continued only in fome Towns in the Southern Provinces, diftant from the Metropolis.

But the Countries in which the proceffions we mention (which certainly are as extraordinary as any ceremony of which any Religion affords an inftance) are moft prevalent, and where they are in a manner natuialized, are, Italy, and Spain.

In the latter Country, in Spain, the flagellating Solemnities we fpeak of, have received a peculiar turn from the peculiar manners of the Inhabitants, and they are (which is certainly extraordinaiy) as well operations or fcenes of gallantry, as acts of devotion. Lovers will frequently go, at the head of a proceffion of friends, and difcipline themfelves under the windows of their Miftreffes: or, when they pafs by chance under thefe windows, with a proceffion to which they belong, they redouble the fmartnefs of their flagellations. All Difciplinants in general, fhew attentions of the fame kind to fuch Ladies as they meet in their way, when thefe Ladies appear to them poffeffed of fome charms; and when the latter engage their attention in a peculiar manner, they never fail, efpecially if the proceffion happens to move flowly or to ftop, by means of the increafed brifknefs of their flagellations and fkilful motions of their difciplines, plentifully to fprinkle them with their blood. Thefe facts are attefted by all Travellers; and *Madame* d'Aunoy among others, a French Lady, of quality who in the laft Century publifhed a relation of her journey into Spain, a Book written with judgment, after giving an account of the fame facts with thofe above to the friend to whom fhe wrote, adds that what fhe relates is literally true, and without any exaggeration. The Ladies who are the caufe of this increafed zeal of the Difciplinants, and to whom fuch an agreeable piece of courtfhip is addreffed, reward the latter by raifing the veil which covers their face, or even are obliged by the Byftanders to do fo (*deftapar*, as they call it) in much the fame manner as the croud which ftands at the door of a Houfe where there is a mafquerade, will, in this Country, oblige the mafks, as they get into, or out of the Houfe, to uncover their faces.

How the Spanifh Ladies can be pleafed with feats of that kind, is certainly difficu't to underftand; unlefs it be that, with Ladies, the bare intention of fhewing them courtefy, is enough to procure their good-will, or perhaps alfo it may be, that the extreme gracefulnefs with which the difciplines we mention, are performed, has the power of rendering them pleafing to the Ladies. An opinion of this kind has been delivered by the Author of Hudibras:

" Why.

" Why may not whipping have as good
" A grace, perform'd in time and mood,
" With comely movement, and by art,
" Raife a paffion in a Lady's heart ?"

This power of the graces to render whipping agreeable, is certainly a ftrong argument in their favour, and well worth adding to thofe urged in their behalf, in a certain celebrated publication of late times.

That Difciplinants in Spain, flagellate themfelves with the extreme graccfulnefs we mention, is a fact about which no doubt is to be entertained : nay, there are Mafters in moft Towns, whofe exprefs bufinefs is to teach the time, mood, comely movements and arts, above defcribed, and in fhort to fhew how to perform difciplines with elegance.——Fielding, in one of his Works, has inferted an advertifement of the celebrated Broughton which had juft made its appearance, by which the latter offered his fervices to the public, to inftruct them in the art of boxing, and all the myfteries of it: that Author thought pofterity would be extremely glad to meet with that interefting and incontrovertible monument of the manners of the times in which he wrote : an advertifement from one of the Spanifh flagellating Mafters we fpeak of, would, in like manner, be extremely proper to be produced in this place ; and if I do not infert here the copy of any fuch advertifement, the reader may be perfuaded that it is folely becaufe I have none in my poffeffion.

When the Gentlemen who propofe to difcipline themfelves in honour of their Miftreffes, are of confiderable rank, the ceremony is then performed with great ftate and magnificence. Madame D'Aunoy relates that the day the Duke of Vejar difciplined himfelf, an hundred white wax-candles were carried before the proceffion: the Duke was preceded by fixty of his friends (vaffals perhaps, or dependents) and followed by an hundred, all attended by their own pages and footmen, and befides them there were no doubt abundance of Priefts and crucifixes.

As thefe Spanifh Gallants have no lefs honour than devotion, battles frequently take place between them, for the affertion of their juft prerogatives, and this, for inftance, feldom fails to be the cafe when two proceffions happen to meet in the fame ftreet: each party think they are intitled to the moft honourable fide of the way, and a fcuffle is the confequence. This happened at the time of the proceffion of the abovementioned Duke of Vejar: another proceffion, conducted by the Marquis of Villahermofa, entered the fame ftreet, at the other end of it: the light-armed troops, otherwife the fervants with their lighted long wax-candles, began the engagement, bedaubing the clothes, and fingeing the whifkers and

hair of each other; then the body of Infantry,
that is to fay the Gentlemen with their fwords,
made their appearance, and continued the battle ;
and at laft the two noble Champions themfelves
met, and began a fight with their difciplines (another inftance of Penitents ufing their difciplines
as weapons, is, if I miftake not, to be found in
Don Quixote) the two noble Champions, I fay,
began a fmart engagement with each other; their
felf-flagellations were for a while changed, with
great rapidity, into mutual ones, and their weapons being demolifhed, they were about to begin
a clofer kind of fight, when their friends interfered, and parted them · the high fharp and ftiff
cap of one of the two Combatants, which had
fallen in the dirt, was taken up, properly cleanfed,
and again placed upon his head ; and the two proceffions went each their own courfe, dividing as
chance determined it.   The whole ceremony was
afterwards concluded with fplendid entertainments
which each of the Noble Difciplinants gave in
their Houfes, to the perfons who had formed their
refpective proceffions, during which abundance
of fine compliments were paid them on their piety, their gallantry, and their elegance in giving
themfelves difcipline.

If fuch acts both of devotion and courtfhip are
performed in Spain, by perfons of the firft rank,
much more may we think that practices of the

fame kind prevail among the vulgar : and on this occafion I fhall produce an extract from the Spanifh Book intitled, the Life of Friar *Gerund de Campazas*. As this Novel, which is of a humorous kind, was written in later times by a native of the Country, and a Man of learning (a Father Jefuit, I think) an extract from it may give a furer infight into the above fingular cuftoms of the Spaniards, than any relation of Travellers perhaps can.

‘ Anthony was then ftudying at Villagarcia, and ‘ already in the fourth clafs, as hath been faid, ‘ and in the twenty-fifth year of his age. The ‘ fortnight vacation for the Holy and Eafter Week ‘ arrived, and he went home to his own town, as ‘ is the cuftom for all thofe ftudents whofe home ‘ is within a fhort diftance. The Devil, who ne- ‘ ver fleeps, tempted him to play the penitent on ‘ Maunday Thurfday; for, as our young Peni- ‘ tent was now well fhot up and his beard grown, ‘ he looked lovingly upon a Damfel that had been ‘ a neighbour of his, ever fince they went to ‘ School together to the clerk of the Parifh, to ‘ learn the horn-book ; and in order to court her ‘ in the moft winning manner, he thought it ex- ‘ pedient to go forth as a difciplinant : as this, the ‘ Reader is to know, is one of the gallantries ‘ with which the Women of Campos are moft ‘ pleafed: for it is a very old obfervation there,

' that the greateſt part of the marriages are con-
' certed on the day of the croſs of the May, on
' the evenings on which there is dancing, and on
' *Maunday Thurſday*: ſome of the Women being
' ſo very devout and compunctious, that they are
' as much delighted with ſeeing the inſtruments of
' diſcipline applied, as with the rattling of the
' caſtanets.

' The rogue of an Anthony was not ignorant
' of this inclination of the girls of his Town, and
' therefore went out as diſciplinant, on Maunday
' Thurſday, as we have above ſaid. At a league's
' diſtance he might, notwithſtanding his maſk,
' and his hood which hung down almoſt to his
' waiſt, have been known by Catanla Rebollo,
' which was the name of his ſweetheart, neigh-
' bour, and old ſchool-fellow; for, beſides that
' there was no other cap in the whole proceſſion
' ſo ſpruce or ſo ſtiff-ſtanding as his, he wore as
' a mark, a black girdle which ſhe had given him,
' upon his taking leave of her on Luke's-day, to
' go to Villagarcia. She never took her eyes
' from him, during the time he was paſſing near
' her; and he, who knew it well, took that op-
' portunity to redouble the briſkneſs of his diſci-
' pline, making her, by the way, unobſerved by
' others, two little amorous obeiſances by nod-
' ding his cap: which is one of the tender paſſes
' that never fail to win the hearts of the marriage-

' able girls, who are very attentive to it; and the
' bumkin who knows how to do it with moft
' grace, may pick and choofe among them,
' though at the fame time he may not be the moft
' expert at the rural games and exercifes.

 ' At length, as Anthony had made too much
' hafte to give himfelf a plentiful bleeding, one
' of the Majordomos who fuperintended the pro-
' ceffion, bad him go home and take care of him-
' felf, before the proceffion was over. Catanla
' took herfelf after him, and being a neighbour,
' followed him into the houfe, where there ftood
' ready the wine, rofemary, falt and tow, which
' is all the apparatus for thefe cures. They well
' wafhed his fhoulders, and applied the pledgets;
' after which he put on his ufual clothes, and
' wrapped himfelf up in his grey cloak. They
' afterwards went to fee the proceffion, except Ca-
' tanla, who faid fhe would ftay with him, and
' keep him company, &c.'

The difciplining ceremonies above defcribed,
are, as hath been obferved, alfo admitted in Italy;
and they are performed there with no lefs regularity and applaufe, than in Spain. Moft Travellers into that Country give fome account of them:
Doctor Middleton, for inftance, defcribes at fome
length in his Letter from Rome, two proceffions
of that kind, to and in the Church of St. Peter,
of which he had been a witnefs.

But, as the ceremonies we fpeak of, have been made in Spain, expeditions of gallantry, in which nicety of honour and amorous prowefs are dif-played by turns, fo in Italy, they have been turn-ed into perfect farces, and fcenes of mimickry.

Father Labat, who has publifhed a relation of a Journey to Spain and Italy, in which he gives accounts of difciplining proceffions in both Coun-tries, recites that in one of thefe proceffions he faw at Civita Vecchia, there were in the firft place to be feen at the head of that proceffion feveral figures or perfons who reprefented Jefus Chrift in the different ftages or acts of his condemnation : thefe different figures are commonly expreffed by technical or cant Latin words ; and among thofe which Father Labat mentions as having made part of the above proceffion, was an *Ecce Homo*, which is a figure intended to reprefent Jefus Chrift when he made his appearance before Pilate, clad in purple robe, with a reed in his hand, and a crown on his head.

Another perfonage afterwards made his appear-ance, who reprefented our Lord going to the place of his death : eight Executioners furrounded him, who teafed him, and pulled the chains with which he was loaded ; and a Simeon of Cyrene walked behind him, who affifted him in carrying his crofs. Several Men followed, who were likewife loaded with heavy croffes, and were meant, I fuppofe, to reprefent the Robbers who fuffered on that day. Among thefe different figures were abundance of Roman Soldiers, armed with cafques and bucklers.

After thefe came a number of perfons who, by their tears and groans, expreffed the deep affliction they felt: and then the train of the Difciplinants made their appearance, who manifefted their grief in another manner, that is, by their flagellations: Among the latter were two particular figures who were thoroughly naked, except thofe parts which muft abfolutely be covered, for which purpofe they wore a kind of fhort apron. Thefe two figures, who were called the two *St. Jeroms*, on account of the blows with which they at times beat their breaft, poffeffed a kind of fkill not very unlike that exerted by Dominic the *Cuiraffed*, who could difcipline himfelf with both his hands at once: they performed both the *upper* and the *lower* difcipline at the fame time, and lafhed themfelves from head to foot, with large fcourges they had provided for the occafion. However, as the two latter perfonages exhibited rather a ftriking appearance, they were, the enfuing year, ordered to do like the other Penitents, and to wear breeches.

In the fame train we defcribe, were alfo the family of Jofeph, with a number of female mourners, and among them Mary Magdalen, with the

Virgin Mary, and, laftly, to crown the whole, there was in the proceffion a figure fitted with a red-haired wig, and a red beard, who reprefented Judas, and held up with great triumph in his hand, a purfe, in which he fhook and jingled a few pieces of money, which were fuppofed to be the reward he had received for betraying our Saviour.

In fine, what much increafes our furprife con-cerning the flagellating ceremonies and procef-fions we defcribe, is the great feverity and earneft zeal with which thofe who perform them, lay thefe difciplines upon themfelves; different, in that, from the Priefts of the Goddefs of Syria mentioned in pag. 87, who, as the Emperor Com-modus, and after him Philip Beroald, fhrewdly fufpected, only performed fham flagellations. The cruel feverities exercifed upon themfelves by the modern Penitents, are facts about which all Wri-ters of Relations agree; all mention the great quantity of blood which thefe Flagellants lofe, and throw to and fro with their difciplines. It is commonly reported, I do not know with what truth, in the places where fuch proceffions ufe to be performed, that thofe who have been accuf-tomed for feveral years to difcipline themfelves in them, cannot leave it off afterwards, without dan-ger of fome great diforder, unlefs they get them-felves bled at that time of the year at which thofe

ceremonies ufe to take place *. Madame D'Aunoy fays that the firft time fhe faw one of thefe
proceffions, fhe thought fhe fhould faint away;
and fhe concludes the account fhe has given of the
gallant flagellating excurfions that have been abovementioned, with faying that the Gentleman who
has thus fo handfomely trimmed himfelf, is often
laid up in his room for feveral days afterwards,
and fo fick that he cannot go to Mafs on Eafter
Sunday. All the above facts fhew how much
hardfhip, practice really may bring Men to bear:
and the feats of the above Penitents are not, after
all, much more furprifing than the prowefs of
the illuftrious *Buckhorfe*, in this Country, who
fubmitted to receive boxes upon any part of his
body, and as ftoutly applied as people chofe to
lay them on, for fix-pence apiece: he only covered his ftomach with his arms acrofs it; and
the whole was meant as an advantageous exercife
for thofe who propofed to improve themfelves in
the art of boxing.

A remarkable inftance of this power of *ufe*, to
enable us to bear hardfhips, and even blows, occurs among the Chinefe. It appears, from the
accounts of Travellers, that there are Men, in

---

* In a certain Spanifh book, the name of which I do not
remember, a Man is reproached with having befmeared himfelf with fheep's blood, in order to make people believe he
had flagellated himfelf in a diftinguifhed manner.

China, who make it their trade, being properly feed for it, to receive baftinadoes in the room of thofe who are fentenced to it by the Mandarine; in the fame manner as there are Men about the Courts of Law, in this Country, ready to bail upon any occafion. As the baftinadoe is inflicted on the fpot, while the Mandarine is difpatching other bufinefs, the thing is to bribe the Officer who is to fuperintend the operation: the real Culprit then flips out of the way; the Man who is to do duty for him comes forth, fuffers himfelf to be tied down to the ground, and receives the baftinadoe; which is laid on in fuch earneft, that a frefh Man, or Executioner, is employed after every ten or twelve ftrokes.

However, there is perhaps fomething in all this, arifing from the peculiar conftitution and frame of the body, befides practice and refolution. This difpofition to bear blows without being difturbed, is greatly valued by Boxers, who fet it almoft upon a par with fkill, agility, and real ftrength. I hope the Reader will thank me if I inform him that this advantageous capability to receive blows without minding them, is technically called by Boxers, *a Bottom*: at leaft as it feems from certain publications of thofe days when the art of boxing was encouraged by the Public in a higher degree than it is at prefent.

7

The ufe that has been made of flagellations in public fhows and proceffions, the different Edicts of Princes for prohibiting or permitting fuch ceremonies, the Bulls iffued by different Popes to approve or condemn them, and the decifions and regulations of a number of Men invefted with the firft dignities in the Church on the fubject of voluntary difcipline, are not the only circumftances that prove the great importance of which thefe practices have gradually grown to be in the Chriftian World : we ought not to omit to fay that they have been the caufe of much difference in opinion among the Learned ; for fomething effential would certainly be wanting to the glory of flagellations, had they not been the caufe of diffentions among Men, and if at leaft Treatifes *pro* and *con* had not been written on occafion of them.

Some among the Learned have, it feems, blamed the pious exercifes here alluded to, without reftriction : fuch were the Cardinal Stephen, and Peter Cerebrofus, who have been mentioned in a former place, as well as certain learned Ecclefiaftics in Rome, againft whom Cardinal Damian likewife wrote. Others have condemned the cruelty with which the fame exercifes were fometimes performed : among them was Gerfon, whofe arguments, together with thofe of the Advocate-General Servin in his fpeech againft the Blue Pe-

C c

nitents of Bourges, are recited at fome length in the Abbé Boileau's ninth Chapter.

Debates have, moreover, taken place among the Learned, concerning the precife views with which difciplines ought to be performed, as well as on the propereft occafions. And difputes have in particular run high, concerning the degree of efficacioufnefs of fuch pious exercifes : on which the Reader may remember what has lately been faid of the doctrines advanced by the Hereticks called *Flagellants.*

Differences in opinion have alfo prevailed with refpect to the manner in which difciplines are to be executed : fome afferting that penitents ought to inflict them upon themfelves with their own hands ; and others being equally pofitive that they ought to receive them from the hands of other perfons ; this was one of the arguments of Gerfon.

In fine, debates have taken place concerning the propereft fituation for penitents to be in, when undergoing fuch mortifications. Some have objected to the difciplining perfons laying themfelves bare for that purpofe, as being contrary to decency ; while others, at the head of whom was Cardinal Damian, have ftrenuoufly declared for a ftate of unlimited nakednefs. The following is one of the arguments of the Cardinal on the fubject,

' Tell me, whoever you may be, who are ac-
' tuated by fo much pride as to ceride the Paffion
' of our Saviour, and who, refuhing to be ftrip-
' ped along with him ridicule his nakednefs, and
' call his fufferings mere dreams or trifles, tell
' me, pray, what you prepare to do, when you
' fhall fee this heavenly Saviour, who was pub-
' licly ftripped and faftened to a crofs, clad with
' majefty and glory, accompanied by an innume-
' rable multitude of Angels, furrounded by in-
' comparable and inexpreffible fplendours, and
' infinitely more glorious than all vifible and invi-
' fible things? what will you do, I fay, when
' you fhall fee him whofe ignominy you pretend
' to defpife, feated upon a Tribunal exalted and
' furrounded by fire, and judging all Mankind in
' a manner both equitable and terrible? Then
' will the Sun lofe its luftre; the Moon will be
' involved in darknefs; the Stars will fall from
' their places, the foundations of mountains will
' be fhaken, only a few fcarce gloomy rays will
' be fent from the fkies, the earth and air will be
' confumed by impetuous fires, and all the ele-
' ments confounded together· what, once more,
' will you do, when all thefe things fhall happen?
' of what fervice to you will thefe clothes and
' garments be, with which you now are covered,
' and which you refufe to lay afide, to fubmit to
' the exercife of penitence? with what pre-

C c 2

' fumptuous audacioufnefs do you hope to partake
' of the glory of Him whofe fhame and igno-
' miny you now refufe to fhare ?'——The above
is certainly the beft argument I have hitherto read
in favour of nakednefs, and it reconciles me to
Cardinal Damian, whom I find to have been no
bad Writer.

This neceffity of nakednefs to complete the merit of Penance, has been infifted upon by other
Men of importance befides him whom we have
juft fpoken of; and without alledging any further
authority on this fubject, it will fuffice to obferve
that the greateft perfonages have fubmitted to that
part of Penitence we mention; feveral inftances
of which have been produced in a former
Chapter.

Nay, the more complete was this privation of
clothes, the more merit there was thought to be
in it: hence we find that feveral Offenders have
proportioned their freedom from habiliments, to
the greatnefs of the fenfe they entertained of their
offences; and on this occafion may be recited the
penance performed by Fulk, furnamed *Grifegon-
nelle*, about the year 1000.

This Fulk, who was a very powerful Man in
France, being the Son of the great *Senefchal* of
the Kingdom, had been a moft bad and violent
Man in thofe times of feudal Anarchy, when
force was almoft the only law that exifted, and

the Nobles and Lords were rather Heads of Robbers, than perfons invefted with any precife dignity. Among other crimes the above Fulk had committed, he had killed with his own hand Conan, Duke of Britanny. He had performed three pilgrimages to the Holy Land; and on the laft, meaning to render his penance complete and perfectly unexceptionable, he caufed himfelf to be drawn naked upon a hurdle, with a halter round his neck, through the ftreets of Jerufalem, Men who had been directed fo to do, lafhed him by turns, with fcourges, and a perfon appointed for that purpofe, cried at certain intervals, *Lord have mercy on the traitor and forfwearer Fulk.* He lived very devoutly afterwards, and founded feveral Monafteries. An account of this Fulk, and his penance, is to be found in Moreri's Dictionary.

Others have carried their notions on the prefent fubject ftill farther, and have thought that bare freedom from habiliments, had fome fanctity peculiar to it, and poffeffed, of itfelf, a great degree of merit. The Cynic Philofophers in Greece, among whom Diogenes was particularly remarkable, frequently made, we find, their appearance in public, without even a fingle rag to cover their nakednefs, and the Indian Philofophers called *Gymnofophifts,* conftantly appeared in the fame light kind of drefs, as we learn from their appellation itfelf, which fignifies *naked Sages*.

Sages of the fame kind ftill continue to exift in the fame quarters we fpeak of; and we have likewife had, in our parts of the World, particular Sages or Sectaries, who have attributed no lefs merit to a ftate of nakednefs. Such were the *Adamites*, mentioned by St. Auftin. Thefe Adamites, thinking they would effectually affimilate themfelves to our firft Parents before their fall, if they appeared in the fame habit, would put themfelves in a complicate ftate of nature during certain folemnities of their own, and either ventured to make their appearance in the public ftreets in that condition, or did the fame, both Men and Women together, in private conventicles or houfes, which, if it was winter time, they took care to have well warmed beforehand.

About the year 1300, a Sect of the fame kind, called the *Turlupins* (which word rather feems to have been a nickname, than a ferious appellation of that fect) made their appearance in France, again declaring themfelves, as well by their example as by their words, for fieedom from accoutrements. To thefe the *Picards*, a century afterwards, fucceeded in Germany, who carrying their opinion on the fanctity of nakednefs, and their abhorrence of fuch unhallowed thing as clothing, farther than the Adamites had done, made at all times their appearance in a perfect state of nature. A certain party of Anabaptists, adopting the doctrine of these Picards, tried, on the thirteenth day of February in the year 1535, to make an excursion in the streets of *Amsterdam*, in the hallowed state we mention, but the Magistracy, not taking the joke so well as they ought to have done, used these Adventurers in rather a severe manner.

In fine, to the instances of nakedness we have just recited, we ought not to omit to add that of Brother *Juniperus*, a Friar of the Franciscan Order: and the merit of this Friar was the greater in that, different from the abovementioned partisans of nakedness, he performed his own processions alone, with great assurance and composure.

' Another time he entered the Town of Vi-
' terbo; and while he stood within the gate, he
' put his breeches on his head, and, his gown
' being tied round his neck in the shape of a load,
' he walked through the streets of the Town,
' where he suffered many tricks from the inhabi-
' tants; and still in the same situation, he went to
' the Convent of the Brothers, who all exclaim-
' ed against him, but he cared little for them, *so*
' *holy was this good little Brother* * .'

---

* *Aliâ vice intravit Viterbium, & dùm esset in portâ, fœ-moralibus positis in capite, habitu in modum fardeli ligato ad collum, sic nudus ad plateas ruit civitatis, ubi multas verecun-*

This account of Brother Juniperus, is extracted from the Book called " Of the Conformities"
(*De Conformitatibus*) or rather from that called the
Alcoran of the Cordeliers, which is an extract from
the former : for this Book of the *Conformities* exifts, it is faid, no longer ; or at leaft only two or
three Copies of it are to be come at, in certain
Libraries, the name of which I have forgotten.
The Book in queftion, which is well known from
other old Books that mention it, was a compilation
made by Francifcan Monks : the defign of it, befides reciting pious Anecdotes relative to the Order, was to inveftigate the *conformities* between
Jefus Chrift, and their Founder St. Francis ;
and the advantage commonly was, in thefe comparifons, modeftly given to the latter. After the
period of the Reformation, the Monks of the
Order we fpeak of, became fomewhat afhamed of
the performance, and have fince fucceeded in fup-
preffing it, only two or three copies, as hath been
above obferved, being now left : a Proteftant Minifter, who procured fight of one of them, has,
in this Century, done the Cordeliers or Francif-
cans the charitable fervice of giving an extract
from the moft remarkable Articles to the World,
under the abovementioned title of the Alcoran
of the Cordeliers.

dias perpeffus eft ; & nudus ad locum fratrum ivit omnibus
contrà eum clamantibus, ipfo tamen de iis parùm curante, tam
fanctus fuit ifte fratricellus.

However, thefe ftark-naked proceffions performed by the Cynic Philofophers, by the Adamites, the Turlupins, the Picards, and by Brother
Juniperus, never met, we find, with any great
and lafting countenance from the Public ; and, as
beatings without nakednefs, that is mere baftinadoes, have generally been confidered as being but
dull and unmeritorious acts of penance, and accordingly never experienced any degree of encouragement, fo, nakednefs without beatings, has
been but indifferently practifed or relifhed. But
when flagellations have been employed, then has
the fcene become cheered and enlivened ; then
have Penitents entertained fufficient confcioufnefs
of their merit, to continue their exercifes with,
perfeverance and regularity ; then have numerous
converts contributed to perpetuate the practice ;
then have the World thought the affair worth en-
gaging their attention, and public fhews, ceremonies, and folemnities, have been inftituted.

Ceremonies of this kind have, however, been
planned with different fuccefs, by which I mean
with different degrees of ingenuity, among different Nations.

The flagellating Solemnities, for inftance, that
took place in Lacedæmon, are not in any degree
intitled to our approbation, very far from it. The
cruel advantage that was taken in them, of the
filly pride of Boys, to prevail upon them to fuffer

themfelves to be cut to pieces, rendered fuch ceremonies a practice of really a brutifh kind; and it
is difficult to decide whether there was in them
more inhumanity, or ftupidity. The fame is to
be faid of the Solemnities of a fimilar kind that
were performed among the Thracians.

Lefs exceptionable than thofe juft mentioned
certainly were the ceremonies exhibited by the
Egyptians, and by the Syrian Priefts of Bellona;
fince it is evident that no kind whatever of compul-
fion took place in them, in regard to any perfon.

The fame obfervation is to be made in favour
of the proceffions of modern Flagellants, in which
every one has the fcourging of his own fkin; and
at the fame time it muft be owned that the gallantry and courtfhip paid to the fair Sex, which
fo eminently prevail in thofe proceffions, are circumftances that greatly recommend them. On
the other hand, the gloomy affectation of fanctity
which is mixed with the feftivity and pageantry of
thofe difciplining folemnities, gives the whole an
air of hypocrify, which is in fome degree difguft-
ing; and the degree of real cruelty with which
they are attended, cannot but compleat the aver-
fion of fuch perfons as ufe has not reconciled to
the thought of them.

The feftival of the Lupercalia that was performed in Rome, had indeed greatly the advantage of
all the ceremonies of the kind that ever were in-

ſtituted. It really deſerved to have been contrived, or continued, by a People more polite and re-·
fined than the Romans, eſpecially in early times,
are repreſented to us to have been.

Among other excellencies the Feſtival we ſpeak
of poſſeſſed, it was performed but once a year,
and only continued a few days : for, ceremonies
of this kind ought to occur but ſeldom, and be
only of ſhort duration : and it was like a ſhort
time of *Saturnalia,* during which each Sex kindly
exhibited to the ſight of the other thoſe perſonal
charms and advantages which they wiſely kept hidden during the reſt of the whole year.

In the ſecond place, the real deſign of the whole
tranſaction was pretty openly and candidly acknowledged : and if we except the few religious
rites by which the ceremony was begun, which
ſerved to give dignity to it, and the notion of the
power of the ſlaps of the *Luperci* to render Women fruitful, which ſerved to give importance to
the whole ſolemnity, it was agreed fairly enough
on all ſides, that no more was meant than tempo-
rary paſtime and amuſement.

In the third place, no cruelty whatever took
place in the performance of the Feſtival we ſpeak
of, nor was it poſſible any ſhould ; and from the
lightneſs and the breadth of the ſtraps which the
Luperci employed, we may judge of their tender
anxiouſneſs not to do, through zeal or other cauſe,

I

any injury to the fair objects who made application to them.

When one of the three bands of Luperci (out of which every Man who wanted an excellent shape or elegant addrefs, was no doubt irremiffibly blackballed) had been let loofe out of the Temple of the God Pan, and after the coming of a Lupercus into any particular ftreet had been announced by the flourifhes of the haut-boys, the clarinets, the trumpets, kettle-drums, and other mufical inftruments that were ftationed near the entrance of it (for we are abfolutely to fuppofe that mufic contributed to embellifh fo chaiming a feftival) fome one of the amiable perfons who propofed to receive benefit from the Lupercus's fervices, moved out of the croud, and threw herfelf into his way.

On fight of her, the whole fiercenefs of the Lupercus became foftened. However kindled his fpirits might have been by the religious rites by which the ceremony was begun, by the courfe he had juft performed, and the fight of the multitude of fpectators who lined the ftreets, whatever in fhort might be that ftate of fever in which Feftus feems to reprefent him, the *februans* Lupercus, at the fight of the lovely creature who obftructed his paffage, felt his agitation fucceeded by fenfations of the moft benevolent fort.

So far from entertaining defigns of a fevere or cruel nature, he fcarcely poffeffed fufficient power to raife his arm, and perform with a faint hand the office that was expected from him. His bofom was filled with the fofteft paffions. Intirely loft in the contemplation of the lovely object that made application to him, already did he begin to have thoughts of employing remedies of a more obvious and natural kind,—already, forgetting all Mankind, did he attempt to inclofe her in his arms, when the acclamations of the fpectators and the fudden explofion of the mufical inftruments, at once recalled him to himfelf; he flew from the amiable perfon who had thus fo thoroughly engaged his attention, and haftened to other objects equally amiable, who likewife came to crave his affiftance. If I was called upon to give my vote for any ceremony of the kind here mentioned, I would give it for the feftival of the Lupercalia, efpecially with the improvements that had been made in it about the time of Pope Gelafius. (See p. 94.)

C H A P. XXIV.

The laſt Chapter, in which the Abbe Boileau is perſonally introduced: he is of opinion that the lower diſcipline is contrary to decency, and the upper diſcipline is liable to bring de-fluxions on the eyes *.

SEVERAL Divines, as we have ſeen, have united in blaming the cruel ſeverity with which certain perſons uſed to inflict diſ-

---

* In order to ſupport his opinion concerning the dangers of diſciplines, the Abbé Boileau has quoted Bartholinus's treatiſe *De medico flagrorum uſu*, and that wrote by John-Henry Meibomius, a Profeſſor at Lubeck, *De uſu flagrorum in re venereâ*. The ſingularity of theſe titles led me to look into both publications, in order to be able to give my opinion about them, and alſo in hope I might pick a few facts and quotations to entertain the Reader with: but I have been diſappointed, both Treatiſes being as dull unconnected farragos as ever were printed. From Meibomius's Trea-

ciplines upon themfelves, by which thofe perfons affimilated themfelves to Idolaters and
Pagans; befides, it is well worth obferving
that, by this very feverity, thofe zealous per-

tife, and alfo from Cœlius Rhodiginus's Book, the
Abbé had however borrowed two ftories, which I
at firft intended to infert in this Chapter, but as
I have found them, upon more attentive examination, to be related in no pleafing nor even probable manner, befides being very long, I have fet
them afide, contrary to the defign of this Work,
as I have explained it in the *Introduction*, which
was to make ufe of and introduce, in the Text, all
the facts and quotations fcattered in the Abbé's
Book: I therefore make my apology to the Reader
for the omiffion.

To the other facts thus fupplied by the Abbé's
Work, I have in this Chapter, conformably to the
promife made at p. 131, added the Abbé's own
expreffions and remarks, not only on account of
their great ingenuity, but alfo in order that the
prefent final Chapter might be a common conclufion of our refpective tafks, and that the Abbé
and me, joining hands again in it, might thus
have an opportunity, as is the cuftom at the end
of Plays, to make our obeifance together, and
take a joint leave of the Public.

formers of difciplines in the iffue obftruct their own piety, and defeat their own ends.

In fact, Phyficians and Anatomifts inform us, that fuch is the fecret, or open, communication between all parts of the human body, that it is impoffible to do any material and continual kind of injury to any, without the other parts being, fooner or later, affected by it : hence it follows that thofe perfons who execute difciplines upon themfelves with the great feverity we mention, in procefs of time fall into ferious diftempers of fome kind or other; fo that they at length find themfelves difabled from continuing thofe practices by which they intended to procure the improvement of their morals.

The next and the moft tender parts are, in the cafes we fpeak of, unavoidably affected by the confequence of the injury that is thus done to the other parts; and from harfh difciplines repeatedly performed upon the fhoulders, at length arife, at the learned Bartholinus obferves, diforders and defluxions on the eyes.

This inconvenience from the exercifes we mention, much perplexed Father Gretzer, who, as hath been before obferved, was a great friend to the practice of difcipline; and in order to be thoroughly fatisfied on that fub-

ject, he one day confulted a Phyfician, a friend
of his, who partly freed him from his fears,
and partly confirmed them. This Phyfician
made anfwer, that difciplines executed on the
fhoulders, when performed with moderation,
were perfectly harmlefs with refpect to the eye-
fight; but then he abfolutely avoided giving
any fuch opinion in regard to thofe which were
performed in a harfh or cruel manner. The
following is the oracle which the Phyfician in
queftion delivered.

‘ The vulgar opinion, that lafhes, applied
‘ to the back, are apt to hurt the eyes, is not
‘ well grounded. It is true that the great
‘ lofs of blood injures the brain, and confe-
‘ quently the eyes, which are called by fome
‘ the *fprouts* of it; and this it effects by the
‘ diminution it caufes of the vital heat. But
‘ there does not arife from difciplines, fuch a
‘ great lofs of blood as that the brain may
‘ thereby fuffer any confiderable deperdition
‘ of its heat: on the contrary; fince fcarifica-
‘ tions on the back are often employed with
‘ fuccefs for the cure of diforders in the eyes,
‘ why fhould bad confequences to them be
‘ feared from a few ftripes? Thofe therefore
‘ alone who are of a weakly habit of body
‘ the exercife in queftion can hurt, but not
‘ perfons of a good conftitution; and when
‘ difciplines are fo moderately inflicted as

D d

' caufe no lofs of blood, and barely to affect
' the colour of the fkin, no detriment cer-
' tainly ought to be feared fiom them.' Such
was the decifion of this excellent Phyfician,
and to it Father Gretzer adds that he willingly and readily fubfcribes *.

All phyficians, however, have not agreed.
with him whofe authority we have juft quoted.
Some have delivered different opinions concerning the harmleffnefs of difcipline with refpect to the eyes; and whether it was that the
Capuchin Friars thought the advice of thefe
latter of greateft weight, or that they intended
their zeal fhould be unreftrained by any apprehenfion, they have adopted the ufe of the
lower difcipline; and the generality of Nuns
have done the fame, from the like intention
of fecuing their eye fight. Determined there-
to by the advice of able Phyficians and pious
perfons, they have given up the method of
flagellating themfelves on their fhoulders, in
order to belabour and flafh their loins and pofteriors with knotted fmall cords and hardened
rods †.

* . . . . ad cujus fententiam, meam libens volenf-
que adjungo.

† Quippecum eâ de caufâ Capucini, multæque Mo-
niales, virorum Medicorum ac piorum hominum con-
filio, afcefim flagellandi furfum humeros reliquerint, ut
fuminates lumbofque ftrient afperatis virgis, ac nodofis
funiculis confcribillent.

But while the perfons we fpeak of have endeavoured to prevent dangers of one kind,
they have incurred others which are ftill worfe.
By moft of the antient Monaftic Rules, religious perfons were forbidden to infpect any
part of their naked bodies, for fear of the
wicked thoughts to which fuch indulgence
might give rife : now, how is it poffible for
perfons who ftrip intirely naked, in order to
take difcipline, to help, however great their
piety may be, having a fight of thofe parts of
themfelves which they have been directed never to look on ? How can Nuns avoid, in thofe
inftants, having at leaft a glance of thofe excellent beauties * which they are forbidden to

* *Ho, ho, Monfieur l'Abbé !* How come you to
be fo well acquainted with beauties of the kind
you mention here, and to fpeak of them in fo pofitive a manner ? For, the Reader muft not think
I here lend any expreffions to the Abbé which are
not his own : *Num probrofum* (fays he), *foli often-
dere lumbos & femora juvenilia, excellenti formâ,
quamvis religionis honeftate confecrata ?* This *Monfieur l'Abbé*, for his excurfion upon objects and
beauties which, one fhould have thought, he out
of his province, richly deferves a lecture of the
fame kind with that which Parfon Adams received
from Lady Booby, when he ventured to expatiate,

D d 2

ſurvey, and which they thus imprudently ex-
poſe to the light of the Sun? By ſubſtituting
one kind of diſcipline to the other, religious
perſons have, I am afraid, only laid themſelves
open, as hath been above obſerved, to dangers
of a ſtill worſe nature than thoſe they meant
to avoid, and have perhaps only fallen from
Charybdis into Scylla ✝.

in her Ladyſhip's preſence, on the beauties of
Fanny.

✝ Theſe dangers ariſing from ſelf-examination
I do not allow myſelf to call in queſtion, ſince,
beſides the Abbé Boileau, the Framers of Monaſtic Rules have taken notice of them; and indeed I find Brantome has entertained thoughts of
the ſame kind, and many facts are to be found in
that Chapter of his which he has intitled *Of Sight
in Love*, that fully confirm the above obſervations.
But beſides theſe ſerious dangers into which a too
curious examination of one's-ſelf may lead, there
are others very well worth mentioning: I mean
to ſpeak of the acts of pride, vanity, ſelf-admira-
tion and complacency, to which the above curio-
ſity may give riſe. Vanity and a diſpoſition to
admire one's-ſelf, are diſpoſitions that are but too
general among Mankind, and there is hardly a
time in life at which we may be ſaid to be perfectly cured of ſuch worldly affections. On this oc-

Neither, if fuch difciplines cannot be performed in fecret without danger, is it very pru-

cafion I fhall produce the following anecdote,
which is related by Brantome.

A certain Lady, who had been very handfome,
and now was fomewhat advanced in years, would
no longer look at her face in the looking-glafs,
for fear of difcovering fome new injury time might
have done to it; but fhe ufed to furvey the other
parts of her body, and then, fuddenly actuated by
the worldly vanity we fpeak of, fhe exclaimed,
" God be thanked, here I do not grow old" *(je
ne vieillis point.)*

Thefe dangers of a too curious examination of
one's own perfon, are extremely well expreffed by
Ovid, in that part of his Metamorphofis where
he defcribes Narciffus fitting near that clear filver
fountain in which he contemplated himfelf:

Fons erat illimis, nitidis argenteus undis.

And the Poet relates, in a very lively manner, the
aftonifhment of the Youth, at the fight of, as he
thought, his own charms and perfections.

. . . . *vifæ correptus imagine formæ*
Adftupet ipfe fibi.

That unexperienced Nuns fhould be led, by
their difciplines, into faults of a fimilar kind, are
therefore very natural apprehenfions. Being thoroughly engaged in the contemplation of thofe
beauties which they expofe to light, it is no won-

7

dent to execute them in the prefence of wit-
neffes. Tertullian obferves, that 'Nature has
'made either fear or fhame, the attendants of
'every evil action.' Now, if we judge from
this rule, we fhall become convinced of the
truth of the obfervations we are making here.
In fact, what Man or Woman could, without
fear or fhame, execute a lower difcipline in
company with other perfons? who could
without reluctance firk their loins and pofteriors with rods, on an exalted place, and in
the middle of a numerous Affembly of People? who could thus undauntedly expofe their
nakednefs to the rays of the Sun, and to the
eyes of a multitude of Spectators * ?

---

der that all their thoughts of a religious kind
fhould vanifh: and they even may very well in
the iffue, inchanted as they are by what they are
beholding, intirely forget and neglect thofe pious
exercifes which they have purpofely retired to
their cell to perform.

 * *Quid turpius excogitari poteft, five viro five fœ-
mina, quàm, lumbis & femoribus ad radios Solis
apertis, feipfum diverberare? .... Quis in edita
& aperto loco, plenis comitiis, in confpectu hominum,
lumbos natefque virgis cædere non pertimefcat?*

This exhibition of nakednefs to the rays of the
Sun, the Poet Lafontaine obferves, is only fit for
the New World. He expreffes this opinion in
that Tale which has been above quoted, *The Pair*

of Spectacles, when he attempts to exprefs the objects which the Nuns exhibited to the fight of
each other, and of the Abbefs : " Niggardly and
" proud charms, which the Sun is allowed to fee
" only in the New World, for this does not fhew
" them to him."

> ——— *chiches & fiers appas*
> *Que le Soleil ne voit qu'au nouveau monde,*
> *Car celui-ci ne les lui montre pas.*

However, notwithstanding the opinion of the
Poet La'ontaine, it feems that an exhibition of
charms and attractions, even fuperior to what takes
place in the New World, is common in Ruffia;
which is certainly a part of our Old World : the
Reader may fee in the accounts given by Travellers, that individuals of both Sexes, after fome
ftay in the hot-baths and ftoves in ufe in that
Country, will rufh out promifcuoufly together,
ftark-naked, playing, and delightfully rolling themfelves in the fnow. If Ruffia had been more vi-
fited by Travellers in the times of Cardinals Damian and Pullus, thefe two great Promoters of
nakednefs would have been fupplied with facts
much to the advantage of their doctrine.

Bartholinus too, from the accounts of the fame
Travellers would have been fupplied with excellent materials for compofing his abovementioned
Treatife, *On the phyfical ufe of Flagellations.* The
Abbé Dauteroche, one of the lateft Travellers
who have publifhed an account of Ruffia, where
he went to obferve the tranfit of Venus, gives a

somewhat accurate defcription of the baths and stoves we mention. The heat is commonly carried in them to so high a degree as the fiftieth of Reaumur's scale (which answer to the 130th of Fahrenheit's; the greateft summer heat in England seldom surpaffes, or even reaches, 80) a suffocating steam is raised by throwing plenty of water upon stones kept conftantly red hot, and, in order to carry the agitation of the blood still farther, flagellations are applied to: a bundle of birchen twigs, with the leaves on, which being dry are soon stripped off, is as conftant a part of the bathing implements and furniture, as a handkerchief or a towel. All thefe different operations being fulfilled, the bathers, as is above faid, rush out into the external air, sometimes ten, or even twenty degrees colder than it was in this Country in the year 1740, and roll themfelves in the snow, or jump into water through holes made in the ice. Thefe are certainly surprifing inftances of what the human body may be brought to bear; much more remarkable than thofe that have been before mentioned; and the boxes of Buckhorfe, the Chinefe baftinadoes, and the flagellations of the Italian and Spanifh difciplinants, are nothing in comparifon to it. But, for a farther account of the Ruffian ftoves, and of the trial the Abbé Dauteroche had the curiofity to make of them, as well as of the unexpected and unwelcome entertainment he received, I muft refer the Reader to the Work itself he has publifhed.

F I N I S.

I N D E X.

E e

lower difciplines defined, 21. The lower difcipline is practifed by a number of Saints of both Sexes, 10. The dangers of thefe two kinds of difciplines, 400, & fq See *Lower Difcipline* Voluntary difciplines, fee *Voluntary Flagellations*.

Dominic the Cuiraffed, a Hero in the career of felf-flagellation, 203, & *feq.*

Du Cange, his Gloffary, quoted, 142, 180, 200.

E.

Edeffe, the familiar manner in which its inhabitants treated the ftatue of the Emperor Conftantine, 288.

Edmund (St) Archbifhop of Canterbury, a great inftance of his virtue, while he purfues his ftudies in Paris, 262.

Elizabeth (Queen), no lover of formality in giving tokens of her difpleafure, 190 Seems to have ufed peculiar methods for rendering her Minifters what they ought to be, 343, 344.

Emprefs, the, wife to Juftinian II. is threatened with a flagellation by the great Eunuch, 173.

Engineer, an, of the Town of Elæa, an officious miftake of his, and atonement for the fame, 149, 150.

Effex (the Earl of) his letter to Queen Elizabeth, quoted, 343.

F.

Fakirs, their aftonifhing penances, which are well-afcertained facts, render every account of that kind credible, 115, 206. Dialogue between one and a Turk, quoted from M. de Voltaire, 207.

Fathers, antient Greek and Latin, are their expreffions about felf-fcourgings and beatings to be taken in a literal fenfe? 122, 123.

Fielding, quoted, 294, 376.

Flagellants, the formation of their proceffions, 345, & *feq.* The fuccefs they met with in different Countries, 350. Defcription of one of their itinerant proceffions in Germany, 351, & *feq.* Their eftablifhment and firft fuccefs in France, 355, 372, & *feq.* are there difcountenanced at laft, 373 Their fraternities muft be diftinguifhed from the fect of Hereticks, called *Flag. llants*, 368. Account of thefe Hereticks, 369. Account of thefe fraternities, 370, & *feq.* Are, as it were, naturalifed in Italy and Spain, 374. Manner in which they perform thefe proceffions in Spain, 374, & *feq.* In Italy, 382, & *feq.* Real cruelty of thefe Flagellants upon themfelves, 384, 385.

Flagellating fanaticifm a kind of, feems to have taken place in England about the time of the Rebellion, 340. Proofs of it, *ibid.*

E e 3

E e 4

comb who had affronted them, 334, *&* *feq.* See *Ladies.*

S.

Sadragefillus, preceptor to Dagobert, heir to the Crown of France, 74. How ufed by his Pupil, 75.

St Loe (Captain) gets the Bofton Magiftrates and Selectmen ferved with a flagellation, 273, *& feq.*

Saints, the frequent tricks the Devil puts upon them, 125, *& feq.* How they have received the advances of the Fair Sex, 261, *& feq.* The expedient of a certain Eaftern Saint to make himfelf cry, 364.

Salluft (the Hiftorian), makes free with Milo's Wife; how ferved by the Hufband, 65.

Sancho, his manner of difcipline, 195, 226.

Sanlec, a French Poet; his Satire on Confeffors quoted, 234.

Scarron quoted, 285.

Scaligerana quoted, 36, 270.

Schoolmafters of modern times are as fond of ufing their difcipline as ancient ones, 71, *& feq.* Are not worth mentioning in fo interefting a book as this, 160, 175.

Scot, a good Story of his, in his *Menfa Philofophica,* 232.

Scythians, their expedient to conquer their revolted Slaves, 51, and fuccefs, 52.

Seneca quoted, 82.

Slaves, the wanton ufage of

them in Rome, 61, *& feq.* 66, *& feq.* See *Mafters.*

Solomon (King), recommends flagellations, 76. His opinion confirmed afterwards by that of Chryfippus, *ibid.*

Sorbona, whence the word is derived, 143.

Sovereigns; inftances of Sovereigns upon whom difciplines have been publicly inflicted, 250, *& feq.*

Spain. An account of the proceffions of Penitents eftablifhed there, 374, *& feq.* Gallantry and nicety of honour that prevail in them, *ibid* The art of performing flagellations with gracefulnefs is taught there by Mafters for that purpofe, 376.

Spirit of Laws quoted, 173.

Stephen (Cardinal), dies fuddenly for his having neglected the ufe of flagellations, 214, 302.

Stylites (St. Simeon), an Anchorite who had fixed his habitation on the top of a column, 114.

Suetonius quoted, 59, 97.

Superanus, a Greek Philofopher; laudable flagellations he inflicts upon himfelf, 98.

Surgeon, great favour and confidence fhewn to him by a great Princefs, 270. His ungrateful conduct, *ibid.* The greatnefs of his guilt difplayed, 271, 272; his punifhment, *ibid.* extreme juftice of the fame, *ibid.*

Syrians, flagellations of a religious kind ufed among them, 86, 87.

T.

Tales, Arabian Tales quoted, 290. Of the Queen of Navarre, 188, 330, 331.

Thracians, flagellations of a voluntary kind ufed among them, 84.

Trefnel (the Marchionefs of), is incenfed at the arrogant competition of the Ladv of Liancourt, a woman of inferior birth, 278. Gets her ferved with a flagellation, 279. More ferious confequences of the affair, 280.

Triumpher among the Romans, the companion he had in his Car, 59.

V.

Venus, the ftrange weapon with which the Antients fupplied her, 60, 319. The Temple which the Greeks erected to her, 283.

Veftals, how punifhed, 167, *& feq.*

Villemartin (Mifs de), is co-fpectatrefs of a flagellation, 280; is admonifhed never to do fo any more, 281.

Virgil quoted, 90.

Virgin Mary refcues an Ufurer from the hands of the Devils, 304. The affiftance fhe gives to a perfon who ufed to pay devotion to her, 308. The remarkable zeal of a Monk to affert her honour, 310, *& feq.*

Vifitation (Nuns of the), difcipline themfelves when they pleafe, 121.

Voltaire (M. de), quoted, 32, 207, 288.

Upper difcipline defined, 21. See *Difcipline.*

W.

Walpole (Sir Robert), his Excife Scheme, preferable, upon the whole, to the fchemes that took place in the times of the Roman Emperors, 124.

Whipcord, the great expence made about it by Government, 344. At what time it began to be ufed, *ibid.*

Wife, Roman Wives not much better than modern ones, 64. Inftance of conjugal love of one whofe hufband offered himfelf to be difciplined in her ftead, 232. Inflict caftigations upon their hufbands, 339, 340.

Witafky, the Buffoon to Peter I. is a good hand at flagellating and cudgelling, 266.

Wurtzbourg, a Sovereign Bifhoprick in Germany; a flagellation is an indifpenfible ftep to procure the inftallation to that See, 256.

CONTENTS.

Lightning Source UK Ltd.
Milton Keynes UK
UKHW022247240720
367133UK00003B/100